ARMS AND THE AFRICAN

A Council on Foreign Relations Book

COUNCIL ON FOREIGN RELATIONS BOOKS

ARMS
and the
AFRICAN
Military Influences on Africa's International Relations

Edited by

William J. Foltz
and
Henry S. Bienen

YALE UNIVERSITY PRESS
New Haven and London

Designed by Margaret E.B. Joyner
and set in Baskerville type
by American–Stratford Graphic Services, Inc.
Printed in the United States of America
by Vail-Ballou Press, Binghamton, New York

Library of Congress Cataloging in Publication Data
Main entry under title:

Arms and the African.

"Council on Foreign Relations books"
Includes index.
1. Africa, Sub-Saharan—Armed Forces—Addresses,
essays, lectures.   2. Africa, Sub-Saharan—Armed Forces—
Political activity—Addresses, essays, lectures.
3. Africa, Sub-Saharan—Military relations—Foreign
countries—Addresses, essays, lectures.   4. Munitions—
Africa, Sub-Saharan—Addresses, essays, lectures.
I. Foltz, William J.   II. Bienen, Henry.   III. Council on
Foreign Relations.
UA855.7.A76   1985   355′.033067   84–40670
ISBN 0–300–03347–8 (alk. paper)

10   9   8   7   6   5   4   3   2   1

355.033
A734

Contents

TABLES

Foreword

The Africa Project of the Council on Foreign Relations was designed to focus both on Africa and on its significance for the United States. Undertaken in response to a perceived need for greater knowledge about African realities on the part of the American foreign policy community, the Project aimed to produce and disseminate original research on Africa's changing role in the international community and to stimulate discussion and debate within the Western, and particularly American, policymaking communities.

The Project proceeded in two ways, each calculated to reinforce the other's impact: through a marked expansion of attention to Africa in the Council's regular activities and through a series of studies and publications. The process aimed at bringing together regional specialists with people in government, business, the professions, and the public media whose views are likely to have an effect on Africa policy. The Africa Project books were designed to fill what the Council saw as a serious gap in information and public understanding, bringing a detailed knowledge of African issues to bear on the larger questions that confront United States citizens and policymakers. Their authors have sought to use their expert knowledge to interpret African developments in a way that addresses the concerns of an informed but largely nonspecialist audience.

This study by William Foltz and Henry Bienen follows Crawford Young's *Ideology and Development in Africa;* I. William Zartman's *Conflict Resolution in Africa* will be published at the same time.

The Africa Project was made possible by generous grants from the Ford and Rockefeller Foundations. Their advice and assistance along the way has proven invaluable.

WILLIAM J. FOLTZ
Africa Project Director

JENNIFER SEYMOUR WHITAKER
Editor, Africa Project Book Series

Preface

Military involvement in African politics is a well-worn theme. Coups and guerrillas have become depressingly familiar parts of the domestic politics of many African countries. Much less noticed, however, is the fact that military factors are now significantly affecting the relations among African states and the relations between Africa and the rest of the world.

The increased militarization of Africa's international relations stems from both Africa's weaknesses and some newfound strengths. It is Africa's military weakness that has brought in outsiders—as arms merchants, mercenaries, training teams, expeditionary forces, and superpowers offering economic and military protection in exchange for military facilities. But some weak African states have now built up armies strong enough to threaten their neighbors, in effect strong enough to overthrow governments not their own. They thus are beginning to play the foreign policy role that armies have historically played in the rest of the world, and the relations among African states have changed in consequence.

The conjunction of a heightened military component in relations among African states and the involvement of outside powers in arming, training, and supporting African military forces produces a volatile mixture. Previously obscure quarrels over seemingly worthless pieces of African real estate can be escalated into symbolic—or even real—superpower confrontations. One need not go so far as Zbigniew Brzezinski's hyperbolic dictum that "SALT lies buried in the sands of Ogaden" to realize that military events in Africa can have consequences far beyond that continent's shores.

To understand both causes and consequences of the militarization of Africa's international relations requires approaching the problem from many different viewpoints, extracontinental as well as African. This volume opens with a broad historic view of Africa's changing involvement in the strategic calculations and miscalculations of the great powers. It considers next the involvement of the two most prominent outside actors in Africa's military affairs—the Soviets and the French. Next it looks at the military capabilities of the black African states and the army's increasingly political role in Africa's military "superpower," South Africa, and then investigates how the spread of military regimes in Africa affects the international behavior of African states. The final chapter pulls together some of the most significant threads of earlier arguments to lay out the policy issues the West, and especially the United States, must face in adjusting to a more heavily militarized Africa in the coming years.

This volume originated in a study group convened by the Africa Project of the Council on Foreign Relations in 1980. The group brought together a mixture of academic and governmental analysts, civilian and military, with widely differing political and analytic approaches to the issues considered. Henry S. Bienen chaired the group meetings, and George E. Moose, then an International Affairs Fellow at the Council, served as group director. The papers published here have been revised—in some cases substantially—to take into account the group discussion and subsequent events. In presenting this book, however, the editors have sought to preserve the characteristic intellectual and analytic style of each contribution. They have encouraged the authors to capitalize on the particular informational and analytic resources at their disposal, even though this has entailed some divergence in style, particularly with regard to citation of sources, between those authors in government service and those in academic life.

The editors would like to thank all the members of the study group for their vigorous participation, Andrew Loewinger for preparing summaries of the discussion, Carol Richmond for secretarial help, and Jennifer Widner for editorial assistance. Particular thanks go to Jennifer Seymour Whitaker for her many substantive and editorial contributions.

The views and interpretations expressed in each chapter are those of the author personally and should not be attributed to the institution for which he works nor to the Council on Foreign Relations.

WILLIAM J. FOLTZ
Director of the Africa Project
Council on Foreign Relations

ABBREVIATIONS

ANC	African National Congress (South Africa)
CAE	Central African Empire
CAR	Central African Republic
FNLA	Frente Nacional de Libertação de Angola
Frelimo	Frente de Libertação de Moçambique
Frolinat	Front pour la Libération Nationale du Tchad
MNR	Resistência Nacional Moçambicana
MPLA	Movimento Popular de Liberatação de Angola
NP	National Party (South Africa)
OAU	Organization of African Unity
PAC	Pan African Congress (South Africa)
Polisario	Front Populaire pour la Libération du Sakiet al-Hamra et du Rio de Oro (Western Sahara)
Renamo	See MNR
SAAF	South African Air Force
SADF	South African Defence Force
SAM	Ground-to-air missile
SLOC	Sea-lane of communication
SSC	State Security Council (South Africa)
SWAPO	South West Africa People's Organization
UNITA	União Nacional para a Independência Total de Angola
ZANLA	Zimbabwe African National Liberation Army (armed wing of ZANU)
ZANU	Zimbabwe African National Union
ZAPU	Zimbabwe African People's Union
ZIPRA	Zimbabwe People's Revolutionary Army (armed wing of ZAPU)

ARMS AND THE AFRICAN

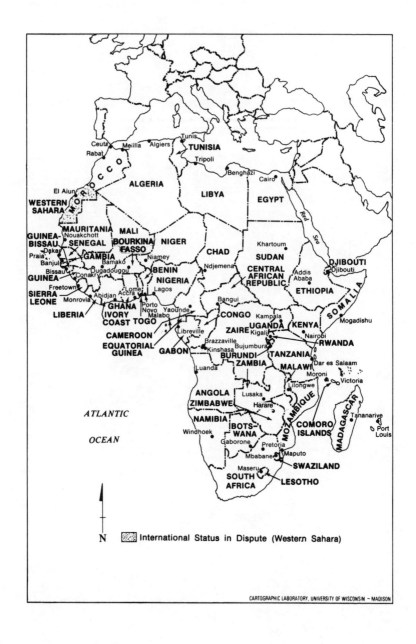

International Status in Dispute (Western Sahara)

N

ATLANTIC
OCEAN

CARTOGRAPHIC LABORATORY, UNIVERSITY OF WISCONSIN – MADISON

I

Africa in
Great-Power Strategy

WILLIAM J. FOLTZ

There seems to be a number of Christopher Columbuses setting out from the United States to discover Africa for the first time. I've got news for them. It's been there a long time.

> Prime Minister James Callaghan,
> May 31, 1978

Africa has a way of phasing in and out of Western consciousness, each time to reappear in a different guise, stimulating a different concern and intriguing or agitating a different set of Western interests and a different set of westerners. Of course, it has rarely been Africa that actively does the phasing, the disappearing and returning; rather, it has been the West that changes its interests, its enthusiasms, and its worries, that from time to time reaches out to embrace Africa, to find it suddenly relevant. As the interests change, Africa recedes again from Western consciousness or becomes the focus of a new group of enthusiasts who reshape its image in the world's eye. And then the process may repeat itself, with Africa reemerging in an old and forgotten disguise, to be greeted once more with the strangely comforting reflection *ex Africa semper aliquid novi.*

The concerns of the world's great powers have changed again, and Africa has perforce emerged anew in an old guise; again it has become a strategic battleground. A glance at history may permit us some perspective on present-day strategic concerns and some

1

opportunity to learn from the abundant miscalculations of others in the past. Although the present strategic competition in, around, and over African territory bears all the outward signs specific to the last quarter of the twentieth century, it has deeper roots that constrain and shape the way that competition is played out. These produce certain continuities and recurrences that are not simply fortuitous. They derive from enduring structures governing Africa's interactions with the rest of the world, notably Africa's geographic position and the military and economic weakness of its peoples in comparison to distant nations able to reach Africa's shores.

AFRICA'S STRATEGIC ROLES

Africa has historically been allotted five roles in great-power strategic calculations: that of physical obstacle (or resting point on the way to someplace important); that of defensive bastion to protect sea-lanes heading elsewhere; that of launching pad for attacks against other territory; that of source of military supplies, and finally, that of surrogate terrain where great powers could compete symbolically without bearing the full costs of destruction.[1]

Obstacle. Viewed from western Europe or the eastern coast of the Americas, Africa is a geographic obstacle whose vast bulk lies athwart direct seaborne lines of access to Asia. The routes eventually developed by western European nations, both around the Cape of Good Hope and through the Suez Canal, have been essential to European expansion and domestic economic development. They have outflanked the lands controlled by Islam and Muscovy, which otherwise would have dominated Western commerce and communication with the East. From the perspective of Moscow and particularly of the Middle Eastern powers, of course, Africa historically has been a useful buffer, protecting them from flanking attacks from western Europe and giving them leverage on European economic activities. Vasco da Gama's opening of the Cape

1. For a comparable catalog, see Chester A. Crocker, "Statement," pp. 126–51, in U.S. House of Representatives, Subcommittee on Africa, Committee on Foreign Affairs, *Hearings on U.S. Interests in Africa,* Ninety-sixth Cong. First Sess., October–November 1979.

route to the Indies produced the first permanent European settlements along the East African coast; they served as refreshment stations on the long voyage, though most European powers found the islands of the Indian Ocean (Madagascar and Mauritius) and the South Atlantic (St. Helena and the Azores) more convenient and certainly less troublesome.

As trade and competition among the European powers increased, the Atlantic islands were depleted of their resources (St. Helena's wild pigs and goats were exterminated by the 1640s), and new sailing technology permitted ship captains to be more selective in their landfalls along the smooth African coastline. Permanent settlement on the African coast became a necessary adjunct to the expansion of Europe's trade with the East and—once the development of the triangular trade with the Americas began in earnest—with the West as well. The African coast became the source of way stations for a trade that principally looked elsewhere for its rewards.

Sea-Lanes. Way stations do not long remain passive installations. Potentially they threaten passage by ships of other nations. The West African forts had cannon facing to the sea, not inland, so that they could protect themselves against attack and deter hostile powers from using the landfall. The 1649 *Remonstrance* to the directors of the Dutch East Indies Company arguing for the establishment of a refreshment station used as its clinching argument the warning "that, if the Cape was not occupied by the Dutch, it might be used by 'our public enemies the Spanish and Portuguese' as a base for attacking Dutch ships."[2] Control over the African coast thus became strategically important to protect seaborne commerce, particularly at such obviously sensitive choke points as the eastern and western ends of the Mediterranean and the Cape. It was on these areas that the British and French—the successors to the Portuguese and Dutch as the great powers of western Europe—concentrated their efforts. It provided impulsion for the French conquest of Algeria and its "protectorate" over Morocco

2. M. F. Katzen, "White Settlers and the Origin of a New Society, 1652–1778," in Monica Wilson and Leonard M. Thompson, eds., *The Oxford History of South Africa,* vol. 1 (New York: Oxford University Press, 1969), pp. 187–232.

and for the complex nineteenth-century rivalry between Britain and France over Egypt, as well as the central rationale for British presence in South Africa.

The opening of the Suez Canal in 1869 extended the stretch of the African coast that became relevant to the strategic protection of the routes of empire, and by increasing trade with the East and lowering transit costs, it heightened European concern with all those coastal parts of Africa that might potentially control the sea-lanes or those inland parts that might affect the stability of the coast. The scramble to divide up Africa in the 1880s had its origins in these European perceptions of strategic imperatives.[3]

Closer to our own era, western control over Africa in World War II played an important role in supporting Allied military operations in the Middle East, as, in effect, air routes replaced or at least supplemented sea routes in strategic importance. The U.S. Air Transport Command flew supplies from the continental United States via an extended route including typically stops in the Caribbean, Natal (Brazil), Ascension, Dakar, Kano, Khartoum, and Cairo to eventual destinations in the Middle East or even South Asia. The African routes declined relatively in importance after 1944 when the United States opened an airfield in the Azores and the Allies reasserted control over the Mediterranean.[4]

Launching Pad. The use of parts of the African littoral for sea-lane protection requires only the most minimal occupation. Most occupation for defensive purposes indeed comes about principally to ensure that someone else will not use the littoral for offensive purposes. For the dominant sea power of any age, denying an enemy use of a littoral is more important than acquiring the land itself; inevitably, though, acquisition will appear to be the surest method of denial, even if it also is the most expensive. For those who would attack, however, acquisition of the coastline, and of enough hinterland to protect the coastline, is essential—particularly if the attacker does not enjoy overall maritime ascendancy.

3. Ronald Robinson and John Gallagher with Alice Denny, *Africa and the Victorians: The Climax of Imperialism in the Dark Continent* (New York: St. Martin's Press, 1961).

4. Simon Rigge, *War in the Outposts* (Washington: Time-Life Books, 1981), p. 22.

The Barbary pirates represented a response by the Muslims of the Maghrib to Christian powers' domination of Mediterranean commerce, a response that put to use their principal strategic resource, firm control of the North African littoral.[5]

In World War II, Germany and Italy sought to use their North African holdings to interrupt Allied Mediterranean communications, and in turn the Allies used North Africa as a launching pad for their conquest of Italy and further advance into Germany itself. This latter role was foreshadowed in the geopolitical writings of Mackinder and Spykman, who came to see a rimland stretching from the southern shore of the Mediterranean across the Middle East and South Asia eventually to Japan as essential to control over the heartland (Germany and/or Russia).[6] With the coming of the cold war, the United States enthusiastically annexed North Africa to the rimland as part of its strategy of containing the Soviet Union.

> From this rimland, nuclear armed B-36 bombers could strike at Soviet military concentrations if required; war supplies could be pre-stocked with assurance they would not fall into adversary hands; Soviet maritime and naval activities could be kept under surveillance; facilities in North Africa and Middle Africa could be used to transport . . . equipment into the Middle East; communications and other intelligence activities could be carried out in comparative security; antisubmarine patrols in the Atlantic, the Red Sea, and the Indian Ocean could be facilitated.[7]

In the early 1950s the United States constructed four air bases in Morocco and built a major strategic base, Wheelus Field, in Libya and a substantial communications and electronic intercept station in Ethiopia. Smaller bases owned by the European colonial powers were informally regarded as useful backup assets for the NATO alliance. U.S. interest in the politics of the area was secondary to its strategic concerns. It negotiated for the Moroccan bases

5. Philip Curtin, Steven Feierman, Leonard Thompson, and Jan Vansina, *African History* (Boston: Little, Brown, 1978), p. 190.

6. Halford J. MacKinder, "The Geographical Pivot of History," *Geographical Journal* 23, no. 4 (1904), and Nicholas Spykman, *The Geography of the Peace* (New York: Harcourt Brace, 1944).

7. William H. Lewis, "How a Defense Planner Looks at Africa," in Helen Kitchen, ed., *Africa: From Mystery to Maze* (Lexington, Mass.: Lexington Books, 1976), p. 278.

with the French, and ignored the Moroccan king; it sponsored Libyan independence as the best way of freezing out the Soviets (who had once sought to exercise a UN trusteeship over Libya) and bringing to power a compliant government under King Idris. These installations have all fallen victim to the combined forces of African revolutionary nationalism and technological change. The former has greatly increased the cost of keeping the installations in place; the latter has diminished their value in comparison to newer technologies.

Strategic Resources. Beginning with the Portuguese in the fifteenth century, great powers have seized parts of the African littoral for reasons of wider global strategy.[8] Once established on the ground, however, they have usually sought to derive secondary benefit from their occupation by exploiting and exporting African resources of strategic interest to the metropole. As the initial geostrategic raison d'être for the occupation waned, the hunt for strategic resources often took over as chief justification for spending the king's purse or the taxpayers' money on a far-flung venture. In strict financial terms, very few of these African ventures paid their way. Most often, the trading companies procured state subsidies on the grounds that they were serving national strategic and political interests, while strategists argued that continued occupation was justified by the promise of future riches and irreplaceable products to be pulled from the soil and the sweat of the local inhabitants.[9] And to those skeptical statesmen, convinced free traders, and socialists who argued that occupation achieved nothing came the reply that "if it was not practical politics . . . to take on more starveling African colonies, neither was it practical politics to let foreign powers annex the fields of their strategic and commercial interests, however small they might be."[10]

8. Bailey W. Diffie and George D. Winius, *Foundation of the Portuguese Empire, 1415–1580* (Minneapolis: University of Minnesota Press, 1977), pp. 407–15.

9. See, for example, the conclusions of Henri Brunschwig, *Mythes et Réalités de L'Impérialisme Colonial Français 1871–1914* (Paris: Colin, 1960), and R. J. Hammond, *Portugal and Africa, 1850–1910: A Study in Uneconomic Imperialism* (Stanford: Stanford University Press, 1966).

10. Ronald Robinson, "European Imperialism and Indigenous Reactions in British West Africa, 1880–1914," in H. J. Wesseling, ed., *Expansion and Reaction* (Leiden: Leiden University Press, 1978), p. 150.

This denial argument is at its strongest when applied to resources and commodities of particular strategic interest rather than to the majority of commodities of more general economic interest, where the efficiency of the free market would dominate. In fact, serious attempts to derive strategic resources from Africa are of quite recent date, and the colonial powers looked first to the Africans themselves. French colonial enthusiasts in the early twentieth century looked to African manpower—*la force noire*—to compensate for France's low birthrate and staff an army capable of recovering the lost provinces of Alsace and Lorraine.[11] Indeed, some 188,000 West African troops fought in France during World War I. Smaller numbers of African troops were used between the wars, in particular for putting down strikers and rioters in France, and later in colonial action in Madagascar, Indochina, and Algeria. The British raised 470,000 African troops in World War II, and some 100,000 of these were involved in the Burma campaign.[12] Though minerals began to be exported from southern Africa in the 1880s, it was not until World War II when uranium from the Belgian Congo helped fuel the Manhattan Project that African mineral production began to become a crucial strategic resource for Western advanced technology and war-making potential.[13] Since then, rapid technological development has greatly increased the importance of African minerals, most of them lying from Zaire's copper belt south to the Cape, even as it has shifted substantially the relative importance of these minerals.

Surrogate Terrain. Great-power expansion into Africa, as we now appreciate, has stemmed from and been maintained by highly complex motives, not easily reduced to any single-factor explanation. Much research has shown that in thinking about their African ventures, great-power statesmen paid more attention to their rivalries with other great powers than to the contemporary or po-

11. Charles Mangin, *La Force Noire* (Paris: Hachette, 1910), and Leland Conley Barrows, "L'Influence des Conquêtes Coloniales sur L'Armée Française 1830-1919," *Le Mois en Afrique*, no. 192-93 (December 1981–January 1982): 97-127.

12. Eugene P. A. Schleh, "The Post-War Careers of Ex-Servicemen in Ghana and Uganda," *Journal of Modern African Studies* 6, no. 2 (1968): 203.

13. Gregg Herken, *The Winning Weapon: The Atomic Bomb in the Cold War, 1945-1950* (New York: Vintage Books, 1982), pp. 102-05 and passim.

tential realities of the African continent itself. Thus Africa came to play a role as surrogate terrain where powers could play out these rivalries at less cost to themselves (if not the Africans) than they could at home or in more economically valuable parts of the world. The advantages obtained were usually more symbolic than tangible, but important nonetheless. Africa provided a scorecard for tallying national prowess, useful for intimidating opponents abroad and political opposition at home.

Within each of the principal European countries, the initiative in African matters was seized by comparatively disadvantaged, peripheral, or newly established parts of the private and public sectors. They saw in Africa a new field of action that was not already preempted by the most powerful and prestigious industries and commercial groups or by the senior branches of government service whose members were recruited from the oldest and "best" families. For parts of the newly vigorous middle class, product of Europe's Industrial Revolution, Africa represented a new frontier of opportunity to display their talents and prowess and thus continue their social rise at home. Against the disdain of the established private and public interests, and over the protests of most spokesmen for the working class that funds for African ventures could better be spent at home, the new groups formed colonial lobbies to preach the strategic importance of Africa and the need to expand national grandeur and defend national honor through bold African ventures. By distinguishing themselves in Africa, these new groups sought to win honor at home, just as they preached that by winning advantage on the African continent, their countries could win prestige in the councils of Europe.

The wiliest of statesmen, Bismarck, at first successfully resisted such blandishments and turned such enthusiasms to advantage by subtly encouraging British and French interests in Africa—thus exacerbating their rivalry and distracting France from its obsession with *ravanche* for the loss of Alsace and Lorraine in 1871. Even Bismarck soon found, however, that for all he might look on African colonial expeditions as *Schwindel* "sham," they stirred an echo in public opinion and had their electoral uses. Once his eyes were turned to Africa, and as Britain, France, and even the king of the Belgians began to assert formal control over more and more of the continent, Bismarck, too, was seized with a *Torschlusspanik,* the fear that the other powers would permanently exclude Germany from access to Africa's supposed vast resources.[14] Germany joined the scramble for African possessions, with its colonial lobby joining in the agitation for a battle fleet, thus setting Wilhelmine Germany on "the ruinous path of *Weltpolitik.*"[15] At the same time, increased German activity in Africa spurred on the British, especially in East and southern Africa, to assert formal control for fear that its new rival would subvert that minimal degree of sullen acquiescence in British designs by local white, Arab, and African elites needed to protect imperial control of its strategic hinterland.

Perhaps the purest use of African ventures for symbolic aggrandizement was Italy's attempt to conquer Ethiopia. The first try failed abjectly in the face of Ethiopian tenacity at Adowa in 1896. The second attempt, under the fascist regime, succeeded—if not really in increasing Italian prestige abroad, then at least in defeating the Ethiopian army and most certainly in sounding the death knell of the League of Nations.[16]

In all these historic cases, the symbolism of an African presence has provided the paramount motive for the newer and weaker powers that sought external acceptance, for unsteady governments that sought popular support, and for colonial lobbyists to advance into the front ranks at home. The dominant great powers, Great Britain in the nineteenth century, like Portugal in the fifteenth, responded not so much to the symbolic challenge (though that was not without its effects) as to perturbations in convenient and low-cost informal arrangements on the African continent and to the possibility that other powers' actions in Africa would threaten strategic interests elsewhere. Direct confrontations between major powers in Africa produced little more than sound and fury at the time, but they helped destroy the informal rules of the game and

14. See Jean Stengers, "British and German Imperial Rivalry: A Conclusion," pp. 337–47, and Henry A. Turner, Jr., "Bismarck's Imperial Venture: Anti-British in Origin?" pp. 47–82, in Prosser Gifford and W. Roger Louis, *Britain and Germany in Africa: Imperial Rivalry and Colonial Rule* (New Haven: Yale University Press, 1969).

15. Hans-Ulrich Wehler, "German Imperialism: Robinson and Gallagher and Bismarck's Colonial Policy," in W. Roger Louis, ed., *Imperialism: The Robinson and Gallagher Controversy* (New York: New Viewpoints, 1976), p. 211.

16. A. J. Barker, *The Civilizing Mission: A History of the Italo-Ethiopian War of 1935–1936* (New York: Dial Press, 1968).

contributed to the breakdown of world peace in 1914 and again in 1939.

Now, the questions should be raised as to whether once again great-power rivalry in Africa can destabilize the informal arrangements on which international peace rests and—more important perhaps to Africans—whether the playing out of great-power rivalries will lead outside powers to attempt to reassert control over the African continent.

WHAT PROMPTS WHICH ROLE?

Great-power focus on Africa has alternated with periods, sometimes long periods, of neglect, in which it appeared that the continent played only a minor role in strategic rivalry. Through most of the eighteenth century, for example, the great powers played out their overseas rivalries in the New World and to a lesser extent in Asia. The Napoleonic Wars briefly drew a few coastal parts of Africa in as minor adjuncts to the larger struggle on the European continent; when European relations were stabilized by the Concert of Europe and the wider seas were brought under Britannia's sway, Africa again became militarily irrelevant. The 1870s, beginning with the assertion of formal British control over Egypt, inaugurated the intense strategic competition played out in the scramble to divide up the continent among the European powers. Although the outbreak of the Great War once again relegated African competition to sideshow status, this phase might be said to have lasted until the formal disposal of the German colonies in the 1919 Treaty of Versailles. The 1935 Italian invasion of Ethiopia returned Africa to the realm of strategic competition, which persisted through World War II and the early years of the cold war. The phasing out of American strategic bases in North Africa and the withdrawal of European powers from formal colonial control in the early 1960s again sharply reduced Africa's military interest to the outside world. The Soviet Union's defeat—at the hands of the United States working through the United Nations—in its attempt to play a military role in the Congo transferred great-power competition in sub-Saharan Africa from the military to the political and economic realms. The collapse of the Portuguese empire in 1974 and the successful projection of Soviet military force in Angola the following year made Africa once again the site of strategic competition—a status that shows no sign of early reversal.

How are we to explain these alterations in great-power strategic competition over Africa and over specific parts of the African continent? What determines which of the aforementioned strategic roles will be thrust upon the continent, what form great-power competition will take, and what the consequences will be for Africa? History suggests that the interactions of four factors can be determinant: the distribution of military power among the great powers, the state of indigenous African political activity, changes in military and industrial technology, and Africa's proximity to other areas of economic importance or to vital transport routes to those areas.

Military Power. Africa's periods of seeming strategic irrelevance, when it was least affected by great-power strategic rivalries, have coincided with periods in which one power or another held undoubted preeminence in the ability to project military power. Conversely, the more equally matched were the powers, the more credible were the threats one could offer to another's world position, the more likely was Africa to become a focus of strategic rivalry, and the greater were the consequences for Africa.

Two qualifications should immediately be entered. First, it would be incorrect to say that from the sixteenth century on Africa has ever been totally strategically irrelevant; rather, through long periods, it has been an obstacle for lesser powers and an important way station and launching pad for the dominant power whose principal interests lay elsewhere. So long as they were not seriously threatened, these stations could be small and lightly armed and needed no significant strategic hinterland. With only minimal levels of coercive power available, the settlements either were established in lightly populated areas (the Cape peninsula) or came to terms on a mutually beneficial basis with collaborating African authorities (the West and East African coasts).

Second, the key element of military strength on which strategic competition in Africa has depended is not the overall military balance among the powers as measured in size of armies, armaments, or military budget but the much more specific ability to project ef-

fective force thousands of miles away from the metropole at a level
that has some hope of effecting military outcomes. In the nineteenth century Africa's insulation from great-power military competition ended not when Germany and France developed great
continental armies but when they developed navies and naval infantry capable of defeating African opposition and at any specific
location of facing down routine coastal patrols from other powers.
In this sense, what is relevant for a peripheral area like Africa is the
acquisition by challenger states of a certain *absolute* level of effective power projection capability rather than the overall strategic
balance among the powers. In the Congo crisis of 1960–61 the Soviet Union quickly learned that it lacked the minimum level of in-
terventionary power to be effective, even locally, in a militarily
competitive situation in tropical Africa. This "lesson of the Congo"
(reinforced perhaps by Khrushchev's failure in the Cuban missile
crisis) kept Africa out of direct great-power strategic confrontation
until the Angolan war of 1975. By then the Soviet Union had acquired the military transport capacity and an effective allied intervention force that allowed it to determine the war's outcome in
the absence of a major military commitment from the United
States—which neither the American Congress nor the American
people was prepared to accept.

African Nationalism. Africa has never been just a passive
plaything of outside interests. Various African groups have resisted
great-power incursions, and others have sought to turn them to
their advantage in local struggles for power and preeminence, in
the process often playing off one outside power against another.
The long period of seeming strategic irrelevance that preceded the
scramble of the 1880s was one in which limited great-power aims,
particularly British, were assured through mostly informal under-
standings with various collaborationist elites. These aims were for
the most part quite limited, as we have seen, and the commitments
and impositions on both sides of the bargain were limited as well.
This particular version of the Pax Britannica began to unravel
when the early stirrings of nationalism on the continent began to
challenge the collaborationist elites' control. First in Egypt, then in
the Boer republics of South Africa, and then throughout the continent, these local struggles for power opened up opportunities for

outsiders to intervene in support of dissident African groups.[17] Concurrently, the hope of attracting outside support stimulated increasingly autonomous action by new African claimants for power. The regionally dominant great powers responded militarily by increasing the repressive forces they committed to their African spheres of influence and diplomatically by turning these informal spheres of influence into formally demarcated areas of direct, sovereign control. These military resources, initially introduced to withstand challenges from other great powers, were then turned to subjugate local African groups and to install effective colonial control on the ground as a means of stabilizing an increasingly chaotic situation.

The rise of modern African nationalism following World War II occurred in a period of unchallenged Western military hegemony in Africa and was accommodated, if not always encouraged, by a United States secure in its sense of regional strategic superiority over the Soviet Union and confident in its ability to maintain the new African states within a broad Western sphere of economic influence. So long as the few important economic links were maintained and the Soviet Union lacked the means to challenge Western strategic superiority, East-West political and ideological rivalry was played out without serious consequences or commitment of resources by either side. Such signs of African disaffection as African socialism, positive neutralism, and the occasional bestowal of Lenin Peace Prizes on African leaders who made appropriate rhetorical noises aroused little sustained concern in Washington, London, or Paris. Similarly, Moscow had little compunction about abandoning self-proclaimed Marxist-Leninist revolutionary groups and establishing friendly state-to-state relations with the most capitalist and neocolonialist regimes.[18] The competition was political, not military, and it aroused only passing inter-

17. Agatha Ramm, "Great Britain and France in Egypt, 1876–1882," in Prosser Gifford and W. Roger Louis, eds., *France and Britain in Africa* (New Haven: Yale University Press, 1971), pp. 73–120, and Deryck M. Schreuder, *The Scramble for Southern Africa, 1877–1895: The Politics of Partition Reappraised* (New York: Cambridge University Press, 1980).

18. William J. Foltz, "Le Parti Africain de l'Indépendance: Les Dilemmes d'un Mouvement Communiste en Afrique Occidentale," *Revue Française D'Études Politiques Africaines*, no. 45 (September 1969):8–35.

est on either side of the cold war.[19] When on rare occasions serious strategic interests were at stake, as during the Cuban missile crisis when the Soviets sought to use the airfield in Guinea as a transit stop, U.S. pressure on Sekou Touré's government sufficed to close the airfield to flights from what was at the time its principal economic and diplomatic patron.

Since World War II, southern Africa has provided the most complicated terrain for great-power relations with African nationalist forces. In South Africa, which from an Olympian point of view can be considered a case of split nationalism, the United States, like other Western powers, has essentially accommodated the white nationalist group in power, while taking occasional, and largely symbolic, steps to avoid a total break with local black nationalist forces. Since for most of the postwar period the whites have appeared securely in power, even these limited steps have been dictated at least as much by a desire to avoid complicating relations with independent black nationalist regimes in the rest of Africa as by any commitment to force a substantial change in the status quo.[20] It has been principally after incidents (such as the Soweto upheavals of 1976) in which black South African nationalists have reminded the world of their potential power that sympathetic groups within the Western states have been able to decrease their governments' level of cooperation with the white nationalist regime, largely by arguing that it would be prudent to start hedging one's bet against the day when a more substantial shift of power takes place.

The one sustained exception to the United States' willingness to accommodate at least some variety of African nationalism occurred in Portuguese-ruled Africa. In this case, those who argued the importance of considerations of global strategy prevailed over those who emphasized longer-range calculations of political advantage in Africa. Not only did Portugal refuse obdurately to advance its African "provinces" to independence, it made clear that

19. Robert Legvold, *Soviet Policy in West Africa* (Cambridge: Harvard University Press, 1970), and Waldemar A. Nielsen, *The Great Powers and Africa* (New York, Praeger, 1969).

20. I have discussed this further in "The United States and South Africa," in Study Commission on U.S. Policy toward Southern Africa, *South Africa: Time Running Out* (Berkeley and Los Angeles: University of California Press, 1981), pp. 340–65.

it expected its NATO allies at least to tolerate its policies in exchange for leasing to the United States substantial naval and air facilities on the Azores Islands. The Azores' importance to the United States was indeed manifest when they served as critical transit points for resupplying Israel during the 1967 and 1973 wars in the Middle East. Southern Africa's place in the hierarchy of the United States' concerns was made clear in 1963 when President Kennedy made the decision to avoid jeopardizing the Azores base through public pressure on Portugal while courting black African opinion through a unilateral embargo on the supply of arms to the Republic of South Africa.[21]

The sudden collapse of Portuguese African rule in 1975 left the United States to face the longer-term consequences of its strategic choice. Having done little to assist the most effective nationalist movements, or even to know well their leaders and aims, the United States was poorly placed to influence their actions. In Angola, where the secretary of state decided such influence was important, the United States was obliged to act indirectly through the South African and Zairian regimes and fully shared the blame for the intervention's failure.

Western inability or unwillingness to back cohesive and majoritarian nationalist movements in southern Africa opened up opportunities for the Soviet Union to intervene and for African groups to draw Soviet military resources to their side in a complex struggle. We know too few details of Soviet decision making on African matters to assess confidently the calculations that have attended their African adventures, but there can be no doubt that pull factors appear to operate independently of any generalized push from within the Soviet government to intervene. The record of Soviet involvement in Angola, for example, shows that the Soviet government initially refused MPLA requests for military advisers and throughout the war responded cautiously to Cuban and

21. Arthur M. Schlesinger, Jr., *A Thousand Days: John F. Kennedy in the White House* (Boston: Houghton Mifflin, 1965), pp. 562–63, 582–83. During World War II the Azores base had been deemed important enough that the United States acceded to Portuguese insistence and provided the first guarantee given a colonial power that a particular part of its empire would remain inviolate after the war. See John A. L. Sullivan, "The United States, The East Indies and World War II: American Efforts to Modify the Colonial Status Quo" (Ph.D. diss., University of Massachusetts, 1968), pp. 162–82.

Angolan initiatives and needs, often with considerable delay.[22] In Angola, as in many other African situations, Soviet involvement appears to have been spurred additionally by a desire to counteract or to preempt Chinese influence within radical African movements, influence felt to be deleterious to Soviet positions elsewhere in the Third World.[23]

Like the United States, the Soviet Union seems to become involved in Africa in response to specific situational pressures and in response to highly ranked considerations of general international political and military strategy at least as much as to any specifically African plan of action. Overall, divisions within African nationalist movements have the effect of drawing in Soviet influence, which in turn often exacerbates the divisions. Within southern Africa, a ranking of African nationalist movements from least to most divided (i.e., Mozambique, Namibia, Zimbabwe, Angola) neatly parallels a scale of increasing Soviet military involvement and influence. There is nothing magical about this tendency; rather, it results from a more general propensity of African movements and governments to invite outside military involvement only when needed for survival. The dramatic reversal of alliances in the Horn of Africa in 1977–78 provides a good example of this propensity. Survival considerations become particularly acute for a nationalist movement when it faces opposition from a rival movement as well as from the objectionable regime in power. In such a case, merely hanging on and continuing the struggle will little avail the movement should rivals, meanwhile, defeat the regime and assume power to the plaudits of the neighboring states that provide the movement sanctuary and support.

In the past decade, then—as was the case a century before—local political competition in Africa has provided opportunities for previously uninterested outside powers to intervene. These opportunities often have taken the form of appeals for assistance from local groups, which then strengthened the case of those within the great power's councils who sought such intervention for their own strategic reasons. These reasons have often had little to do with the

22. William M. Leo Grande, *Cuba's Policy in Africa, 1959–1980* (Berkeley: University of California Institute of International Studies, 1980).

23. Colin Legum, *After Angola: The War over Southern Africa* (New York: Africana, 1978).

details of the specific African situation, and actions predicated on them often led to unforeseen and unintended consequences.

Changes in Technology. Africa first became an active factor in great-power calculations with the development of sailing technology that permitted reasonable assurance that ships sent out along the coast would eventually return home. Penetration and conquest of the interior took place only when the machine gun and modern medicine made them possible at low cost.[24] In our own time the development of physical and electronic communications technology has made virtually all the continent accessible to outsiders and therefore potentially strategically relevant. However, the rapid succession of new technologies has produced (usually with some perceptual lag) equally rapid shifts in strategists' attention to different parts of the continent. The United States' immediate postwar interest in North African strategic bases waned when the rimland-basing strategy was made obsolete by the development of intercontinental ballistics missiles, which could be based at home, and shorter-range missiles, which could be effectively concealed beneath the sea in submarines ranging widely from a few secure home ports. Whereas the French relied on Saharan sites to test their first primitive nuclear weapons, advances in monitoring techniques allowed them subsequently to shift their operations to less politically sensitive areas of the Pacific. Similarly, the development of increasingly sophisticated and reliable satellites allowed the United States to phase out its communications and listening installation in Ethiopia and has reduced the importance of a ground-based listening establishment like South Africa's Project Advokaat. Although the previous African basing mode might still have been technically viable, once political costs were added into the strategic calculations, the strategic appeal of African geography was no longer competitive with other options. As the political costs are not likely to diminish, nor is the development of remote sensing devices likely to be reversed, this aspect of technological change is likely to reduce Africa's strategic importance.

By contrast, changes in industrial technology have increased

24. John Ellis, *The Social History of the Machine Gun* (New York: Pantheon Books, 1975), and Daniel R. Headrick, *The Tools of Empire: Technology and European Imperialism in the Nineteenth Century* (Oxford: Oxford University Press, 1981).

Africa's strategic relevance to the great powers, particularly to those of the West. When the industrial world ran on coal and iron, the continent of Africa hardly entered into great-power thinking as a provider of strategic materials for their factories and war machines. Through most of World War II Africa's principal commodity contributions to the Allied war effort were agricultural—vegetable fats, oils, and rubber—and all eminently replaceable by production elsewhere in the world or by substitute products. Copper and chrome were also significant, but Africa was one among many sources of Allied supply. Uranium was the first African mineral whose supply from the then Belgian Congo in the closing years of World War II was deemed essential to Western security. The Congo was quickly replaced as the prime uranium source by South Africa—which had previously treated the mineral as an exotic and uneconomic by-product of gold mining. Greatly increased demand soon led to worldwide prospecting and proving of reserves to the point now where no single uranium provider or geographic region can expect to obtain any significant political or economic leverage independent of the play of a broadly based world market.

The development of space-age technology in the past quarter-century has, however, greatly increased the importance for industrial production, and especially military production, of a few minerals whose principal sources of current supply and presently known reserves are concentrated both in Africa south of the equator and within the Soviet sphere of control. Those of undoubted importance for which reliable and efficient substitutes or adequate alternative sources of supply are unlikely to be produced during the 1980s are chromium (found in Zimbabwe and South Africa), cobalt (found in Zaire and Zambia), and manganese (found in Gabon and South Africa). Much public attention had recently been focused on these strategic minerals—not a little of it orchestrated by the South African information services and by London and New York commodity brokers who have discovered a common interest in raising a specter of the West's being threatened with a mineral "resource war."[25]

25. For examples, see *The Resource War and the U.S. Business Community: The Case for a Council on Economics and National Security* (Washington: Council on Economics and National Security, 1980), and Dirk T. Kunert, *South Africa: Supermarket of the World's Minerals* (Johannesburg: Southern African Forum, 1981).

If one sets aside the heady, but short-term, concerns of the commodity traders and views the issue from the longer-range perspective of security concerns, two points seem important. First, the overwhelming strategic interest of the Western powers lies in assuring continued *access* to these minerals (as opposed to a specific corporation's interest in their ownership) and to the maintenance of stable conditions of production and evacuation so that world market pricing mechanisms are not artificially disrupted. On recent evidence, such access and production have proved to be highly resilient, surviving sanctions, guerrilla war and dramatic political change in Zimbabwe, and two disruptive invasions into Zaire's cobalt-producing Shaba Province. No African government of whatever ideological or dermatological complexion has shown the slightest hesitation in selling its production to the highest reliable bidder, nor is any African economy in such robust shape that any national leader is likely to attempt to do so. What would threaten access and production would be a total collapse of social and economic order in the subequatorial region to the point where neither production nor evacuation routes could be maintained or, somewhat more plausibly, the widespread physical destruction of productive infrastructure, such as would follow from an all-out conventional, main-force military confrontation that turned into an extended war of attrition. Such eventualities would reflect gross political mismanagement on the part of those nations interested in continued access to southern Africa's minerals.

The second major point is that there is a substantial imbalance between the concerns of the East and the West in the strategic mineral resources of southern Africa. Western industry must import these minerals; the Soviet Union produces enough for its own needs and for export. Although it is conceivable that the Soviet Union could profit from significantly disrupting Western access to southern African minerals, such disruption would require substantial efforts on its part. Either it would have to engage directly in main-force military confrontation or it would have to acquire thoroughgoing political domination, backed up with massive economic support, over a substantial part of the region, including the Republic of South Africa. This would require an effort substantially

---

For a calmer perspective, see Michael Shafer, "Mineral Myths," *Foreign Policy*, no. 47 (Summer 1982): 154–71.

greater than any the Soviets have expended anywhere beyond their immediate borders and would divert resources needed to control those borders.

Petroleum, of course, is in a class by itself as a modern strategic resource by the scale of world requirements rather than by virtue of its scarcity or the limited number of its suppliers. As in the case of the minerals just discussed, great-power concern is unbalanced, since the Soviet Union at present meets all its domestic requirements and is likely to meet the bulk of them through the remainder of the decade. Africa has been a significant petroleum provider only since the mid-1960s. The continent is currently the source of 8 percent of world petroleum production, three-fourths of that coming from just three countries, Libya, Algeria, and Nigeria. Recently increased exploration suggests that the West African littoral on either side of Nigeria from Ivory Coast through Angola may become a significant factor in world production by the end of the 1980s. Although a specific African country may at a particular moment enjoy a privileged position as a supplier to a particular Western country, the African producers as a group are not likely to attain significant independent leverage on the importing countries. The more African countries become important producers and increase the world supply, the less leverage any single producer or group of producers can exercise and the greater the political and practical difficulties African and other nations will encounter in trying to constrict supply artificially. Of all present African producers, only Libya has a scale of production large enough in relation to its population and basic economic needs to allow it credibly to threaten to withhold production from the world market. But so long as Libya's leader persists in his penchant for expensive arms purchases and quixotic foreign policy adventures, that country will remain dependent on a steady flow of earnings from selling oil to the West. The Western powers thus have an economic interest in furthering the expansion of African petroleum production and multiplying the number of states contributing to that production. If the Soviet Union is obliged to enter the world market for petroleum by the end of the 1980s, as the U.S. Central Intelligence Agency has predicted, it most probably will share that interest.[26]

26. Thane Gustafson, "Energy and the Soviet Bloc," *International Security*, Winter 1982, pp. 65–89.

Overall, the Western powers' strategic interests in the minerals of Africa south of the equator would seem to be under no immediate or even foreseeable threat and are best safeguarded through prudent policies calculated, on the one hand, to avoid massive Soviet military implantation in the region and, on the other, to facilitate at least a minimal level of stability throughout the area. Where such stability is impossible, the West should facilitate change in a manner that avoids large-scale physical destruction of productive resources and transport lines.

Changing Proximity to Strategic Routes and Resources Elsewhere. Africa's geographic location has not drifted more than a few feet in modern history, but its geographic significance has varied with changes in the economic and strategic importance of other parts of the world to the great powers and with changes in the vulnerability of the sea-lanes of communication (SLOCs) around its coasts. As we have seen, protecting the SLOCs near Africa has been a long-standing aim of any age's dominant trading nation. At present, most attention has been focused on the petroleum routes: up to 65 percent of western European and 28 percent of American oil imports pass along the Cape route in some six hundred tankers each month.[27] It is therefore understandable that many should echo the British Royal Commission on Imperial Defense, which in September 1881 proclaimed "This route must be maintained at all hazards and irrespective of costs."[28]

Maintaining a sea route, however, differs fundamentally from maintaining an interstate highway. The latter requires the frequent attention of men and machines; the former is, on balance, better assured by their absence. The danger to the SLOCs of the 1980s, as to the sea routes of the 1880s, is presumed to come from interference by another power's hostile naval forces, which would impede shipping. This was legitimately a major concern in the two world wars, which were extended wars of attrition determined ultimately by the ability of the two sides to sustain industrial production while hostilities continued. Today, a major commitment of

27. Larry Bowman, "The Strategic Importance of South Africa," *African Affairs* 81, no. 323 (April 1982): 159–92.
28. Schreuder, *The Scramble for South Africa*, p. 19.

great-power resources to defend or attack sea-lanes around Africa would make sense only under the presumption that a major confrontation would take the form of sustained combat with conventional arms. Even then effective disruption of commerce would require massive and sustained attack focused on one of the narrow passageways in which shipping would be concentrated: the Straits of Hormuz (the only passage narrow enough to permit a blockade), the Madagascar Channel (and the alternative Madagascar-Mascarene passage), the Cape of Good Hope, the Cap Vert–Cabo Verde passage, and the Canarie–Cape Bojador passage. Except for the Straits of Hormuz, which could be air mined from land bases in the USSR, the rest would require massive deployment of naval resources—pulled from tasks in more vital areas—and of air power, which would have to be land based, either in Africa or on one of the Indian Ocean or Atlantic islands. Although such a scenario seems farfetched indeed, it does point up one very important aspect of current great-power rivalry: acquisition of a major military base in or adjacent to Africa would add far more to Soviet strategic capabilities than acquisition of comparable facilities would to Western capabilities. Western strategists might therefore pay particular attention that their actions not increase the likelihood that any state along the Indian or Atlantic Ocean littoral might feel obliged to welcome a major Soviet base on its territory.[29] This asymmetry of interests is not likely to change.

Of more immediate strategic concern than the SLOCs is the continued production of oil by the nations of the Middle East and the maintenance of Western access to that oil. As Iran demonstrated, the governments of these states—and thus Western interests—are threatened at least as much by internal disruption as by external invasion, and a major great-power military presence on their soil can contribute to that disruption. The northeastern corner of Africa thus has come to be viewed as a possible base area, a return to Africa's old role as launching pad, this time for a rapid deployment force. Africa's importance for the Middle East lies both in its proximity and in the fact that it is *not* the Middle East. Thus, the rulers of oil-producing Arab nations may relax in the

29. Crocker, "Statement."

security of a great-power protective force in the neighborhood without having to suffer the symbolic humiliation of having the force quartered on their terrain or the practical fear that their own citizens may rise in fundamentalist wrath to expel the infidel presence and the regime that invited it in. The risks of such humiliation and upheaval are borne by their African neighbors. It should not be presumed that the risks of upheaval are necessarily any less, but any such untoward events are less likely to contaminate the broader Middle East environment and more likely to remain confined to intrinsically less valuable pieces of real estate. Thus, the United States has begun work in rehabilitating the former Soviet air and naval installations in Berbera, in stockpiling material and maintenance crews in Mombasa and Nairobi, and in increasing its quiet use of French naval facilities in Djibouti. The Soviet Union has countered by developing a protective anchorage and dry dock in the Dahlak Islands off Eritrea and by stockpiling material in Aden, across from Berbera. None of these facilities appears designed for strategic forces directed against the other side's homeland. Rather, they are designed to reassure friendly nations while giving others something to think about. They show the flag in the best nineteenth-century manner.

The eastern coast of Africa borders an additional area of great strategic concern, the Indian Ocean itself. This time the importance resides not in the commerce that passes over its waters but in the strategic missiles carried in submarines on patrol beneath the multiple thermal layers and currents that confuse sonic antisubmarine warfare detection systems. The United States' Trident submarines are capable of carrying missiles with a six-thousand-mile range, and this potentially makes all the Indian Ocean useful as a launching platform for the most secure and reliable nuclear delivery system the West possesses. The expansion of Soviet naval activity in the Indian Ocean that began in the late 1960s is in substantial part related to the Soviet Union's desire to search out American missile-bearing submarines.[30] In turn, the United States' development of Diego Garcia as a naval base is in substantial part

30. For informed discussions, see Bowyer Bell, "Strategic Implications of the Soviet Presence in Somalia," *Orbis* 19, no. 2 (Summer 1975): 402–11, and Michael MccGwire, Ken Booth, and John McDonnell, *Soviet Naval Policy: Objectives and Constraints* (New York: Praeger, 1975).

caused by the need to track Soviet antisubmarine forces.[31] In current doctrine, the strategic rimland has now become the ocean itself. The effect on the African mainland has yet to be determined.

WHAT NOW?

Will Africa develop further into a major focus for East-West strategic competition and conflict in the 1980s? What strategic roles might different parts of the continent play? If the precedents discussed here maintain their validity, it would seem indeed that the historical elements are present that could make some of these roles possible, though not imperative.

The decade of the 1980s is one in which no power or group of allies can exercise near-effortless sway over far-flung lands. No great power's informal dominion over any part of Africa is immune from challenge, not only by an opposing great power, but by indigenous forces as well. In this sense, the effective strength of the great powers is in decline. This is clearest for the United States as the brief era of the Pax Americana disappears below the horizon; it seems also to be the case for the Soviet Union, which has been sacrificing and scrimping at home to emulate the military ways overseas of the only great power with global reach it has known. Like its American role model, the Soviet Union has found its gigantic power tied down in foreign sands by lilliputian threads of tangled local and regional politics. Britain's formal empire was produced as a result of just such a decline of effective power, when informal pressures no longer sufficed to guarantee imperial interests against the ambitions of local leaders and European rivals.[32] Although formal empire in Africa seems indeed to have been consigned to history's dustbin, the imperial impulse survives in the temptation to tidy up Africa's ambiguities by dividing strategic parts of the continent into mutually hostile dependencies of the "free world" and the "socialist camp."

31. See U.S. House of Representatives, Subcommittee on the Near East and South Asia of the Committee on Foreign Affairs. *Hearings on Proposed Expansion of U.S. Military Facilities in the Indian Ocean.* Ninety-third Cong., Second Sess. (Washington: U.S. Government Printing Office, 1974).

32. Bernard Porter, *The Lion's Share: A Short History of British Imperialism* (New York: Longman, 1975), pp. 353–54.

Africa of the 1980s does not lack regimes unhappy with their neighbors nor rebellious population groups ready to assume a convenient ideological guise and to solicit military support from outside powers. However, it is not easy for even great powers to deliver decisive military force and also to profit substantially from having done so. Decisive military commitments are likely to be expensive; the day is past in most of Africa when a technologically superior power could send in a lightly armed group and expect the opposition to flee in terror. Most African states are quite capable of sinking gunboats off their shores, and irregular bands of mercenaries have had their wings clipped. For an outside power to operate effectively in Africa, it must operate at the invitation of a national government or recognized liberation movement. Such entities have demonstrated considerable independence and have a singular record of ingratitude toward outside patrons whose services are no longer urgently required. Africa is not, in fact, filled with puppet states and subservient neocolonies, whatever conservative U.S. senators and radical dependency theorists may think.

The provision of arms and even of substantial military encadrement to established African governments does not seriously affect the strategic balance between the major powers. What would make a serious difference, however, would be the establishment by either side of a major independent military base, the equivalent of a Wheelus Field or a Subic Bay, from which a great power could project decisive military power over a wide region. The only foreign installation on the African continent that even marginally approaches this is the French base at Djibouti, and in size and technological development this is hardly in a class with those cited. Under contemporary conditions of national sovereignty and inter-African diplomacy, such a base could be established only with the accord of an established government, which would be moved to agree only if it felt that nothing else would ensure its survival. Even then, it would appear that such a base would be at best a quick-fix solution for both the host regime and for the great power involved. Major bases are rightly feared as sources of instability, both within the host countries themselves and within their regions. They give rise to domestic opposition and invitations from nervous neighbors for an opposing power to do likewise.

The development of modern military technology has on balance decreased great-power need for military installations on African soil, while once again making smaller installations on the islands off Africa more attractive. As we have seen, however, developments in industrial technology have given the Western nations a major stake in the orderly production and marketing of minerals from central and southern Africa. Logically, this should lead the Western nations to policies that would support the power and effectiveness of central governments in that large region and a high degree of peaceful cooperation among them. At a minimum, it should call for policies designed to avoid the worst possible outcome, the massive destruction of physical infrastructure in the region. The negotiations to end civil strife and to produce majoritarian regimes in Zimbabwe and Namibia reflect, if somewhat belatedly, awareness of this interest throughout the Western Alliance.

It is in this context that South Africa poses a strategic problem for the West and a strategic opportunity for the USSR. Current South African military action is highly disruptive of regional stability, and should such action expand to the point at which neighboring regimes are seriously worried about their own survival, those regimes will have a serious incentive to take the political risks of inviting the Soviet Union to establish a major military presence and thereby to implicate them fully in the defense of the regime. So far, not even the hard-pressed Angolans have done so—or if they have tried, the Soviets have not responded—but one can expect that some level of continued threat would produce such an invitation, and some constellation of interests within the Soviet government could bring forth a positive response. Such a turn of events might well do the Soviet Union's net strategic position little good, but it doubtless would do the West's a fair amount of harm. It is surely evident that any Western attempt to set up a military base in South Africa would greatly increase the pressure on the Soviet Union to do likewise in one of the neighboring states.

The significance of Middle Eastern petroleum to the West is not likely to diminish in the next decade, and therefore the West's strategic concern with Northeast Africa is likely to remain high. The situation here is somewhat the reverse of that in southern Africa: the United States has the greater temptation to establish a major military base in Northeast Africa, whereas the Soviet Union has much to lose by a mutual escalation of strategic resources—if only because the region is so much closer to the Soviet Union than to the United States. Even then, the disruptive effect of a major American base in the region would raise costs to the West, particularly if Kenya were to dissolve in domestic turmoil. For this reason, Western interests would logically be best served by the smallest possible American presence on mainland Africa consistent with supporting some sort of rapid deployment force, should such a force continue to seem necessary to reassure the governments of the Arabian peninsula.

During the rest of the 1980s increased great-power strategic competition in Africa is decidedly possible, but far from imperative. It is difficult to make a sound rational-actor case for either superpower to decide upon a major commitment of strategic resources to the African continent. Although it might be rational for the United States and the Soviet Union to appear to be willing under some circumstances to establish a major strategic base—in order to make its opponent think twice about doing so—it would be irrational to take the lead in actually setting one up. To make such a course of action rational, it would have to be carried out as part of a massive global strategy of unremitting hostility and harassment toward the other side. Such a strategy would be based on historically dubious premises, that is, that without continued dominance over the Third World, capitalism would in short order collapse, and its counterpart, that overextended Soviet military commitments would lead to an internal revolt against Communist rule and the overthrow from within of the Soviet state. Neither regime, even now, seems seriously to believe in the utility of such a strategy.

The more realistic danger for the coming decade lies in one, and then both, of the superpowers being drawn into a major confrontation by desperate regimes or factions on a highly disordered corner of the continent. In such a situation the Africans would be, once again, certain losers. Almost as certainly, so too would be the great powers.

2

Soviet Military Policy and Arms Activities in Sub-Saharan Africa

LOUIS GEORGE SARRIS

In Moscow's view of its priorities in the Third World, sub-Saharan Africa clearly ranks below the Middle East. Nevertheless, direct Soviet involvement in Black Africa, although it coincided with the African independence process in the 1960s, increased sharply with the Angolan civil war in the mid-1970s. Soviet activities in the area are driven by pragmatic military and political interests as well as a broad strategic view of the Third World. But to a considerable degree, the pattern of Soviet conduct has been one of opportunistic action and reaction.

In his excellent overview of Soviet policies during the 1960s and 1970s, Seweryn Bialer pointed out that this was the period that the USSR "became a truly global power" and did so essentially through "low-risk and low-cost adventures without confronting a major danger of confrontation with the U.S."[1] In the turmoil besetting the less-developed world, Bialer further notes, Moscow's basic approach was to exploit "targets of opportunity." Perhaps in no area of the globe is Professor Bialer's thesis of Soviet low-cost, low-risk strategy more demonstrable than in sub-Saharan Africa.

In such a vast and complex area, the opportunities for the Soviets have indeed been many and varied. Sub-Saharan Africa only recently was the colonial domain of several Western powers, while

1. Seweryn Bialer, "Soviet Policies in the 1980s," *Foreign Affairs* 9, no. 5 (Summer 1981).

29

the Soviet Union's colonial sphere lay elsewhere. Britain and especially France still retain important political, economic, cultural, and military interests in the region, and the Soviets have attempted, with perhaps some measure of success, to portray these interests as a continuation of Western imperialism and colonialism. Whatever success the Soviets may have achieved is largely the result of efforts to identify themselves with "national liberation struggles," which remain at the core of the political dynamics of Black Africa, or, as in the case of Mengistu's Ethiopia, with "social revolution." The attractiveness for the Soviets of these opportunities is even greater when judged, on the one hand, by the relatively small albeit growing economic, political, and military investment required of Moscow and, on the other, by the absence of a serious and direct challenge from the West.

However limited Moscow's investment and opportunistic its involvement in Black Africa, there have been reverses, and even in places where the Soviets seem to be succeeding, they must have some concern for the future.

- They have been expelled from Somalia and Equatorial Guinea (and, north of the Sahara, from Egypt), have seen their military operations curtailed in Guinea, had their nationals sent home from (and their relations broken with) the Central African Republic in 1980, and have not yet been able to capitalize on their "revolutionary" involvement in Zimbabwe since independence and the formation of a government under the avowedly Marxist Robert Mugabe.[2]
- In Ethiopia, where in 1974 Addis Ababa was containing the rebellions in the north with an army of about twenty-five thousand, the war continues unabated, despite more than $3 billion in Soviet aid and an army of two hun-

---

2. Indeed, the handwriting on the wall to a Soviet failure in Zimbabwe was clear to all except Moscow in the late 1970s. Soviet efforts to modify its policy of favoring Joshua Nkomo's armed faction over Robert Mugabe's were too little, too late, and outpaced by events leading to a negotiated settlement. There is, moreover, considerable evidence that the success achieved at Lancaster House in 1979 came as a surprise to Moscow. The February 1980 elections scored a stunning defeat for Nkomo, who won only twenty seats, in contrast to Mugabe's fifty-seven.

dred thousand to three hundred thousand. The Cuban presence apparently is being drawn down significantly.

• In Mozambique, Moscow has witnessed President Samora Machel's volte-face toward South Africa in the security pact of March 1984. However galling that may be, the Soviets have not been prepared to take significant risks in Mozambique, either on their own or with the introduction of even larger numbers of Cuban military personnel, given the possibility of a strong South African military reaction.

• In Namibia, where the South West African People's Organization (SWAPO) might win in any future election, how much confidence can Moscow have that it can translate this into continuing influence—given South Africa's ability to carry out a variety of economic, political, and military measures to retain its predominant position there?

• And in Angola, despite a strong Soviet warning, continued South African aid to the UNITA insurgents and direct military attacks have brought the Luanda government into a serious negotiation with Pretoria, including talks on mutual troop withdrawals and a phasedown of the Cubans.

In short, even a pragmatic policy of opportunistic reaction does not necessarily assure the Soviets easy success or, for that matter, lessen the prospect of significant political setbacks. Moreover, as African countries are obliged by drought and hunger to focus on economic problems, the Soviets may find themselves on weaker ground, given their demonstrated inability or unwillingness to undertake long-term development assistance, required by most Black African regimes regardless of their political persuasion or ideological orientation.

SOVIET MILITARY INTERESTS AND OBJECTIVES

Reacting pragmatically to opportunities, Soviet military policy in sub-Saharan Africa has consistently pursued three basic objectives: access to military facilities to fulfill Soviet security requirements; expansion of political influence to advance Soviet prestige as a global power; and reduction of Western and other inimical foreign

influence. The relevance of one or more of these objectives to various parts of sub-Saharan Africa has varied, as have the methods
and the intensity of effort applied to achieve them. A central and
common ingredient in Soviet tactics, however, has been the provision of military assistance, openly or covertly, whose magnitude is
conspicuously greater than any economic or developmental assistance.

Soviet military interests in sub-Saharan Africa focus on access
to naval and airfield facilities. In East Africa, for example, Soviet
access to Somali naval, airfield, and communications facilities
prior to President Siad's termination of military relations with
Moscow in late 1977 strengthened Soviet naval and air deployments and surveillance capabilities in the Indian Ocean. The loss
of access to Somali facilities was compensated for by gains in Ethiopia. The use of the Asmara airfield and the dry-dock and bun-
kering facilities at Dahlak Island have the potential of extending
Soviet naval presence into the Red Sea and Soviet surveillance
into the Indian Ocean.

In West Africa, Guinea's termination in 1977 of long-standing
Soviet TU-95 flights out of Conakry reduced Soviet reconnaissance
capabilities over the North and South Atlantic. The Soviets have
partially resolved this problem by periodic deployment of TU-95s
to Angola, although the transit distance for the Angola-based operations is now more than double. The flights require more time
and effort to complete and may not cover as large an area as the
Guinea-based ones.

Perhaps the most significant immediate military advantage
gained from Soviet access to bases in sub-Saharan Africa is the reinforcement of Moscow's ability to airlift and sealift supplies and
personnel to the region. Access to facilities and transit rights in
Angola, Benin, Congo, Guinea, Mali, and Cape Verde, for example, have facilitated the movement of Cuban troops and Soviet
arms to other parts of southern and western Africa. The importance of these facilities for logistical purposes was demonstrated by
the size and decisive character of the Soviet airlift and naval re-
supply effort during the Angolan civil war.

Moscow, in pursuing its main political objectives of advancing
Soviet and countering Western influence in sub-Saharan Africa,
also attempts to project an image of support for countries that seek

to maintain the integrity of their national border or that are engaged in liberation struggles against neocolonialism. These motives are particularly applicable in southern Africa, where the political and military efforts against minority rule in Namibia and South Africa continue. Moscow has reason to believe that continued confrontation in Africa is inevitable, that the forces supported by the Soviet Union (despite any temporary setback) will be the ultimate inheritors of power, and that neither the Western powers nor the People's Republic of China (PRC) is willing or able to provide assistance on a sustained and sufficient scale to satisfy Black African military interests.

These motives are basic to Soviet actions in Ethiopia and Angola, which have been the focal points of Moscow's strategy in East and West Africa. In addition, its policy also aims at fostering ideologically based affinities with the revolutionary character of the Ethiopian and Angolan regimes, which proclaim Marxist-Leninist inspiration. Despite Mozambique's recent overtures to the West, these apply also in Maputo, where President Machel has announced the goal of establishing a socialist state. Assisting these states strengthens Moscow's claim of being in the vanguard of world socialism as well as national liberation. (Indeed, Mengistu seems to believe that Marxism-Leninism is a model for governing a multinational state, and the Soviets are helping and urging the construction of an Ethiopian Communist party, the Commission for Organizing the Party of the Working People [COPWE].) In the case of Ethiopia and Angola in particular, the size of the Soviet investment in arms and the introduction of combat forces by Moscow's Cuban ally are seen by some Third World countries as a measure not only of Moscow's determination to assist Africa but also of its ability to challenge the West directly.

Initially at least, competition with the People's Republic of China probably reinforced the USSR's other motives in sub-Saharan Africa. Moscow's initial decision to back Neto's Popular Movement for the Liberation of Angola (MPLA) during the Angolan civil war may have been partly motivated by the Soviet desire to prevent the Chinese from gaining important influence in Angola. The speed with which Moscow pursued its relationship with Ethiopia may have been influenced by a desire to prevent a major Chinese role in Addis Ababa. Similarly in Tanzania,

Moscow's accelerated arms assistance may have reflected an attempt to counter a long-standing and, until about 1974 at least, apparently successful Chinese relationship.

It is important not to overemphasize competition with China as a force driving Soviet policy in Africa. Although Beijing has since 1980 shown renewed interest in identifying itself with Black African and Third World causes, it has been unwilling or unable to back its rhetoric up with substantial material assistance. The Soviets must be well aware that China has no intention of repeating any aid effort on the spectacular scale of the railway from Zambia to the sea it built in the late 1960s. Far more important than any preemptive reaction to Chinese initiatives is Soviet exploitation of opportunities presented within Africa itself.

In pursuing its objectives in sub-Saharan Africa, Moscow has turned to some of its East European allies for assistance. In 1981, 767 East European military technicians were reported in sub-Saharan Africa. Coordination between Soviet and East European efforts is attractive, particularly since Eastern Europe can provide weaponry, spares, and ammunition compatible with Soviet systems. Indeed, in certain instances Soviet and East European countries, it should be noted, are also concerned with promoting their own individual interests and objectives. East European interests in Africa, in contrast to those of the Soviet Union, appear more commercial than geopolitical, according to some observers. They cite in particular activities in East Germany and Bulgaria (in Mozambique and Angola), Romania (in Angola and Zambia), and Poland (in Angola) and point out that every East European country except Czechoslovakia has concluded cooperation agreements with FRELIMO and that Romania is a participant in twenty joint economic partnership arrangements in sub-Sahara.[3]

With regard to Cuba, Havana's most significant involvements—in Ethiopia particularly, but also perhaps in Angola—are now being drawn down. To the present, in any case, there can be little doubt that its activities in sub-Saharan Africa have been closely coordinated with those of the Soviet Union. On the other hand, Havana is not involved in the area solely because of its ties

3. See Christopher Coker, "Adventurism and Pragmatism: The Soviet Union, COMECON, and Relations with African States," *International Affairs*, August 1981.

with Moscow. Cuba's African policy has grown out of an activist revolutionary drive and, perhaps more important, Castro's almost fanatic commitment to diminish U.S. and other Western influence in the Third World. Nevertheless, Cuba is so dependent on Soviet military and economic support that one must assume that Havana can little afford to get too far ahead of Moscow's Africa policy.

Whether or not (or to what extent) the Soviets have actually made good on Cuban losses of material, we must assume that virtually all the material cost of the Cuban presence in Africa can be borne by the USSR. It is perhaps no coincidence that from 1976 through 1981 annual Soviet seaborne deliveries to Cuba doubled to twenty thousand metric tons from ten thousand metric tons annually in 1969–75.[4] Although these deliveries reflected other Cuban requirements, the need to support the increasing Cuban military involvement in Africa presumably was also a factor. Soviet arms to support the Cubans are also shipped directly to Africa. The intricacy of the Soviet-Cuban logistical connection is illustrated by the dispatch of a considerable number of Soviet pilots to Cuba to augment Cuban air defenses in 1976 and 1978—at a time when Cuban pilots were sent to Angola and Ethiopia.

Castro regards his actions in Africa as enabling him to play a major international role as a supporter of revolutionary movements and of progressive governments, thus fulfilling a long-standing and until recently frustrated ambition. Like the Soviets, he must see Africa as a region in which historical Western influence is vulnerable, particularly in those areas where conflict situations are susceptible to external Communist intervention. Castro obviously seeks to exploit residual anticolonial feelings as well as the vulnerabilities of African political institutions and to promote the image that the West has failed or is unwilling to respond to the perceived needs of African revolutionary movements in particular.

Within the broad policy context, Cuban actions also are highly opportunistic. Castro seems willing to take risks while avoiding major military commitments where chances of success are doubtful. Cuban forces have yet to experience a major military setback; except for a few engagements against South African forces in An-

---

4. See U.S. Department of State, Bureau of Public Affairs, *Cuban Armed Forces and the Soviet Military Presence*, August 1982.

gola in 1975 and in January 1984, their involvement has been against inadequately trained and ill-equipped forces capable of inflicting frequent casualties but unable to threaten seriously the Cuban military presence. It must be assumed that Castro remains sensitive to African views of Cuban activities and is aware of a general African propensity to support or acquiesce in Cuban policy only as long as it can be justified as supporting such basic African principles as black majority rule, opposition to white minority regimes, and the sanctity of existing borders.

SOVIET ARMS AND MILITARY TRAINING ASSISTANCE

Trends and Highlights.

Arms Assistance. The provision of arms became a dominant component of Soviet relations with Africa during the 1970s. The Central Intelligence Agency (CIA) has estimated that, as of the end of 1978, the Soviets delivered almost $2.8 billion in arms and related equipment and services to the area—or more than 10 percent of total Soviet arms and related deliveries to the non-Communist less-developed world. According to the CIA, the Soviets had about $1.1 billion in military equipment and services still to be delivered to sub-Saharan Africa based on agreements already concluded.[5]

The Soviet Union has become the world's leading arms supplier to sub-Saharan Africa—a fact consistently supported by the comprehensive statistics published in recent years by the Arms Control and Disarmament Agency (ACDA). As of the end of 1980, Soviet deliveries of equipment alone to the region exceeded $3.9 billion and constituted more than 46 percent of the global delivery level, as shown in tables 2.1 and 2.2. This increase of 18 percent over the 1978 level was due mainly to greater Soviet arms shipments to Angola, Ethiopia, and Mozambique. France has been the second leading supplier during this period ($875 million), followed by the Federal Republic of Germany ($545 million) and the United States ($385 million).

Although more recent figures on actual arms *deliveries* are not publicly available, the U.S. Department of Defense has estimated

5. Central Intelligence Agency, *Communist Aid Activities in Non-Communist Less Developed Countries, 1978*, Washington, D.C., September 1979.

the total value of Soviet arms sales *agreements* with sub-Saharan Africa at $5.6 billion between 1977 and 1982. Sixty percent of that total was with Ethiopia.[6]

The first Soviet arms accord in the sub-Sahara was with Guinea and Mali in the early 1960s. The largest single arms accords have been since 1975 with Angola, Ethiopia, Somalia, and Tanzania; arms accords with Zambia in 1980 valued at about $90 million gave Lusaka its first MIG-21 fighters and T-55 tanks. A sizable portion of Soviet arms, particularly during the 1960s, has been offered as either outright grant aid or substantially discounted—obviously intended to facilitate Soviet penetration of the area and impress recipients with Moscow's generosity and support. We can also assume that actual sales involved equally liberal interest rates and repayments periods.

In terms of regional and country distribution, about two-thirds of Soviet arms in recent years has gone to East Africa, mainly to Ethiopia, Somalia, Tanzania, and Uganda (see table 2.1). Central Africa is next with almost 17 percent, mainly to Angola. Deliveries to West Africa, largely Guinea, Mali, and Nigeria, total about 11 percent. Other major recipient countries include Congo, Mozambique, and Zambia, but even in such other countries as Benin, Equatorial Guinea, and Guinea-Bissau, where the Soviet arms supply effort has been on a much smaller scale, the impact has been substantial.

Soviet arms activities in sub-Saharan Africa have increased sharply in recent years. According to ACDA statistics, Soviet arms deliveries to the region averaged more than $774 million annually in 1976–80, compared to about $74 million in 1967–76 (see tables 2.1 and 2.2). Although a major reason for this surge has been the massive assistance to Ethiopia, it is sufficient to observe that Moscow has expanded its arms efforts progressively and significantly throughout the area since its involvement in Angola in the mid-1970s. In its 1979 study, the CIA noted that its preliminary estimates indicated an even sharper jump to $1,220 million in Soviet deliveries in 1978—almost equal to the entire amount supplied during 1973–77. Moreover, Soviet deliveries to sub-Saharan Africa in 1978 exceeded those to any Third World area, including the

6. U.S. Department of Defense, *Soviet Military Power*, August 1983, p. 91.

Table 2.1. World Arms Deliveries to Sub-Saharan Africa, 1967–76[a]
(in million current dollars)

	GLOBAL	U.S.	USSR	FRANCE	UK	FRG
GRAND TOTAL	2,433	214	739	463	149	47
CENTRAL AFRICA	626	5	216	14	10	11
Angola	315		190			
Burundi	10			1		5
Cameroon	15	5		5		
CAR	5			1		
Congo	20		1	1		
Equatorial Guinea	5		10			
Gabon	11		5	5		
Rwanda	5			1		
Sao Tome/Principe						
Zaire	240		10		10	5
SOUTH AFRICA	607	30	25	365	22	6
Botswana						
Lesotho						
Malawi	5				1	1
Mozambique	20		15			
Namibia						
Rhodesia (Zimbabwe)	1				1	
South Africa	500	30		365	10	
Swaziland					10	5
Zambia	81		10		10	

	737	142	342	26	51	13
EAST AFRICA	737	142	342	26	51	13
Comoros						
Djibouti						
Ethiopia	190	135		10	5	5
Kenya	51	5		5	35	1
Madagascar	5		1	1		
Mauritius						
Seychelles						
Somalia	185		181	10	5	5
Sudan	100	1	65		1	1
Tanzania	125	1	30		5	1
Uganda	81		65			
WEST AFRICA	463	37	156	58	66	17
Benin	10		1	10		
Cape Verde						
Chad	10		5	5		5
Gambia	1					
Ghana	35		50	1	15	
Guinea	55		5			
Guinea-Bissau	5					
Ivory Coast	30	1		15		
Liberia	5	5				1
Mali	25		25			1
Mauritania	21			5	1	
Niger	5			1		1
Nigeria	221	31	70	1	50	5
Senegal	5			5		
Sierra Leone						
Togo	25			5		
Upper Volta (Bourkina Fasso)	10			10		5

Source: ACDA, *World Military Expenditures and Arms Transfers, 1967–76*, Wash., D.C., July 1978.
a. Statistics cover only arms, spare parts, ammunition, and support and other equipment considered primarily military in nature.

Table 2.2. World Arms Deliveries to Sub-Saharan Africa, 1976–80[a]
(in million current dollars)

	GLOBAL	U.S.	USSR	FRANCE	UK	FRG
GRAND TOTAL	8395	385	3870	875	285	545
CENTRAL AFRICA	1470	50	635	180	10	15
Angola	950		550	10	10	10
Burundi	20		10			
Cameroon	20	20				
CAR	10					
Congo	70		60			
Equatorial Guinea	20		10			
Gabon	110		5	60		
Rwanda	30					
Sao Tome/Principe						
Zaire	240	30		110		5
SOUTH AFRICA	1220	20	400	210	90	10
Botswana	20				20	
Lesotho						
Malawi	30			10	10	5
Mozambique	280		180			
Namibia	NA	NA		NA		
South Africa	460	20	NA	200	NA	NA
Swaziland						
Zambia	340		220		20	
Zimbabwe	90				70	5
(Rhodesia)						

EAST AFRICA	4415	270	2480	100	65	385
Comoros	NA	NA	NA	NA	NA	NA
Djibouti	NA	NA	NA	NA	NA	NA
Ethiopia	2300	80	1900	10	40	5
Kenya	180	50		30		
Madagascar	80		60	10		
Mauritius	NA	NA	NA	NA	NA	NA
Seychelles			150	40	10	10
Somalia	750	140	10	5		360
Sudan	575		320	5	10	10
Tanzania	470		40		5	
Uganda	60					
WEST AFRICA	1245	45	355	385	120	135
Benin	30		20			
Cape Verde	50		50	50		
Chad	10		5	5		
Gambia	5					
Ghana	130				5	50
Guinea	50		50			
Guinea-Bissau	30		30			
Ivory Coast	250	5	200			
Liberia	10					10
Mali	120			110		
Mauritania	90			40		
Niger	40			40		10
Nigeria	330	40	90		110	50
Senegal	70			30		
Sierra Leone	5					
Togo	40			20		5
Upper Volta (Bourkina Fasso)	30				5	10

Source: ACDA, *World Military Expenditures and Arms Transfers, 1976–1980,* Washington, D.C., 1983.
a. Statistics cover only arms, spare parts, ammunition, and support and other equipment considered primarily military in nature.

Middle East ($1,095 million), North Africa ($1,175 million), and South Asia ($260 million). For the entire period of 1976 to 1980, ACDA statistics show that Moscow's $3.9 billion in arms shipment to the sub-Sahara rank third after the Middle East ($12.5 billion) and North Africa ($7.4 billion), and significantly ahead of South Asia ($2.8 billion), East Asia ($2.8 billion), and Latin America ($2.0 billion).

There has been another and perhaps more fundamental change in Soviet arms assistance activities in sub-Saharan Africa. In the 1960s, Soviet arms to the region seem to have consisted largely of relatively inexpensive, second-line ground forces equipment—for example, a varied assortment of small arms, ammunition, explosives, and vehicles. In recent years, however, Moscow has shown little if any reticence in providing main-line and sophisticated weapons systems—including advanced jet fighter aircraft (MIG-23s to Ethiopia); missiles (SAMs to Angola, Ethiopia, Mali, Mozambique, and Tanzania); guided missile boats (Osa IIs, with Styx missiles to Ethiopia and Somalia); and a wide range of tanks, armored personnel carriers, and long-range heavy artillery. This trend toward Soviet-advanced, main-line equipment to the sub-Sahara is sharply reflected in a Department of State study released in August 1982 and noted in table 2.3. In 1977–81, for example, Soviet shipments of supersonic fighter aircraft, SAMs, tanks and self-propelled guns, heavy artillery, and major and minor surface warships increased significantly and in some cases more than doubled.[7] This particular development has raised serious concern about the stability and security of the region on the part not only of Western nations but also many African leaders who see their own largely Western military equipment as increasingly inadequate for defense.

Other Communist countries have also provided arms, including Cuba, Czechoslovakia, East Germany, Poland, and the PRC. The Chinese, with some $140 million in deliveries in 1975–79 mainly to Tanzania, Zaire (both have received Shanghai patrol boats), and Zambia (which has also received MIG-19 fighters), are the main suppliers, but their African activities have decreased in recent years. Czech arms assistance during this period came to

7. U.S. Department of State, *Conventional Arms Transfers in the Third World, 1972–81*, August 1982.

Table 2.3. World Arms Deliveries to Sub-Saharan Africa
(by number of weapons and percentage of regional share)

SUB-SAHARAN AFRICA
(number of weapons and regional share [%])

WEAPON	1972–76 No.	%	1977–81 No.	%	1972–76 No.	%	1977–81 No.	%
% of Third World supply for decade	TANKS AND SELF-PROPELLED GUNS 1.3%				SUBMARINES 1.3%			
Suppliers								
USSR	475	62.9	1,140	60.5				
Other European Communist	10	1.3	230	12.2				
U.S.	10	1.3	25	1.3				
Major West European	55	7.2	40	2.1	1	100.0		
Minor West European								
Other	205	27.1	450	23.8				
Total	755		1,885		1			

WEAPON	1972–76 No.	%	1977–81 No.	%	1972–76 No.	%	1977–81 No.	%
% of Third World supply for decade	LIGHT ARMOR 12.4%				SUPERSONIC COMBAT AIRCRAFT 7.8%			
Suppliers								
USSR	910	61.6	1,590	48.9	120	60.0	220	68.7
Other European Communist	35	2.3	85	2.6				
U.S.	30	2.0	50	1.5				
Major West European	355	24.0	920	28.3	50	25.0	20	6.2
Minor West European			85	2.6			25	7.8
Other	145	9.8	515	15.8	30	15.0	55	17.1
Total	1,475		3,245		200		320	

Table 2.3. (Continued)

SUB-SAHARAN AFRICA
(number of weapons and regional share [%])

	1972–76		1977–81	
	No.	%	No.	%
ade	3,700 100.0 6,745 59.2 1,165	100.0	1,585	99.3

WEAPON

ARTILLERY (OVER 100MM)
19.1%
% of Third World supply for decade

Suppliers	1972–76		1977–81	
	No.	%	No.	%
USSR	1,595	43.1	3,510	52.0
Other European Communist	105	2.8	515	7.6
U.S.	20	0.5	255	3.7
Major West European	235	6.3	300	4.4
Minor West European	90	2.4	55	0.8
Other	1,655	44.7	2,110	31.2
Total	3,700		6,745	

SUBSONIC COMBAT AIRCRAFT
% of Third World supply for decade 10.8%

Suppliers	1972–76		1977–81	
	No.	%	No.	%
USSR	60	60.0	80	69.5
Other European Communist	10	10.0	5	4.3
U.S.				
Major West European	10	10.0	30	26.0
Minor West European	5	5.0		
Other	15	15.0		
Total	100		115	

MAJOR SURFACE WARSHIPS
% of Third World supply for decade 12.0%

Suppliers	1972–76		1977–81	
	No.	%	No.	%
USSR	1	25.0	5	18.5
Other European Communist				
U.S.				
Major West European	3	75.0	16	59.2
Minor West European				
Other			6	22.2
Total	4		27	

HELICOPTERS
8.7%

Suppliers	1972–76		1977–81	
	No.	%	No.	%
USSR	40	21.0	125	43.1
Other European Communist			20	6.8
U.S.	5	2.6		
Major West European	110	57.8	120	41.3
Minor West European	25	13.1	10	3.4
Other	10	5.2	15	5.1
Total	190		290	

WEAPON % of Third World supply for decade	MINOR SURFACE WARSHIPS 23.0%						OTHER MILITARY AIRCRAFT 12.3%	
Suppliers								
USSR	24	17.9	45	45.4	20	5.0	70	22.5
Other European Communist	7	5.2			10	2.0	35	11.2
U.S.			30	30.3	10	2.0	40	12.9
Major West European	38	28.3	13	13.1	250	62.5	100	32.2
Minor West European	31	23.1	11	11.1	100	25.0	40	12.9
Other	34	25.3			10	2.0	25	8.0
Total	134		99		400		310	

WEAPON % of Third World supply for decade	GUIDED-MISSILE PATROL BOATS 4.6%						SURFACE-TO-AIR MISSILES 7.7%	
Suppliers								
USSR	2	100.0	4	80.0	600	51.5	1,575	99.3
Other European Communist								
U.S.					385	33.0		
Major West European			1	20.0			10	0.6
Minor West European								
Other					180	15.4		
Total	2		5		1,165		1,585	

Source: U.S. Department of State, *Conventional Arms Transfers in the Third World, 1972–81*, Special Report no. 102, August 1982.
Note: Countries in this region are Angola, Benin, Botswana, Burundi, Cameroon, Cape Verde, Central African Republic, Chad, Congo, Djibouti, Equatorial Guinea, Ethiopia, Gabon, Gambia, Ghana, Guinea, Guinea-Bissau, Ivory Coast, Kenya, Lesotho, Madagascar, Malawi, Mali, Mauritania, Mauritius, Mozambique, Niger, Nigeria, Rwanda, Sao Tome and Principe, Senegal, Seychelles, Sierra Leone, Somalia, South Africa, Sudan, Swaziland, Tanzania, Togo, Uganda, Upper Volta, Zaire, Zambia, and Zimbabwe.

Table 2.4. Communist Military Personnel in Sub-Saharan Africa 1981[a]

	USSR AND EASTERN EUROPE	CUBA[b]	TOTAL
Angola	1,600	23,000	24,600
Ethiopia	1,900	12,000	13,900
Guinea	50	10	60
Guinea-Bissau	50	50	100
Mali	205		205
Mozambique	550	1,000	1,550
Other	945	850	1,795
Total	5,300	36,910	42,210

Source: U.S. Department of State, *Soviet and East European Aid to the Third World, 1981,* Washington, D.C., February 1983.

a. Minimum estimates of the number of persons present for a period of one month or more. Numbers are rounded to the nearest 5.

b. Including combat units in Angola and Ethiopia.

about $45 million and was extended largely to Ethiopia (mainly small arms), while the Poles provided about $30 million worth of equipment mainly to Angola (largely tanks).

Training Activities. In part because of the sharp increase in Soviet arms exports to sub-Saharan Africa, particularly of advanced weapons, Moscow has stepped up its military training assistance efforts in the area. According to CIA statistics, there were approximately fifty-three hundred Soviet and East European military advisory and technical personnel in sub-Saharan Africa as of the end of 1981 (see table 2.4). Thus far, Soviet advisers have emphasized training indigenous military personnel in the operation and maintenance of weapons systems and in military doctrine and tactics. In addition, thousands of sub-Saharan military personnel were undergoing training in the Soviet Union by the end of the 1970s, primarily on advanced weapons systems. Indeed, since the mid-1950s, more than ten thousand sub-Saharan military personnel have trained in the Soviet Union, more than one thousand in Eastern Europe, and twenty-seven hundred in the PRC (see table 2.5).

The main Communist military presence in sub-Saharan Africa, however, is Cuban—estimated in 1983 before the Ethiopian drawdown at thirty-seven thousand training, technical, and combat personnel. In 1983 the Cuban military presence was several times the size of French training and regular forces, estimated at eleven

Table 2.5. USSR and Eastern Europe: Training of Sub-Saharan African Military Personnel in Communist Countries, 1955–81[a]

COUNTRY	NUMBER OF PERSONS
Angola	180
Benin	120
Congo	630
Equatorial Guinea	200
Ethiopia	2,095
Ghana	180
Guinea	1,005
Mali	495
Mozambique	530
Somalia	2,600
Sudan	350
Tanzania	2,125
Zambia	600
Other	1,840
Total	13,800

Source: U.S. Department of State, *Soviet and East European Aid to the Third World, 1981,* Washington, D.C., February 1983.

a. Data refer to the minimum number of persons departing for training; numbers are rounded to the nearest 5.

thousand in 1982,[8] which constitutes the largest non-Communist foreign military contingent in the region. Training assistance to sub-Saharan Africa by other Communist countries has also increased. Two relative newcomers are East Germany and North Korea; the latter, for example, trains Ugandan troops and in Mozambique trained the Fifth Brigade, which was in 1983 deployed against Joshua Nkomo's forces in Matabeleland.

Some observers continue to insist that Cuban involvement in combat operations in Black Africa is minimal. The fact that roughly 70 percent of the Cuban troops who have served in Africa apparently are believed to be reservists[9] may tend to reinforce the view that Cuban forces are used mainly in rear-echelon and garrison positions. In Angola and Ethiopia, however, these forces went

8. François Soudan, "L'Armée de Mitterrand en Afrique," *Jeune Afrique,* December 1982.

9. U.S. Department of State, *Cuban Armed Forces and the Soviet Military Presence.*

far beyond their training and advisory missions and actually played key roles in the fighting that brought the Neto regime to power in Luanda in 1975 and defeated Somali forces during Ethiopia's war in the Ogaden in 1978. Although Cuban forces in recent years have for the most part avoided challenging the South African military pressure in southern Angola, it is also true that up until 1978–79, at least a substantial portion of the Cuban force in Angola was deployed in forward combat missions. Indeed, the first Cuban unit introduced in Angola was an airborne battalion,[10] and Xan Smiley, a highly informed observer, recalls that in 1976 he found himself "retreating in front of an oncoming wave of Cuban tanks."[11] Moreover, it is acknowledged that the commitment of Cuban pilots to Angola very clearly has been a major factor in strengthening Luanda's military punch. It is hardly conceivable that the use of air power, including helicopter gunships, was left then (or is now) entirely in the hands of Angolan pilots, notwithstanding the training they have received in this complex aspect of tactical warfare.

Support of Insurgencies. Another major feature of Communist military activities in sub-Saharan Africa is arms assistance to insurgent or guerrilla groups. These have included primarily Joshua Nkomo's Zimbabwe African People's Union (ZAPU) virtually from its inception in 1961, which fought to end white minority rule in Rhodesia, and SWAPO, fighting to establish an independent Namibia. Soviet arms to ZAPU included some heavy equipment and main-force military training. In contrast, Chinese assistance to Mugabe's Zimbabwe African National Union (ZANU) was primarily guerrilla-oriented equipment and training, which proved to be more effective. In any event, assistance to insurgent groups constitutes a relatively small portion of the total Communist arms efforts in sub-Saharan Africa and consists largely of small arms, ammunition, and light field artillery. Although dollar estimates of this aid are difficult to assess, it has been sufficient to support an expanding guerrilla effort in the area and in recent years has included armored cars, an increasing array of automatic weapons, and heavier artillery. Arms for the guerrilla forces have been sent

10. Ibid.
11. Xan Smiley, *Inside Angola, New York Review of Books* 30, no. 2 (February 17, 1983).

directly or funneled through states supporting the insurgent struggle. An important part of the assistance has taken the form of training, which includes a strong ideological component.

Soviet Losses and Gains: A Net Assessment. Soviet military involvement in sub-Saharan Africa has produced a mixture of gains and losses for the Soviets. They have lost and gained access to military facilities and have been praised as well as criticized for their military policies and arms assistance. Although military activities have doubtless enhanced the Soviet Union's political role in Africa, even many of those African leaders who rely heavily on Soviet arms remain suspicious of Moscow's ultimate intentions. There is little doubt that these suspicions have constituted the main barrier to further Soviet successes in the area.

Access to Bases. In East Africa, Soviet successes in Ethiopia would appear to have more than offset losses in Somalia. The break with Mogadishu canceled the use of Somalia for TU-95 BEAR reconnaissance flights over the Indian Ocean, but upgrading of airfields and lengthening and paving of runways in Ethiopia could permit heavier aircraft, including the TU-95, to operate. Moreover, Asmara provides the Soviets an important regional airfield from which to operate maritime reconnaissance aircraft. Indeed, the Soviets have been flying IL-38 MAYs out of Asmara on a routine basis since the early part of 1980. Ethiopia also provides the Soviet navy with a major support facility at Dahlak Island, which in the past three years has been substantially improved. The Soviets would appear to have virtually unrestricted use of Dahlak to carry out all routine and emergency repair and replenishment tasks for all their surface ships and submarines in the region. Facilities at Dahlak include fuel storage tanks and a floating dry dock (towed from Somalia after the Soviet expulsion). A repair ship is maintained permanently at Dahlak, and submarine tenders regularly call there to service Soviet submarines. Other floating pier sections also have been towed by tug for the construction of two floating piers.

The significance of Soviet military presence in Ethiopia extends much further than just East Africa. In fact, when seen in conjunction with their activities in South Yemen, the Soviets have now developed an important strategic position to support their efforts in both the Red Sea and the Indian Ocean. Aden itself has excellent port facilities for replenishment operations of deployed Soviet ships, and since 1979 I1-38 MAY reconnaissance flights out of Aden's international airport have become a permanent feature. These aircraft, according to the U.S. Department of the Navy, have frequently tracked U.S. naval units in the Arabian Sea, and at certain periods as many as six MAYs operated from Aden and Ethiopia.[12] Additionally, the island of Socotra off the coast of South Yemen and Somalia has become the primary anchorage for the Soviet Indian Ocean fleet. Several Soviet ships are usually anchored there, and the majority of Soviet naval exercises are conducted in the vicinity of Socotra.

In southern Africa, Moscow concluded a Treaty of Friendship and Cooperation with Mozambique in 1977. In addition, since early 1977 Soviet combatant and noncombatant ships' visits to the Mozambican ports of Nacala, Maputo, and Beira have been fairly frequent. Nonetheless, Moscow has remained frustrated in its attempts to gain permanent facilities in such countries as Tanzania, Zambia, and Mozambique. And the Mozambique–South Africa security pact should dim immediate hopes for greater access.

In West Africa, the Soviet Union suffered a major setback in June 1977 when Guinea curtailed relations with Moscow and revoked long-standing rights for TU-95 BEAR reconnaissance aircraft in Conakry. (Periodic BEAR deployments from the Soviet Arctic to Conakry had flown surveillance missions against U.S. Navy ships in the Central Atlantic.) However, the Soviets shifted their maritime surveillance (and some of their naval activities) to Luanda; since 1981, BEAR reconnaissance flights from Luanda have allowed the Soviets to cover most of the South Atlantic.[13] In addition, Soviet access to Conakry for transport flights to Angola may still be available, and Soviet naval craft apparently continue to make limited use of Guinean shore facilities.

In Mali, the Soviet Union still has access to the airfields, most of them built by the Soviets. An air route through Mali to southern

12. U.S. Department of the Navy, Office of the Chief of Naval Operations, *Understanding Soviet Naval Developments*, Washington, D.C., January 1981.
    13. Ibid.

Africa could afford the Soviets an alternative route shorter than the one through Guinea that has been used in the past.

In Cape Verde, Amilcar Cabral Airport on the island of Sal has been used by Cuban and Angolan aircraft to ferry Cuban military and other personnel to Luanda. (Paradoxically, the airport also serves as a refueling stop for South African Airways flights to New York.) Some observers feel that the Soviets are interested in increasing their presence in Cape Verde and in establishing regular access to air as well as naval facilities. Thus far, however, there is no evidence of much progress toward these objectives.

REACTION TO SOVIET-CUBAN MILITARY ACTIVITIES

African attitudes toward the increasing Communist military involvement in the area are essentially pragmatic, shaped not only by colonial experiences but also by the economic, political, and military priorities set by the African leaders themselves. Thus, African views vary widely—from deep fear and distrust of Communist involvement and qualified support of Communist assistance efforts for legitimate self-defense purposes to relatively unqualified support of any Communist action that can be seen as designed to end white rule in southern Africa.

Few African countries, however, adhere exclusively or entirely to any of these basic attitudes. Even among some of the strongest Black African supporters of Soviet-Cuban involvement in the area, there are clear signs of concern over long-term Communist objectives and about the role and conduct of Soviet, East European, and Cuban Communist military advisory personnel in their own countries. Indeed, for virtually all African countries, support for Soviet-Cuban military activities does not constitute a license to either Moscow or Havana for unrestricted military access and political influence, nor does Communist assistance, economic or military, preclude aid from Western sources.

The strongest African criticism and fears of Communist military activities come from Francophone and other states—including Zaire, Sudan, Senegal, Ivory Coast, Gabon, and even Nigeria—who see the Soviets as exploiting the area to enhance their global power and to undermine and overthrow unsympathetic regimes. Some of these countries depend heavily on Western and particularly French assistance and have suggested that the West must become discreetly involved in combating Communist influence in Africa.

At the other end of the spectrum, such states as Angola, Ethiopia, Mozambique, and Madagascar support the view that Soviet-Cuban involvement is essentially a response to African requests for assistance for self-defense purposes or to bring an end to white domination in southern Africa. These nations see any Western involvement, even at the request of such African states as Zaire or Chad, as another attempt at neocolonialism. However, while they give considerable support to Soviet-Cuban activities, they remain sensitive to any Communist intervention in internal affairs. Nor does Communist assistance necessarily entail support of Soviet or Cuban policies elsewhere. Tanzania, for example, has condemned Soviet occupation of Afghanistan. Mozambique, despite its heavy dependence on Soviet and Soviet-bloc assistance, appears to be making efforts to expand economic ties with the West. Zambia, despite purchasing heavy military equipment from the Soviets, has sought to remain nonaligned in international forums; President Kaunda has made a point of visiting London and Washington in an effort to improve economic relations with the West.

Perhaps a greater number of sub-Saharan states would fall into a middle position: uncritical of Communist military involvement but largely on the basis of the right of any country to request outside assistance to defend itself. Although some states holding the two extreme positions would also accept this position, territorial sovereignty is in fact one of the few principles with which virtually all members of the Organization of African Unity (OAU) are at least in theoretical agreement.

Some leaders with views that fall into this middle position see the Soviet Union as an indispensable source of support for national liberation in southern Africa. Their incentive to accept or ask for Soviet assistance is further enhanced by the absence of Soviet colonial involvement in the area and the reluctance of the West to back armed liberation movements. At the same time, these leaders remain particularly sensitive to any Soviet interest in establishment of a permanent presence or sphere of influence in the area.

African preferences between Soviet as opposed to Cuban military involvement also vary. Whereas some moderate states apparently do not differentiate between Soviet and Cuban involvement, other Black African leaders seem to make the distinction. For them, Cuba is essentially a catalyst to force the West to exert greater pressure on the white regimes in southern Africa without provoking a direct U.S.-Soviet confrontation. In addition, they regard Cuba as a Third World leader and a nonwhite nation with a long history of colonial domination.

OUTLOOK

For the foreseeable future, sub-Saharan Africa will remain high on the list of Soviet priorities in the Third World. Moscow may believe that, despite its setbacks, there has been a net gain for the USSR and that the opportunities for Soviet policy in the area will justify the associated burdens or costs on Soviet resources. The Soviets almost certainly calculate that the overall odds for success are good or at least worth the risk as long as their actions continue to focus on guidelines generally acceptable to most sub-Saharan countries:

- Support of national liberation movements
- Majority rule
- The inviolability of national boundaries
- Opposition to Western policies perceived by Africans as neocolonialist in character

While remaining concerned over the possibility of a major Western response to Soviet actions in sub-Saharan Africa, the Soviets may feel that the West lacks the political credentials to gain widespread African support for their policies. Moreover, the Soviets seem to regard the West as short in military determination to act decisively to counter their military efforts in distant Black Africa.

Moscow must realize that there are factors it cannot control and developments it cannot anticipate that may increase future political costs for the USSR and work against Soviet objectives in Africa. The perception on the part of some moderate African leaders of a Soviet grand design in the area could lead to a more favorable environment for the creation of African regional cooperation as in West Africa and to a strengthening of Western influence. For many African leaders, moreover, Moscow's apparent lack of commitment to Black Africa's long-term economic problems could become increasingly important. And a more pervasive Communist physical military presence might well provoke African popular resentment considerably beyond the sensitivities that have already surfaced in Angola, Ethiopia, and elsewhere. Indeed, among the major factors inhibiting Communist influence will continue to be the intense nationalistic orientation of the leadership and the complex political dynamics of sub-Saharan Africa.

There is no evidence that Yuri Andropov's and then Konstantin Chernenko's accession to power in Moscow have produced any shift or disruption in Soviet policy toward sub-Saharan Africa. Like Andropov, Chernenko was a member of the inner sanctum of the Politburo under Brezhnev and presumably, therefore, one of the architects of present policies. For the foreseeable future, the Soviets seem likely to refrain from launching new, costly adventures and continue instead to look for exploitable opportunities and to counter perceived threats to their own (and their clients') interest. In short, radical changes or departures from current policies, notwithstanding past failures, are not expected.

Ethiopia and Angola probably will remain centerpieces of Soviet and Cuban interests and strategy in sub-Saharan Africa. The level of future Soviet arms transfers to Addis Ababa will depend on several factors, including Somali success in obtaining Western military assistance, Ethiopia's capacity to use additional weaponry, and Soviet (and Ethiopian) perceptions of the requirements in Eritrea and of Somalia's ability to support renewed fighting in the Ogaden.

In Angola, the outlook for Soviet and Cuban activities involves other issues. South African deep-penetration raids and military occupation of part of southern Angola, continued economic difficulties, and insurgent attacks in central and southeastern Angola for some time have given the Soviet and Cuban presence the appearance of a permanent fixture. Indeed, the Luanda authorities are no closer to achieving effective control over Angola than they were in 1976; in many respects the situation may be worse. However, the Reagan administration's policy of linking a Namibian settlement to withdrawal of Cuban troops presents the Angolan government—and the Soviets and Cubans—with a difficult choice. Should South African troops definitely withdraw from Angola and their forward Namibian bases, the Angolan government would still face internal threats that might well bring the government down.

While Moscow's financial investment in Angola is much less than it has been in Ethiopia, it cannot easily walk away from what has been a major international commitment. Suffice it to say that the collapse of the present regimes in either Addis Ababa or Luanda would bring into serious question the effectiveness of Soviet-Cuban military assistance throughout the whole continent.

Elsewhere in sub-Saharan Africa, bringing about the end of minority rule in Namibia and South Africa through militant means will continue to be a major objective. Moscow's main efforts also will focus on Tanzania, Zimbabwe, Zambia, and Mozambique. However, these countries, although among the most influential in the area and among the strongest proponents of the struggle against minority rule, are not likely to want to confront South Africa militarily, since they obviously would suffer most from such a confrontation. Although they will continue to accept Soviet arms and even military training assistance, the acceptance of Soviet or Cuban combat troops does not appear likely.

Future Soviet military policy toward Zimbabwe may have to make some adjustment. Moscow was clearly surprised by Robert Mugabe's massive electoral victory and disappointed at the showing of Joshua Nkomo whose ZAPU was a major recipient of Soviet military assistance. Whatever the immediate impact on Soviet strategy, Moscow may still feel that its connections and record with Nkomo are not necessarily spent cards over the longer term. For now, however, the Soviets seem to be quietly working to improve their relationship with Mugabe while soft-pedaling their past association with Nkomo. The Soviets probably would like to establish some sort of arms relationship with Mugabe, particularly in view of his efforts to create a conventional armed forces structure. But Mugabe remains highly suspicious of Moscow and, given any reasonable alternative, will resist dependence on Soviet military supplies.

Moscow can be expected to devote considerable effort to improving its access to military facilities in sub-Saharan Africa. For example, the Soviets almost certainly want to expand their access to facilities in Ethiopia. This could conceivably result in arrangements that would recover, even more than has already occurred, the military access they lost in Somalia. On the other hand, Moscow may have difficulties in realizing its maximum expectations. The importance to Moscow of access to naval and air facilities in West Africa is not likely to diminish; it could increase in line with the advantages that Moscow hopes to derive from the operations of its naval patrol squadron in the region, reconnaissance over the Atlantic, and continuing arms assistance to southern Africa. Transit facilities in West Africa also will increase in importance if armed strife grows in the Caribbean region.

The recent patterns of arms flows to the area, the continuing potential for expanded armed conflict, and the desire of many African leaders to modernize their armed forces along conventional lines suggest that Moscow will continue to take every opportunity to maintain a high volume of arms assistance. Moreover, despite the exceedingly limited African absorptive capacities, Soviet armaments are likely to involve increasing amounts of advanced systems. Even clients that are considering lessening their military dependence on the Soviet Union might feel compelled to continue to rely on Soviet hardware if supplies were not forthcoming from the West.

However, although the Soviets presumably are willing to continue to offer arms as gifts or at concessionary prices, this premise may be increasingly questionable in the future, particularly when the demand is pointed more and more toward advanced weapons systems. In this connection, the economic and industrial aspects of arms transfers may be especially instructive. In 1977, for example, Soviet arms transfers were about one-half of total Soviet industrial exports to the Third World; these arms sales earned the USSR $1.5 billion in hard currency revenues and helped reduce its balance of payments deficits and in turn finance the purchase of much-needed Western imports. It is assumed, of course, that these revenues came primarily from transfers to the Middle East and North Africa. However, the sharp rise in the USSR's export of advanced weaponry to Africa south of the Sahara and the likelihood in the future of an even greater African demand for such equipment suggest some limitation on liberal Soviet arms pricing activities in the region—heretofore a factor in the preference for Soviet military hardware. In addition, the prices of Soviet weaponry (particularly advanced systems) are becoming increasingly aligned with the prices of Western equivalents, presumably dulling further the price appeal of Soviet hardware for African and other Third World countries.

The outlook, therefore, for Soviet military policies in sub-Saharan Africa is essentially for a continuing pattern of gains and losses, but with Moscow probably remaining confident of its ability to exploit opportunities and advance its image in the Third World as a great world power. Moreover, the militant role that Moscow seems willing to play—coupled with the complex, diverse, and dynamic nature of issues in the area—suggests that sub-Saharan Africa will remain high on the priority list for international attention and concern.

On the other hand, Soviet adeptness in capitalizing on events notwithstanding, purely African exigencies are likely to be more operative factors in military developments in the region—for example, regional rivalries and conflicts (quite apart from those associated with liberation struggles), the political goals and priorities set by African leaders themselves, and African nationalism and sensitivities to external influences whatever the source. The acquisition of sophisticated arms may be seen as desirable in order to modernize African armed forces and to lessen dependence on the West—but also to underscore politically the continuing development of African states as viable modern political entities. But the acceptance of modern armaments clearly is not transferable into a political carte blanche for Moscow—just as it has not been for the West.

Whatever differences may have marked their approaches to Soviet and African issues, the Carter and Reagan administrations have had to recognize the independent sources of key African decisions. As Carter's under secretary of state for political affairs, David Newsom, told the House Subcommittee on Africa in 1979, "Africa's search for international alignments is driven by premises that further Africa's own central priorities." Chester Crocker, Ronald Reagan's assistant secretary for African affairs, put it thus: "I don't sense that many African governments are anxious to see an increase in Soviet presence or influence or arms shipments into the region. . . . That does not mean that they are all of a sudden capitalists, or pro-American, or pro-Western. They are pro-African."[14]

14. Interview in *SAIS Review*, 3, no. 1 (Winter–Spring 1983):93.

3

French Military Policy in Africa

GEORGE E. MOOSE

No survey of the military scene in Africa would be complete without a reference to the continuing French military role on the continent, a role whose broad outlines have survived the transition from Gaullist to Socialist government at home and major crises and upheavals in Africa. Two decades after the French defeat in Algeria hastened the end of French colonial rule in Africa, France remains the only Western nation to station its own troops on the continent and maintain security agreements with many of its former colonies. It is the major Western supplier of arms to African states.

In contrast, Britain, the principal rival to French colonialism in Africa, has yielded to its own narrower vision of its role in the world over the years; its political and military withdrawal from Africa was markedly hastened by African indignation over its failure after 1965 to end the unilateral declaration of independence by the white minority regime in Rhodesia. (Having erased that massive blot on its colonial copybook by its success in Rhodesia, it remains unlikely that the British will seek to capitalize on their new prestige in order to revitalize their role on the continent.) The Germans, never a major contender in the race for African colonies even before their defeat in World War I and understandably chastened by Hitler's rampant militarism in World War II, have maintained under both domestic and international constraints a profound aversion to the development of their potential military strength both at home and abroad. Belgium's flight from the

Congo in the early 1960s was abrupt, and its interventions since have been timid, largely calculated to protect its immediate economic and humanitarian interests in its former colony, now known as Zaire. Portugal and Spain, consumed by the recent transformations of their own societies, are ill-equipped and little disposed to reassert anything approximating their previous roles in Africa.

For its part, the United States, confronted by more serious and immediate security concerns in Europe, Asia, and the Far East, was largely content to leave Africa to the ministrations of its European allies. Following the successful (from the U.S. perspective) resolution of the Congo crises, it was not until 1975—in response to a perceived Soviet-inspired challenge to the existing global balance of power in Angola—that the United States again involved itself directly in an African military conflict. The intervention was quickly aborted by a skeptical American Congress. A new presidential administration, not unmindful of the Angolan experience, set a course that it hoped would keep Africa free of similar great-power rivalries and confrontations by seeking to eliminate the major causes of tension on the continent that might in turn tempt Soviet adventurism or require a countervailing U.S. military response.

The French, however, have given the appearance of being immune to either the domestic foibles or the international constraints that have led other Western nations to eschew an active military role in Africa. Whereas the traumatic experiences of decolonization in Indochina and Algeria might understandably have led to a headlong French withdrawal from its colonial heritage, the French have instead been remarkably resilient and persistent in the pursuit of their interests abroad, particularly in Africa. At the heart of that persistence lies the fact that the French, more than other European nations, see their own national destiny—in terms of security, economic prosperity, and France's political role in the world—as being intimately tied to that of Africa. Perhaps even more remarkable, however, is the evidence that in a period when neocolonialism and dependency head the list of expressed Third World concerns and enemies, the French role in Africa has, if anything, become more active and visible.

Beyond that, however, it would be a mistake to assume that the French role in Africa has not changed in the years since French colonies achieved their formal independence or that France has remained wholly immune to the same constraints, domestic and international, that have affected the willingness and ability of other outside powers to project their security concerns and military influence onto the African continent. Indeed, the appearances created by recent French activism notwithstanding, the current trend is one likely to lead over the next few years toward a reduction in the French military role in Africa—a reduction that may in fact be hastened by the very activism France has displayed in recent years.

FRENCH POLICY IN AFRICA

It is all but impossible to understand contemporary French policy in Africa without recalling France's history as a world power and an imperial nation with colonial possessions in four continents. Ties of sentiment and interest virtually ensured that even in the postcolonial era Africa would remain a primary focus of French concern.

Culturally, Africa would remain for the French an area where the blessings of French civilization could be demonstrated. Economically, France's postwar recovery and future prosperity were seen to depend heavily on access to Africa's rich natural resources and to its ready markets for French exports. Given its geographic proximity, Africa and the Mediterranean would continue to rank behind only Europe and the United States as areas of French strategic thinking, which reasoned that Africa represented the most likely route for a Soviet military challenge to European security. But it is perhaps geopolitically that Africa has acquired the greatest importance to French political leaders. From de Gaulle to Mitterrand, French leaders have viewed the maintenance of French influence on the African continent as a cornerstone of France's ability to continue its role as a major power in a world now dominated by the United States and the USSR.

FRENCH MILITARY TIES TO AFRICA

As part of the complex pattern of relationships by which the French sought to preserve their influence on the African continent,

France negotiated in the immediate postcolonial period two kinds of military cooperation agreements with many of its former colonies. First were bilateral defense agreements that permitted the French to intervene militarily at the request of the African government in question. Eleven such agreements were signed between 1960 and 1963, of which five—Central African Republic (CAR), Gabon, Ivory Coast, Togo, and Senegal—remain in force.[1] (A sixth agreement was signed with Djibouti following its independence in 1978.)

In addition, virtually all Francophone states signed military technical assistance agreements under which France agreed to provide assistance and training to the newly formed military and paramilitary forces. Twenty-two such agreements were in force as of 1979, including two with the former Belgian trust territories Rwanda and Burundi and one with the former Belgian colony Zaire. Many of the original agreements have been renegotiated since the mid-1970s, partly in response to African demands for more favorable and flexible terms. But the renewal of these agreements by seven African states since 1974 (plus the signing of new agreements with Rwanda, Burundi, and Zaire) also attests to a continuing African interest in assured access to French assistance and training during a period of continuing concern among African leaders over potential threats to their stability and security.

Military Supply Relationship. By virtue of the military technical cooperation agreements, the French have retained the role of principal arms supplier to most (but not all) of their former African colonies. Of the twenty-one former French African colonies, only four have sought significant supplies of arms from sources other than France—Guinea, Mali, Congo (Brazzaville), and Benin.

Despite France's near monopoly, however, the scale of French military transfers has remained relatively modest, and actual deliveries of military equipment have generally lagged considerably behind supply agreements. Of the estimated $715 million in military equipment that France shipped to the continent between

1. Pierre Lellouche and Dominique Moisi, "French Policy in Africa: A Lonely Battle against Destabilization," *International Security* 3, no. 4 (April 1979).

1973 and 1977, $455 million was destined for South Africa and Rhodesia. (French arms sales to South Africa were officially terminated in November 1977 after the UN Security Council instituted a mandatory arms embargo.) Another $130 million was accounted for by shipments to Zaire, largely consisting of a sale of Mirage aircraft in 1977. The remaining $130 million in deliveries was divided fairly evenly among some seventeen African recipients. The cost of weapons to developing African countries has clearly been a factor in French restraint with regard to both the quantity and the sophistication of its arms deliveries. Until recently most of the equipment France has provided to its former territories has been on a grant basis, and most consisted of small arms and communications and transport equipment for basic infantry and paramilitary forces.

Scattered evidence suggests that particularly since 1978, French arms transfers have significantly increased in both quantity and sophistication. Although this increase may reflect in small part a push factor on the part of the French armaments industry (which is heavily dependent upon its export market to underwrite the cost of its weapons development and production), most of the increase appears to be in response to African demands for more, and more advanced, weaponry. Recent arms delivery agreements include transport aircraft, helicopters, armored vehicles, and, in a few instances, jet trainers and fighter aircraft. Togo, for example, has acquired French Alpha jet fighters in which the Ivory Coast has also shown an interest; and Gabon has purchased Mirage V fighter aircraft.

While the African market will remain important to the French arms industry, its principal significance to France is likely to continue to be political. Although the French have, by necessity rather than virtue, become more tolerant of arms relationships among their former colonies and other outside suppliers (including Communist countries), they are unlikely to yield readily one of the principal means of retaining their political influence. This would suggest that as the trend toward greater African interest in expanding and improving their military establishments continues, the French will seek to be responsive to African demands, albeit within what France considers the capacity of recipient states to pay for and absorb new and more sophisticated arms.

Military Training. In addition to making France the principal arms supplier to its former colonies, the military cooperation agreements have also enabled France to play a major role in the development and training of their armed forces. In mid-1980, according to French government figures, some sixteen hundred French military personnel were assigned to twenty-five African countries to perform training and technical assistance.[2] This figure does not include French combat troops stationed in various African countries, whose mission often includes some training functions as well. In addition, some eight hundred to one thousand African military personnel are currently being trained in France each year. Significantly, this represents a doubling of the number of African officers trained annually in France prior to 1976.

French Military Presence. By far the most significant feature of the military cooperation and mutual defense agreements between France and its former colonies is that which has allowed the French to maintain a sizable troop presence on the continent itself. In the immediate postcolonial period, France had an estimated thirty thousand troops stationed in sub-Saharan Africa (not including, of course, the estimated four hundred thousand troops in Algeria who were withdrawn between 1962 and 1964). Although the size of the troop presence was largely a carryover from the colonial period during which France was principally responsible for the internal and external security of the colonies, it also reflected the concerns of French military planners over the fragility of the emerging states and Africa's potential as a route for Soviet military advance against Western Europe.

By the early 1970s, the French troop presence had fallen to about seven thousand. The decline reflected a shift in French military priorities away from Africa and toward European security. As Lellouch and Moisi have noted, the priority that France placed on both the transformation of its army into an effective conventional force and the development of its independent nuclear capability resulted in a reduction in the priority assigned to French military interests in Africa.[3] This shift in priority also necessitated

2. French Government Information Ministry Press Release, 80/55, July 1980.
    3. Lellouche and Moisi, "French Policy," pp. 114–16.

a new French military strategy for meeting the obligations under the mutual defense pacts France had signed with several of its former colonies. The result was the French decision after 1967 to develop a flexible, mobile intervention force based in France that could be deployed rapidly to meet contingencies in Africa or elsewhere in the world. With the establishment of this force, coupled with the anticipated increase in the capabilities of the new French-trained African armies, it was possible for France to reduce significantly the size of its own troop presence in Africa.

The decline in the French military presence also coincided with a general rise in African nationalism, whose principal hallmarks were a desire to end as quickly as possible the last vestiges of colonial rule, a growing belief that many of the new African nations' problems were a result of the continued colonial forms and dependencies, and a faith that left to their own devices, Africans could insulate themselves from larger world conflicts and effectively solve their own problems. Although many independent governments in Francophone Africa continued very warm relations with the former metropolis, for a few, France became an object of open hostility, for example, Guinea beginning in 1958 and continuing until 1979, Mali from 1960 at least until 1967, Algeria after 1969, and Mauritania after 1979. It is also significant that the period of the late 1960s and early 1970s saw little in the way of direct French military intervention on the continent, despite the number of developments that seemed inimical to French interests and in stark contrast to the immediate postindependence period, which saw a succession of French interventions to restore order on no fewer than ten occasions.[4]

The decline in the French military presence in Africa through the late 1960s and into the early 1970s began to reverse itself after 1975, particularly following the Soviet-Cuban intervention in the Angolan civil war. The specter of Cuban troops in Angola, supported by Soviet logistics and weapons, was no less alarming to most Francophone leaders than it was to France's newly elected president, Valéry Giscard d'Estaing. As a consequence, both the French and their principal African clients began to perceive in each new crisis on the continent a potential opportunity for Com-

4. Ibid., pp. 117–18.

munist exploitation. Thus the French response, with general Francophone African endorsement, to the outbreak or resumption of
hostilities in Chad, Zaire, Western Sahara, and the Horn was a
steady increase in the number of French troops on the continent.
By late 1978, there were an estimated thirteen thousand French
troops and military support personnel operating in eight African
countries, not counting the roughly one thousand French military
technicians and advisers stationed throughout the continent. In
most cases the French did not regard this presence as permanent;
they were concerned by the resource and manpower implications
of maintaining a large overseas military contingent, as well as by
its political impact in Africa. The nature of current tensions on the
continent and French concern over them will strongly militate
against a unilateral French decision to reduce dramatically its
present troop levels.

FRENCH POLICY AIMS

All the above indices reflect the increase in French concern over
the security situation in Africa, especially since 1975. The same increased concern has been reflected in a series of statements by
French officials and has also found an echo in the statements of
several Francophone African leaders. Whereas, for example, the
1975 Franco-African summit conference in Bangui was dominated
by discussion of aid, trade, and development issues, the meeting in
Paris a year later was overshadowed by security issues, even
though these were not formally on the agenda. Reflecting the concerns of many of the assembled Francophone leaders over the implications of the 1975 Angolan civil war, French president Valéry
Giscard d'Estaing told the final session of the conference that the
"only competition which is in accordance with Africa's interests is
that which promotes economic, social, and cultural development."[5]

By the time the Franco-African summit convened in Dakar in
April 1977, Giscard's views had evolved into a comprehensive policy line from which the French have departed little since. Addressing that conference, Giscard warned that Africa's aspirations

5. *Le Monde*, May 11, 1976, p. 1.

for economic growth, development, and self-sufficiency could only be realized if there was stability and peace. "Over the past few years," he noted, "we have seen the dangers increase, not without concern on our part. Conflicts are multiplying, feelings of antagonism are becoming more and more entrenched, and Africa runs a growing risk of being caught up in conflicts which divert its strength from the goal of development." Lending his endorsement to Article 3 of the Organization of African Unity (OAU) charter on the inviolability of national frontiers and territorial integrity, Giscard concluded by affirming the conformity of French policy with African aspirations for independence and a middle road—that is, between East and West—and by pledging French assistance to the development and security of African states, regardless of their ideological proclivities. In his press conference the same day, Giscard referred to France's commitment to maintaining "an active presence in Africa," noting that France, "more than any country, is the one that makes decisions, the one capable of pursuing a genuine policy in Africa."[6]

The two themes—"no development without security" and France's commitment to assisting African states in the maintenance of their security from all outside interferences, "beginning with those having their origin outside the African continent"—have been the persistent hallmarks of French policy statements since 1976. The French have justified their military role in Africa first on the basis of their security and cooperation agreements with their former colonies, but more generally by references to France's historical ties to and special affinities with the continent. The French do not disguise the fact that they see their own national political and economic interests as inextricably bound with those of Africa. In the words of French foreign minister Jean Francois-Poncet in a May 1979 address to the French Assembly,

> There is undoubtedly no region of the world where the interests and sentiments of France are so profoundly engaged as in Africa. Linked to this neighboring continent by ties of history, geography and culture; and dependent upon it as it is upon Europe for its prosperity and security, France pursues in regard to the continent a policy which is disinterested and courageous.... If the

6. *Le Monde*, April 14, 1977.

government has intervened militarily and with a determination everyone today recognizes, it has been to respond to the requests of weak and unarmed African states obliged to face attacks launched from outside. These actions, limited in scope and duration, have never had any other goal than to permit that freely debated political solutions might put an end to tensions and conflicts. The results have conformed to the intentions.[7]

FRENCH MILITARY INTERVENTIONS

As with the official pronouncements made by all governments, French descriptions of its African policy have had a self-serving quality, and it has not always been easy to square the often altruistic and disinterested rhetoric with the actions taken. More importantly, the as yet incomplete historical record does not permit as definitive an answer as French officials might suggest to the question of whether recent French actions have in fact made a lasting contribution to peace and stability on the continent. What the record does attest to, however, is the level of French concern over stability and security in Africa, and the extent of French willingness to engage in the often murky international and intra-regional politics of the continent. Since 1977 the French have intervened directly in Africa on no fewer than five occasions. The circumstances surrounding these interventions have been varied and the results to date somewhat mixed.

Zaire 1977. As the largest French-speaking country in Africa and potentially one of the most powerful and prosperous, Zaire had long exercised an attraction on French political thinkers and commercial interests. Given Belgium's prior claims and French preoccupations elsewhere, the French interest was not actively pursued in the period following the Congo civil war. It was not until 1975 that President Giscard d'Estaing, elected in May 1974, began to take a personal as well as official interest in Zaire. Spurred by events in Angola, which he saw as a harbinger of renewed Soviet adventurism in Africa and a potential threat to French interests there, Giscard visited Zaire in August 1975. By the

7. French Government Information Ministry Press Release, May 1979.

end of the year, France was channeling through Zaire's president Mobutu Sese Seko assistance for the FNLA, one of two non-Communist movements in the Angolan civil war, whose leader, Holden Roberto, was related by marriage to Mobutu.[8] Already the principal suppliers of military equipment to Zaire, the French substantially increased their deliveries after 1975, to include Mirage fighter aircraft, helicopters, and other transport aircraft.

On March 8, 1977, Zairian dissidents based in Angola attacked across the border into Zaire's western Shaba Province. Given the initial confusion over the source, cause, and magnitude of the attack, the first response in Western capitals was one of caution. Even after it became apparent that Zaire's armed forces were unable to cope with the invasion, all three of the most directly concerned Western governments—the United States, Belgium, and France—found themselves constrained in one way or another by domestic political factors. The French particularly were preoccupied with municipal elections in which a coalition of French Communists and Socialists, as predicted, was scoring major gains against Giscard's government. Three weeks after the invasion began, with the Zairian military showing signs of imminent complete collapse, Mobutu's appeals for Western help in the face of what he characterized as a concerted Soviet-Cuban plot to overthrow his government had brought little more than a promise of stepped-up deliveries of previously ordered military supplies.

By early April, however, Mobutu's position began to show marked improvement with Moroccan King Hassan II's commitment to send fifteen hundred troops to aid in Zaire's defense. The first contingent arrived April 8. Two days later, Paris announced that it would provide eleven French aircraft to assist in the airlift of Moroccan troops and equipment. Hassan's decision was undoubtedly influenced by the French and reportedly the Saudis, out of their concern over Soviet and Cuban penetration in Africa. The French involvement, though limited, did not go uncriticized at home, especially among leftist politicians who questioned what they characterized as blatant intervention in support of one of

8. John Stockwell, *In Search of Enemies: A CIA Story* (New York: Norton 1978), pp. 191–212 and passim.

Africa's more unsavory and least stable regimes.[9] Giscard himself was obliged to go on television to explain and defend French logistical support to the Moroccan airlift, which he justified on the basis of the limited scope of the involvement and France's commitment to combat the subversion of friendly African countries.[10] In a deliberate ploy to disarm both Gaullists and Socialists, who were concerned that Giscard might be surrendering France's vaunted foreign policy independence in favor of closer cooperation with the United States and NATO, Giscard stressed that French actions had been taken without consultation with the Carter administration, and he refrained from identifying the Soviets or the Cubans as the source of the troubles in Shaba.

Despite the pointed questioning of leftist and other politicians, the French public's reaction to the French-supported Moroccan intervention in Shaba was generally favorable. From the outset the operation could be considered a success, and less than three months later the situation was sufficiently in hand that the last Moroccan troops could be withdrawn. French decisiveness, especially when contrasted with the appearance of timidity in Washington and Brussels, had won Giscard praise from moderate African leaders and new respect at home.[11]

Zaire 1978. The generally favorable domestic reaction to Shaba I was no doubt a factor in the more vigorous French response when fighting again broke out in Shaba a year later on May 13, 1978. The fact that the rebel attack began at Kolwezi—a major mining center housing some 2,500 Belgian, French, and American expatriates, which the rebels had not reached in their 1977 campaign—added urgency to the situation. Concern was quickly fueled by fragmented reports from the isolated town that the rebels, contrary to their behavior a year earlier, were targeting Western expatriates, particularly the French, presumably because of Western assistance to Mobutu in putting down the 1977 invasion. Within three days, both the French and Belgians had independently reached the conclusion that direct military intervention was required to protect their citizens. Differences over the timing

9. See, for example, the comments in *L'Humanité*, April 11, 1977.
10. The broadcast text is in *Le Monde*, April 24, 1977.
11. *Le Monde*, April 23, 1977.

and conception of the intervention, however, prompted the French to take the first move independently of the Belgians. French Legionnaires landed north of Kolwezi the afternoon of May 19; the first Belgian troops arrived the following morning. Despite their heavy stake in Shaba's mining sector, the Belgians set for themselves the limited objective of evacuating their estimated four thousand citizens from the province and withdrawing their forces within seventy-two hours.

The French, on the other hand, saw their task as not only the immediate securing of the expatriate community's safety but also the reestablishment of order in Shaba that would permit the continued functioning of the mining sector and end the threat the invasion had posed to the very existence of the Zairian government. In this they were supported by the Carter administration, which saw the second Shaba invasion as an opportunity to demonstrate to critics at home and doubters abroad its determination to oppose Soviet-Cuban adventurism, which some at least were inclined to see as the source of Shaba's recurring difficulties.[12] That perception influenced President Carter's decision to accede to both French and Belgian requests for airlift support, without which the intervention probably could not have succeeded.

The success of the initial rescue operation left unresolved the same issues that had been unsuccessfully addressed following the 1977 invasion: namely, how to ensure against yet another recurrence and the threat posed to Zaire's fragile economic and political stability. Given the demonstrated ineffectiveness of the Zairian armed forces, the immediate problem was to provide for the military security of Shaba Province. Neither the French nor the Belgians were prepared to accept a long-term security role. Both governments were under domestic political pressure to withdraw their forces, in keeping with their contention that the purpose of their intervention was humanitarian. In addition, the French were concerned about commitments elsewhere, especially in Chad and Djibouti. The immediate security problem was resolved when Giscard, at the 1978 Franco-African summit meeting in May, secured the agreement of Morocco, Senegal, Ivory Coast, Togo, and

12. An excellent published account of the 1978 crisis and U.S. policy-making is the series of articles by Martin Schram, *Newsday*, August 30–September 1, 1978.

Gabon to provide contingents for an inter-African force to replace the departing French Legionnaires and Belgian paratroopers.

Although the inter-African force solved the immediate security problem, it could not address deeper causes of Zaire's economic and political instability. The United States, France, and Belgium, as well as Britain and Germany who were drawn into consultations on Zaire's future, were generally agreed that fundamental reforms in the way Mobutu had run the country were essential. But they differed over how extensive those reforms should be and how much pressure should be exerted on Mobutu to undertake them. The Americans, on the one hand, were inclined to see Mobutu's political and economic mismanagement as a principal cause of Zaire's continuing instability and seemed prepared to withhold additional assistance to Zaire until Mobutu had put both his economic and his political house in order. On the other hand, the French and to some extent the Belgians were inclined to view such pressures as threatening to the rule of the one man whom they believed capable of holding Zaire together. In the resulting Western disunity, Mobutu skillfully played one power against the other, acceding to some reform measures while willfully thwarting others. As a consequence, despite two major military interventions and massive Western military and economic assistance, Zaire's future stability seems no more assured today than it was in 1977 when the first Shaba invasion occurred.[13]

Chad. The situation in Chad offers an example of how a consistent French military policy pursued over a number of years fell far short of its objective of helping stabilize an African country. The war in Chad dates from the mid-1960s, when Moslems from the North began to challenge the government, dominated since independence by Christians from the South, for a redistribution of political power. Libya threw its support behind the Moslem Front for the National Liberation of Chad (Frolinat) in 1975, principally as a means of advancing its claim to a disputed strip of territory along the Chad-Libya border, reputed to be rich in uranium and manganese.

Throughout this period France continued to support the Chad-

13. M. Crawford Young, "Zaire: The Unending Crisis," *Foreign Affairs* 57, no. 1 (Fall 1978):169–85.

ian government. In 1968, de Gaulle responded to a Chadian government request for French troops and military assistance. Although the troops remained for three years, Frolinat remained undefeated. French assistance to Chad was briefly interrupted in 1975, when General Malloum, who had ousted and succeeded President Tombalbaye, terminated the bilateral defense agreements as part of an effort at national reconciliation. Within six months, however, pressures from Frolinat forced Malloum to seek new agreements under which the French would rearm and retrain the Chadian army.

By 1978, Frolinat, with Libyan backing, had gained the upper hand in northern Chad, and Malloum, faced with a direct military threat to his capital, again appealed for French troops. Anxious to avoid a dispute with Libya, a major supplier of oil to France, Giscard initially sought to work out a cease-fire arrangement, and an agreement favorable to Frolinat and Libya was signed in Benghazi on March 27. But when Frolinat renewed its offensive a few weeks later, France responded by dispatching fifteen hundred French Legionnaires and four squadrons of French fighter aircraft to Chad, ostensibly to protect the large French expatriate community.[14]

Despite initial French battlefield successes, the war appeared no more winnable than when de Gaulle had intervened in 1968. The French were obliged to assume de facto administrative control of the country since the Malloum government had all but ceased to function. Moreover, mounting French casualties had become a cause for concern in France. Giscard was thus faced with the dilemma of either incurring mounting political disaffection at home because of French involvement in a costly and unwinnable war or appearing to renege on his oft-stated commitment to the defense and stability of France's African client states.

Muammar al-Qaddafi himself seemed to offer the French a way out of their dilemma when in May 1978, following a major French victory over Frolinat forces, he agreed to further negotiations. In August agreement was reached with the aid of the then-OAU chairman, President Gaafar Mohammed al-Nimeiry of Sudan, on the formation of a new government of national unity,

14. See the report by Geoffrey Godsel in *Christian Science Monitor*, April 27, 1979.

with Malloum remaining as president and Frolinat leader Hissene Habre becoming vice-president. Like its predecessors, however, that agreement quickly began to collapse. When Habre denounced the territorial claims of his former Libyan sponsors, Qaddafi quickly shifted his support to Goukouni Oueddei, a rival to Habre within the Frolinat coalition, who renewed the fighting. By February 1979 the Malloum-Habre coalition had itself collapsed. Under renewed attacks from Habre's forces, Malloum withdrew from the government. When Habre and Goukouni subsequently achieved a reconciliation and jointly denounced Libyan aggression in the North, Qaddafi again switched his support to a loose coalition of northern splinter groups eager to continue the war.

Faced with the continued disintegration in Chad, the French announced in March 1979 their intention to begin the withdrawal of their estimated two thousand troops from the country. The announcement undoubtedly reflected growing concern in France over the costs of the Chadian venture at a time when French troops were simultaneously engaged in Djibouti, Lebanon, Zaire, and Mauritania.[15] But it may also have been calculated to give impetus to a new Nigerian initiative to end the Chadian war. Both Goukouni and Habre voiced concern over what they saw as a precipitate French withdrawal. That threat may have encouraged them to participate in talks with dissident northern groups and the remnants of Malloum's forces, which the Nigerians managed to arrange in Kano in April.

The first Nigerian-sponsored agreement, under which Nigerian troops were to supervise the mutual withdrawal of all armed factions from Ndjaména, collapsed within a matter of days. An estimated five thousand people were killed in renewed fighting in the capital, and Malloum fled the country. A subsequent Nigerian-sponsored agreement in August 1979 involving a total of eleven Chadian groups in a proposed national reconciliation government under the supervision of a joint Congolese-Beninian-Guinean peacekeeping force fared no better.[16]

What began as a civil war between northern Moslems and

15. See the report by Paul Lewin in *New York Times*, March 21, 1979, and Paul Webster, "French Bluff Called," *Manchester Guardian Weekly*, June 11, 1978.

16. See Virginia Thompson and Richard Adloff, *Conflict in Chad* (Berkeley: University of California Institute of African Studies, 1981).

southern Christians and animists had been transformed into an internecine conflict among rival Moslem groups. In May 1980, France withdrew its remaining eleven hundred troops from the country, a move that perhaps more than any other symbolized the apparent hopelessness of the situation. By the time of their withdrawal, the role of French troops had changed dramatically from that of defender of one side in a civil war to that of peacekeeper, albeit an ineffective one, among the various factions. Before the Habre victory, Jean-Pierre Cot, Mitterrand's minister of cooperation, summed up French policy toward Chad in the following terms: "We have obtained the withdrawal of [Libyan] troops, we have supported the OAU in putting in place the inter-African force, and we continue our efforts toward reconstruction, but we have no intention of going further."[17] This role suited the African parties involved. None of the Chadian factions, whatever their past views, seriously wanted the French to withdraw, and even African states, such as Nigeria, that had criticized French involvement were troubled by the vacuum left by France's departure. At the same time, despite Chad's uncertain future, France continued to get credit both at home and among moderate Africans for its stand against destabilization.[18]

France has sought to maintain its role as peacekeeper in Chad. Just over two years after the departure of French troops in 1980, the government in Ndjaména fell to Habre's northern army reportedly aided covertly by the United States against French wishes,[19] and Oueddei fled to Cameroon. The new Habre government was implicitly recognized by the OAU on June 9, 1983. Only thirteen days after the new government took its place in the OAU, however, rebel forces under Oueddei, backed by Libyan troops, captured the oasis town of Faya-Largeau.

The Mitterrand government quickly sent weapons and ammunition in support of Habre and increased its material assistance during the first week in July. It refrained from sending military personnel, although members of the French Secret Service (DGSE) were reported to have directed logistical (supply) operations.[20]

17. *Marchés Tropicaux*, April 9, 1982, p. 971.
18. Lewin, in *New York Times*.
19. *West Africa*, August 22, 1983, p. 1931.
20. *Africa Research Bulletin: Political and Cultural Series* 20, no. 7 (July 1–31, 1983): 6904.

Paris also ordered 165 paratroopers to Kousseri in Cameroon, just across the river from Ndjaména.[21] Meanwhile, Habre stepped up his calls for French intervention and accused two of Mitterrand's top officials—roving ambassador Guy Penne and French envoy to Algeria Guy Georgy—of belonging to a pro-Libyan business lobby. Habre's forces recaptured Faya-Largeau but were forced to withdraw again on August 11 in the face of Libyan air attacks. France sent 340 military advisers, 150 paratroopers, antiaircraft weapons, and helicopters to Chad, but they came too late. The rebels completed the siege of the oasis town just hours before French forces arrived in Ndjaména.

Still cautious, however, the Mitterand government launched Operation Manta, a measured military response designed not to help Habre's forces advance but rather to keep Libyan forces from proceeding south beyond the fifteenth parallel—the "ligne rouge"—and to create enough stability to permit negotiation. Close to three thousand French troops were eventually deployed under this scheme, primarily to Abeche and Salal, with some stationed at forward bases.[22] Backup forces included fighter planes and tanks. Minister for Defense Charles Hernu entered into direct negotiations with Habre. The deployment was described by Paris as "a warning to Colonel Qaddafi."[23] French troops were to back up Chadian commando units, but not become directly involved in combat themselves. Mitterand emphasized that "France will not allow herself to be led where she does not want to go,"[24] but added that his government would not allow Chad to be partitioned.[25]

French ambivalence about becoming involved in the fighting has continued. In early September 1983 Paris refused to become involved in fighting near Oum-Chalouba near the fifteenth parallel. Subsequently, following the shooting down of a Jaguar patrol plane, France reinforced its air strength and moved its troops sixty miles north to the sixteenth parallel and seemed to be settling in for a long stay, should that prove necessary.

Western Sahara. In the dispute between Morocco and the Algerian-backed Polisario Front for control of the ex-Spanish

21. Ibid., p. 6905.
22. *West Africa,* August 22, 1983.
23. Ibid.
24. *Le Monde,* August 25, 1983, p. 1.
25. *Le Monde,* Edition Internationale, August 25–August 31, 1983, p. 1.

Sahara, the French have again assumed a role as a major player in an equally complex international conflict and with equally uncertain prospects for a successful resolution.[26] When post-Franco Spain precipitately withdrew from the territory in 1975, it ceded its control to Morocco and Mauritania, each of which asserted long-standing claims to the territory. The move provoked defiance on the part of the Polisario, which had waged a long but desultory struggle for the independence of the lightly populated territory and whose claims to all or part of the territory were given some legitimacy by an International Court of Justice ruling supporting their right to self-determination. The assertion of their claims imposed heavy burdens on both Morocco and Mauritania. The latter suffered most from the initial escalation of the conflict. When the Polisario launched attacks into northern Mauritania, disrupting the mining industry which is the mainstay of the economy, Morocco dispatched some nine thousand troops to help bolster Mauritanian defenses. The escalating cost of the war was a factor contributing to the military coup that ousted Mauritania's president Ould Daddah in July 1978 after eighteen years in office. The new Mauritanian leadership quickly made known its interest in extricating itself from the conflict, much to Moroccan dismay, even at the cost of ceding its territorial claims in the Sahara. In an effort to keep Mauritania in the war, the Moroccans refused to withdraw their troops from northern Mauritania. Moreover, Morocco has steadfastly refused to abandon its absolute claim to the Sahara, despite the growing Polisario military strength and international support, or to act on UN and OAU resolutions urging an internationally supervised referendum to determine the territory's future. While King Hassan's campaign in the Sahara remains a highly popular cause among Moroccans, the growing costs of the war have confirmed in the eyes of many observers that Morocco's economy could ultimately collapse under the strains generated by the dispute.

In the face of conflicting interests and pressures, French policy in the Saharan war has undergone notable shifts. France's studied neutrality in the dispute came under mounting pressure from Senegal and Saudi Arabia, both concerned that Polisario successes

26. A good introduction to this perplexing quarrel is Arnold Hottinger "La Lutte pour le Sahara Occidental," *Politique Etrangère* 45, no. 1 (March 1980):167–80.

would bolster and encourage Algeria and other African radicals. In June 1977, France signed a new military agreement with Mauritania and dispatched a squadron of fighter bombers to Cap Vert in neighboring Senegal to aid Mauritania's defense. When the Polisario retaliated by kidnapping a group of French mining engineers from northern Mauritania and demanding French recognition as the price for their release, Giscard responded by charging Algerian complicity in the kidnapping, reinforcing French forces at Cap Vert, and ordering intensified bombing attacks on the Polisario. Despite French intervention and the rapid expansion of the Mauritanian military from three thousand men in 1975 to more than fifteen thousand by 1978, Mauritania's position continued to worsen. At home, French opposition politicians on both the Left and the Right began to question the costs of French involvement and the risks to the safety of French citizens, particularly in light of the dubiousness of Moroccan and Mauritanian territorial claims.[27] The consequent deterioration of French-Algerian relations, which Giscard himself had made a commitment to improving, fueled concern among both politicians and commercial interests over the loss of France's privileged trading position. And opposition politicians, seeking to build support for their coalition in advance of the next presidential elections, echoed criticism from a number of African states over this new evidence of Giscard's neocolonial ambitions in Africa.

Thus, the July 1978 Mauritanian coup was seen by French officials as an opportunity both to ease Mauritania out of its costly involvement in the war and to reduce the economic, military, and political liabilities of France's own involvement. Clearly pleased by the change of government and attitude in Mauritania and by French encouragement of Mauritanian withdrawal from the conflict, Algeria dispatched its foreign minister to Paris in August 1978 for talks with Giscard. In May 1980, Mauritanian leaders went a major step further in seeking to improve relations with Algeria and the Polisario by insisting that France withdraw all its remaining two hundred troops from the country, much to French dismay. Despite this setback, French officials remained hopeful

27. Webster, "French Bluff," and James Markham, in *New York Times*, July 15, 1979.

that Mauritania's withdrawal from the conflict coupled with increasing international pressure might prod King Hassan into participating in a new effort to settle the dispute.

Publicly and privately France has encouraged various efforts by Ivory Coast president Houphouët-Boigny, the OAU, and even Libya to mediate among Algeria, Morocco, and the Polisario. With broad and militant support at home for the assertion of Morocco's historical claims to the Sahara, Hassan has thus far spurned all settlement proposals, including the OAU's recommendation for a referendum to determine the territory's future. Despite Moroccan obduracy, France has continued to support Morocco politically and militarily, without, however, endorsing Morocco's territorial claims. After October 1979, French-supplied Mirage fighter bombers were employed by the Moroccans against the Polisario in the Western Sahara. At the same time the Carter administration brought its own position closely in line with that of the French by offering to sell OV-10 reconnaissance aircraft and helicopter gunships sought by the Moroccans for use in their fight against the Polisario, but without endorsing Morocco's territorial ambitions. The rationale for the decision, like that given by French officials in support of their military aid, was that although the war must ultimately be settled politically, through negotiation, Morocco would come to the bargaining table only if it was assured of Western support and could do so from a position of relative strength.[28]

Djibouti. French interests in Africa and the Middle East converge sharply in Djibouti. A May 1977 referendum in which a majority of the territories' 250,000 residents chose independence from France came at a time when Soviet influence was gaining on both sides of the Red Sea, sending shudders of alarm through Western capitals. It was feared that the territory would become a microcosm of the growing tensions between Somalia and Ethiopia and that Somalia's assertion of its irredentist claims to Djibouti could provoke an Ethiopian move to take over the territory in order to protect its access to the port of Djibouti. Such a move, if successful,

28. This line of argument is criticized by Steven J. Solarz, "Arms for Morocco?" *Foreign Affairs* 58, no. 2 (Winter 1979–80):278–99.

would give Ethiopia's Soviet backers a foothold on both sides of the narrow Strait of Bab el-Mandeb, which controls the southern access to the Red Sea.[29]

Concern in France over possible involvement in a bloody conflict in Djibouti sparked vocal but disorganized opposition to any continuing French presence in the territory following its independence. Over this opposition and with the urging of its Western allies, France signed military defense and cooperation agreements with the independence government led by Hassan Gouled. France further agreed to retain some three thousand troops in the territory, both to assure peace between the country's two rival ethnic groups and to discourage Somali and Ethiopian territorial ambitions. French officials have also given Hassan Gouled close counsel on maintaining his tenuous political neutrality.

Since 1978, the French have quietly increased their troop presence to an estimated forty-five hundred men. Simultaneously they have gradually increased their naval presence in the Indian Ocean and the size of their garrisons at Réunion and Mayotte, in part to be able to react to any possible outbreak of tensions in Djibouti or elsewhere in the area. Nevertheless, French officials are aware that any serious conflict in Djibouti could again provoke sentiments at home for a withdrawal.

Central African Republic. Of all its recent interventions in Africa, France's involvement in the August 1979 coup that ousted Emperor Jean-Bedel Bokassa has proved to be the most controversial, certainly in Africa, but also in France. While criticism in Africa logically focused on this latest apparent manifestation of French imperial and neocolonial tendencies, the debate in France centered largely on the evidence of personal ties between Giscard and Bokassa and their impact on official French support, right up until the coup, for Bokassa's increasingly brutal dictatorship.

After seizing office in a 1966 coup and styling his rule after his conception of General de Gaulle, Bokassa achieved his crowning glory in December 1977 when he appointed himself emperor of the renamed Central African Empire (CAE). The extravagant corona-

29. Philippe Leymarie, "Début d'Indépendance Difficile à Djibouti" *Revue Française d'Etudes Politiques Africaines* 154 (October 1978):43–58.

tion was heavily subsidized by France. Bokassa's fortunes took a sharp turn for the worse, however, after rumors began circulating of his personal involvement in the April 1979 massacre of more than a hundred schoolchildren detained in the aftermath of an outbreak of anti-Bokassa demonstrations. French officials initially dismissed the reports by Amnesty International and others as "pseudo events."[30] But the persistence and increasing credibility of the evidence led Giscard to support an investigation by a commission of African jurists.

The jurist commission's report, far from exonerating Bokassa of complicity, amassed further evidence of his likely involvement. The criticism also spilled over to France, whose budgetary subventions over a period of thirteen years to Central Africa's civil service and military payrolls were deemed responsible for keeping Bokassa's repressive regime in power. In response, Paris announced a cutoff of all assistance to Bangui that was not of a humanitarian nature, though budgetary subsidies continued.

The jurist commission's report, coupled with the shift in French attitudes and growing opposition in Bangui, stirred undisguised activity among exiled Central African opposition leaders, including Bokassa's former prime minister Ange Patasse in Paris and Abel Boumba, head of the socialistically minded Ubangian Patriot Front, in Benin. Even more alarming to French officials were Bokassa's fresh attempts to get financial and military help from Libya, which Qaddafi seemed prepared to give in exchange for access to Central Africa's rich uranium deposits and the establishment of a military base on CAE soil. French officials justifiably saw such a prospect as threatening to expand Libya's influence and troublemaking in the area, as well as interfering with French access to Central Africa's uranium. In 1976, the CAE's uranium reserves were estimated at fifteen thousand tons; France had majority ownership in a consortium to produce uranium concentrate and export five hundred tons a year.[31]

When Bokassa journeyed to Tripoli in September 1979 for further discussion with Qaddafi, the French seized the moment to as-

30. See the report by Ronald Koven, *Washington Post*, September 22, 1979.

31. U.S. Department of State, *Background Notes on Central African Empire, 1977.*

sure the installation of their own preferred successor, former Central African president David Dacko, whose elected government had been ousted by Bokassa in 1966. The French dropped all pretense of noninvolvement after Dacko's own statements acknowledging the French role in planning and executing the coup and reports that Dacko's return to Bangui was simultaneous with the arrival of some four hundred French paratroopers. French collaboration in the coup was further dramatized when Bokassa flew from Tripoli and landed at a French military air base at Evreux north of Paris to seek asylum, basing his claim to French citizenship on his prior service in the French army. The French government refused to allow Bokassa to leave the aircraft (though after fifty-six hours it did provide a plane to carry him to exile in the Ivory Coast) and later issued a legal brief refuting his claims to citizenship.

At the same time, French lawyers presented an equally controversial brief denying permission to one of Dacko's principal political rivals, former prime minister Patasse, to leave Paris for Bangui, on grounds that his Central African Empire passport had ceased to be a valid travel document with the reversion of the country's name to the Central African Republic.

The cumulative evidence of French maneuvering in the installation of Dacko stirred protests among students, intellectuals, and professionals in Bangui and prompted the French to increase their military presence from four hundred to one thousand troops. While Foreign Minister François-Poncet was assuring a skeptical National Assembly that the "presence of our soldiers in Central Africa will be strictly limited in time and purpose," Dacko was asserting in Bangui that the French army would "remain for more than ten years" if the country required it.[32] While French officials were seeking to square their actions with their official policy of "Africa for the Africans," a number of African governments predictably were showing their disdain for what they regarded as this most blatant exhibition of French imperial behavior and hypocrisy. Considering the principles and issues at stake, however, the African reaction was uncommonly mild. In contrast to the uproar that followed the Soviet occupation of Afghanistan and the over-

32. Ronald Koven, in *Washington Post*, October 14, 1979.

throw of its government, which bore at least superficial similarities to the French action, there was no concerted attempt by the Africans to bring the matter before the United Nations or even to debate it seriously in the OAU.

Meanwhile, the events in Central Africa were also generating public and press criticism in France, but for largely unrelated reasons. Instead, Giscard was variously attacked for his alleged personal ties to and support of Bokassa long after the repression of his rule had become clear to all; the clumsiness and lack of secrecy with which the coup was carried out; the selection of Dacko, deemed the weakest and least capable of the contenders to succeed Bokassa; and the consequent responsibility France had incurred for a seemingly open-ended commitment to the support of Dacko's regime.[33] Ironically, the most highly publicized and politically embarrassing issue to confront Giscard in the wake of the incident concerned neither the wisdom nor the legality of his government's action but rather the allegations in the French press of his acceptance, while finance minister under Pompidou, of a gift of diamonds from Bokassa, coupled with renewed press interest in the commercial activities in Central Africa of Giscard's relatives.[34]

Undoubtedly more worrisome to French officials than either the African or the domestic criticism was the cool reaction from France's closest friends in Africa. Dacko initially claimed that his takeover with French support had been endorsed in advance by several West African presidents, but he later qualified his statement after Houphouët-Boigny and others categorically denied any prior knowledge of the coup plans. In private, French officials reportedly acknowledged that many of "their best friends" had disapproved of the French action, seeing in this example of French intervention to overthrow a government recognized by Paris a dangerous precedent that might some day be applied to them.[35] Only two African leaders publicly defended the French action: President Léopold Senghor, whose staunch support of the French role in Africa has put him at odds even with many of his own

33. Paul-Jean Franceschine, "Hypocrisy and Irresponsibility," *Christian Science Monitor* 14 (October 1979).

34. In particular, see the *Canard Enchaîné*, no. 3076 (October 10, 1979):3.

35. Ronald Koven, in *Washington Post*, September 23, 1979, and October 14, 1979.

Francophone peers; and, ironically, Zaire's Mobutu, who perhaps
has more reason than any other African leader to be concerned
over a future replay of the Central African precedent.

On the surface, the French intervention in the CAR seemed to
bear little relation to its other recent actions, its role in Zaire,
Chad, and Mauritania, for example. Critics of French Africa policy, however, looking at the historical record, are more inclined to
see actions such as that undertaken in the CAR as an inevitable
corollary of French policy, citing as recent evidence the alleged
French involvement in the successful coup in Mayotte in 1978 and
in the abortive coup attempt by French mercenaries in Benin in
1977. Editorializing on the lessons to be drawn by Africans from
the events in Afghanistan, the influential journal *West Africa* probably came closest to summarizing the concerns that many Africans
feel over French actions in Africa generally and in the CAR in particular:

> The lessons to be drawn at a distance from all this are several:
> that the sufferings of the people of Afghanistan make it clear
> that it is dangerous to have a powerful neighbor or friend (the
> people of Ethiopia might reflect on this); that the close and in-
> volved support of a big power is unlikely to be disinterested and
> could be dangerous (the whole of Francophone Africa could re-
> flect on this); . . . and, finally, and most important, that the need
> is more urgent than ever for Africa to be as self-reliant as possible
> both economically and militarily, and able, through the OAU to
> settle by itself its conflicts and border tensions.[36]

CONTRADICTIONS AND CONSTRAINTS

The foregoing record of recent French military actions in Africa
demonstrates the French government's determination to protect its
interests and pursue its broader policy objectives on the continent.
It also suggests some of the limitations and constraints on French
action. Some of these are clearly rooted in French domestic politics
and in the related area of how scarce resources, both financial and
military, are allocated. Perhaps more serious in the long term,

36. "What Kabul Means to Lagos," *West Africa*, 3259, (January 7,
1980):3.

however, are the constraints emerging out of the political dynamics in Africa itself and the conflicts among various interests France is seeking to pursue.

Domestic Political Constraints. In 1962, in the aftermath of the domestic political chaos over Algeria that paralyzed the Fourth Republic, de Gaulle was able to amend the French constitution to provide for the direct election of the president. In so doing, he secured for the office formidable legal powers in the conduct of foreign policy. As a consequence, the occupants of the Élysée Palace have become the secret envy of a succession of American presidents who have found their own freedom of international action increasingly constrained by an elaborate system of congressional checks and balances. Lacking de Gaulle's charismatic popular appeal, his successors have nevertheless been aided in protecting his exercise of presidential foreign policy prerogatives from possible parliamentary encroachment by the divisions among French political parties. Unlike de Gaulle, however, they have been obliged to contend with criticism both from the opposition and from within their own parties. Giscard's African policies faced particularly vigorous attacks from traditional Gaullists within his own governing majority and from the resurgent Socialist and Communist parties.

Gaullist attacks rested on three principal grounds: (1) the wisdom of Giscard's pursuit of military strategies in Africa to the alleged exclusion of political solutions; (2) the danger of Giscard's emphasis on countering Soviet-Cuban adventurism would align France more closely with the United States, thereby jeopardizing both the autonomy of French foreign policy and Paris's relations with Moscow, as well as with large and important segments of Africa and the Third World; and (3) the risk that Giscard's actions would result in open-ended commitments to fragile African regimes at a cost that France could not afford. The sharpness of the criticism was given added weight by the prominence of the critics. Gaullist leader Jacques Chirac led the attack in Parliament following the 1978 interventions in Shaba, Chad, and Mauritania, accusing Giscard variously of souring the climate for the pursuit of important French political and commercial interests in Algeria and Libya, undermining Moroccan security by encouraging its involvement in Shaba, setting back de Gaulle's early efforts at détente with Moscow, and becoming "a scout for the Americans" in Africa. Pompidou's former foreign minister, Michel Joubert, joined the attack by contrasting de Gaulle's earlier support for "solid leaders" with Giscard's open-ended commitments to Mobutu and other unsavory regimes. And de Gaulle's former prime minister, Couve de Murville, added his weight by warning of the repercussions Giscard's policies could have for France's relations with the Third World.[37]

To the voices of Gaullists were added those of the French Left. Socialist party head François Mitterrand and Communist leader Georges Marchais, despite differences on other issues, were in harmony in criticizing what they regarded as Giscard's neocolonialism and condescending paternalism in Africa. Mitterrand repeatedly denounced Giscard's African interventions, calling them "operations in catastrophe."[38]

Despite these periodic and highly personal attacks, however, and his sensitivity to them, Giscard's policy toward Africa remained generally popular with the French public. Parliamentary debate on foreign policy, while occasionally vigorous, was sporadic and pro forma. As a result, Giscard was not obliged to engage in more than minimal consultations domestically, and policymaking remained highly concentrated in the presidency. Despite their distrust and disenchantment with Giscard's activism, the Gaullists were unsuccessful in articulating a clear line that would capture the public imagination. The Communist party's apologia for the Soviet invasion of Afghanistan discredited its voice in all foreign policy matters, and the Socialist attacks concentrated more and more on domestic issues as the spring 1981 elections approached. Nevertheless, the political climate introduced a serious measure of caution and constraint into Giscard's actions and, in turn, on his ability to sustain in particular circumstances the commitment to security and stability in Africa that his broad policy statements imply. Those pressures were reflected in the eagerness with which the Élysée sought to have the French Legionnaires replaced by an inter-African force in the aftermath of Shaba II, in the announce-

37. See the articles of Paul Webster in *Manchester Guardian Weekly*, June 18, 1978, and Maurice Duverger, "Le Gendarme Africain de l'Occident," *Le Monde*, December 28, 1977.

38. *Africa Research Bulletin*, May 1981, p. 6055.

ments beginning in early 1979 of French intention to withdraw from Chad, and in the efforts made to ease Mauritania out of the Western Sahara conflict following the coup of July 1978.

The May 1981 election brought to power a man who had vigorously condemned Giscard's more adventurous African policies and a party that prided itself on its informal alliance, through the Socialist International, with numerous Third World socialist regimes. Understandably, the election generated expectations of increased French support for African development efforts and heightened sympathy for left-wing African political groups.

Mitterrand has moved cautiously in changing African policy, however—so much so that *West Africa* deemed the actions of the new government "hardly a radical departure from Giscard's policies."[39] The emerging policy bears less resemblance to campaign rhetoric than to the moderating influence Mitterrand exerted as minister of overseas France in 1950. At that time he enticed the Ivory Coast political leader Houphouët-Boigny away from alliance with the French Communist party and induced his Rassemblement Démocratique Africain to cooperate with the French government. For all that the Mitterrand entourage may include a sometime revolutionary enthusiast like Régis Debray, such influence is balanced by the formidable presence of men associated with a long sweep of French African policy, notably Gaston Defferre, also a former minister of overseas France and the prime architect of the structure of states under which most of France's African possessions assumed independence. As Mitterrand firmly stated, France "will remain loyal to the arrangements that she has already established with African countries."[40] The pronouncement apparently included South Africa, to which the Mitterrand government approved delivery of a 900m-watt nuclear reactor, despite the Socialists' strong criticism of that state prior to the election.[41]

The new government's stance on intervention appears to differ from its predecessor's primarily in nuance. The name of the highly mobile military units headquartered in France has been changed from *forces d'action extérieure* to the more benign *forces d'assistance ra-*

39. *West Africa*, August 24, 1981, p. 1920.
40. Ibid.
41. *Africa Research Bulletin*, October 1981, p. 6173.

pide, but the continuation of General Lacaze, known familiarly as "Monsieur Para," as chief of staff has indicated that basic military policy remains unchanged.[42] The government's stance on intervention received its first test on September 1, 1981, when David Dacko, whom the French had installed as leader of the Central African Republic, was ousted by General André Kolingba. Although Mitterrand's then minister of cooperation and development, Jean-Pierre Cot, called the coup "a defeat for the process of democracy which was under way,"[43] it was known that the French government had been both embarrassed by Dacko's crackdown on dissenters in July and worried about Libyan support of opposition leader Ange Patasse. With no immediate and clear French interests at stake, Mitterrand ordered that the eleven hundred French troops in the CAR remain impartial. It was announced that the troops would act only if needed to protect the lives of the two thousand French citizens living in that country.

Unlike much of his domestic program, Mitterrand's African policies have not been under serious attack from the Right. Rather, grumblings have been heard from within his own coalition that Socialist principles have been sacrificed to expediency. Several Socialist party activists and Cooperation Minister Cot openly objected to Mitterrand's lavish welcome to President Sekou Touré of Guinea in September 1982. Touré was considered by many to have seriously violated human rights in repressing domestic opposition and, what in the eyes of a few may be even worse, to be a backslider from Socialism engaged in courting good relations with a Republican American administration. Cot resigned his post in December 1982. In what appears to be a reversion to previous presidents' practice, control over African policy seems to have gravitated to the Élysée, where it is directly in the hands of Guy Penne, assisted by the president's son, Jean-Christophe Mitterrand, a former journalist based in West Africa.

Rather than breaking decisively with previous policy, Mitterrand's government appears to be carefully adapting France's actions to the same underlying constraints that affected his prede-

42. George H. Wittman, "Political and Military Background for France's Intervention Capability," *AEI Foreign Policy and Defense Review* 4, no. 1 (1982):15.

43. *Africa Research Bulletin,* October 1981, p. 6173.

cessor's initiatives. In this aspiration, Mitterrand displays no less a concern for maintaining a special relationship with Africa as a cornerstone for France's overall foreign policy.

Resource Constraints. Of all the charges raised against French Africa policy under both Giscard and Mitterrand, the one that has raised the most anxiety with the French public is the risk of over-commitment. The absence of detailed public scrutiny conceals the actual costs of French military involvement in Africa; but at a time when the French economy is experiencing great difficulty, the average French citizen is not unaware that the maintenance of French troops in Africa and the possibility of further military ventures is not cost-free.

As important as the potential political liabilities of a costly French military involvement in Africa are the more immediate constraints that limited resources have imposed on French military capabilities. Ever since de Gaulle, French African policy has been predicated on the maintenance of an effective and flexible French intervention force. But this objective has to contend with others, more important to overall French foreign policy objectives, in the competition for limited government resources. Among these are (1) the continued French commitment to a costly independent nuclear capability, including both land and submarine-launched missiles, which de Gaulle postulated as the cornerstone for French autonomy in foreign policy and which remains a cardinal article of faith across the entire French political spectrum; and (2) the equally important commitment to the modernization of conventional military capabilities in Europe, with the rational goal of ensuring French security in the face of a potential threat from the Warsaw Pact and the less rational but nonetheless real preoccupation with the revival of German power on the Continent.[44]

Because of declining economic growth, inflation, and competing domestic priorities, French defense spending between 1964 and 1982 has consistently fallen short of project goals with no prospect of significant improvement in the near future. As a result, the cost of military operations in Africa and the Middle East (Lebanon) is

44. Alan Ned Sabronsky, "French Foreign Policy Alternatives," *Orbis* 19, no. 4 (Winter 1976):1435–37.

likely to increase. One estimate placed the anticipated cost of extraordinary military operations, primarily in Africa, between 500 million and 800 million francs in 1978 alone.[45] As a result, the forces available for use in Africa are relatively small in number, consisting of the fourteen thousand to fifteen thousand troops of the Eleventh Parachute Division and the Ninth Division of Marine Infantry.[46]

By early 1978 the French military had virtually reached the limits of its capability to deploy forces in Africa. With much of its regular intervention force already committed in Africa and Lebanon, the military was reluctantly obliged to call on the services of the French Legionnaires in responding to the 1978 invasion of Shaba. The Shaba intervention also revealed the deficiencies in French logistical capabilities and equipment. Shortages in long-range military transport aircraft forced the French to rely on the United States and chartered commercial aircraft for the transport of their men and equipment to Zaire. The parachutes used in the drop into Kolwezi were borrowed from the Zairian military. The embarrassing setbacks suffered by the French military in Chad in 1978 also revealed the deficiencies of French weaponry in the face of increasing sophistication of rebel groups in Africa.

The conflicting priorities and limited resources explain why the French military establishment, far from being an advocate of a more activist African policy, has been among the more cautious voices in the French domestic debate. Following the 1978 Shaba intervention, Chief of Staff General Guy Mery, head of the French military and formerly Giscard's personal military adviser, was quoted as saying, "Our defense forces have not been conceived or organized to face specific, far-off missions. We don't have the officer reserves allowing us to face unexpected demand, nor the reserve equipment. Our military schools have only a certain volume and in this area we are approaching our limits. *But I put confidence in the Government to adapt its policy to our means.*"[47]

African and International Constraints. If limited military capabilities have given French military commanders grounds for

45. David S. Yost, "French Defense Budgeting," *Orbis* 23, no. 3 (Fall 1979):579–608.

46. Lellouche and Moisi, "French Policy in Africa," p. 128.

47. Quoted in Webster, June 18, 1978; emphasis added.

caution, a host of broader diplomatic considerations apparently prompted the professional diplomats at the Quai d'Orsay to inter-ject a similar cautionary note into their counseling of the more ac-tivist Africanists at the Élysée.

While France's activist military policy increased French stature in the eyes of moderate Arab and African countries concerned about the threat of Soviet-Cuban penetration in Africa, it also put at risk other French interests in Africa and the Third World. In the narrowest terms, French interventionism has complicated efforts to maintain cordial relations with states where France has historical and important political and economic relationships, notably Alge-ria and Libya, which remain important sources of imported oil. Beyond this, French activism has complicated French diplomatic efforts aimed at broadening relations with other important African states, notably Nigeria, Angola (where France has been seeking ac-cess to Angolan oil), and Tanzania.

Perhaps more important in the broad scope of French policy is the risk to France's self-appointed role as leader in the effort to bridge North-South differences. From de Gaulle on, French presi-dents have sought to identify France with Third World aspirations as part of a broader diplomatic strategy to enhance the French po-sition in Western Europe and to strengthen France's international role vis-à-vis the two superpowers. The claimed special relation-ship with Africa has become one of the keystones to French claims of international relevance. The loss of this presumed special rap-port with Africa would undermine the basis of French claims to an international leadership role independent of the superpowers. To be successful, however, French policy must seek to accommodate the interests of both "moderate" and "radical" African states. It is therefore to some extent hostage to broad African concerns and cannot be seen to run counter to them for long periods without jeopardizing these broader foreign policy goals. But whereas French attacks on U.S. imperialism in the 1960s and 1970s (Viet-nam and Latin America) served to enhance French stature in Africa generally, Giscard's tilt toward military activism in support of African moderates made France the principal target of revived anti-neocolonial, anti-imperialist sentiment on the continent.

At the same time, a policy whose claimed purpose was to re-duce the potential for East-West tension and confrontation in Africa instead tended to contribute to the polarization of the continent along East-West lines. The most evident contradiction in French African policy is that while claiming to offer a "third way" between East and West, France cannot avoid its identification with the West. As a Western capitalist country and moreover a former colonial power, French interests in Africa are inevitably perceived as consonant with overall Western interests, and French military actions are viewed as serving those interests. That perception is only heightened when, as in the aftermath of Shaba II in 1979 and in supporting the 1982 Chad peacekeeping force, France actively coordinates its policies with those of the United States and other Western allies. As a consequence, French military interventions have provoked growing opposition in Africa not only from those ideologically disposed to distrust all Western aims but also among those concerned with insulating the continent from all external intervention, whether by East or West.

Of more immediate concern, however, are the pressures France's activist military policy has placed on the very states such activism is intended to reassure, particularly the moderate Francophone states. Although France's closest friends and strongest supporters in Africa—Senegal, Ivory Coast, Gabon, and Cameroon especially—may privately applaud and welcome France's demonstrated commitment to African security and stability, they find it increasingly difficult and risky to do so publicly, as their general silence in the wake of Bokassa's overthrow shows. Apart from the criticism they could expect from other African states, they have also to be concerned over exposing themselves to attack from critics and opponents within their own borders. The pervasive French economic, political, and military influence in Francophone Africa has provided indigenous opponents of the present regimes and aspiring, ambitious minor functionaries with a ready target. When, for example, Ivory Coast's 1978 independence day celebrations appeared threatened by groups demanding the ouster of the French from the country, Houphouët-Boigny was obliged to request that additional French paratroops be sent to augment the substantial numbers already present, thereby underscoring in the eyes of his opponents his regime's ultimate dependence upon and subservience to French power.[48] But the incident appears also to

48. George H. Rosen, "The Ivory Coast: Folklore, La Prosperité," *Atlantic* 244, no. 6 (December 1979).

have underscored for Houphouët the political liabilities of relying on French military intervention to protect his regime against internal political threats. This perhaps serves to explain why the Ivory Coast has increasingly sought not only to diversify its economic relations and place limits on France's substantial economic and political influence but also to acquire the military means for its own defense.[49] Just as France has felt uncomfortable in having to rely on the U.S. nuclear umbrella for its own national defense, it is not unreasonable to expect African governments to want greater control over their means of protection.

In addition, the likely demise over the next few years of the first generation of postindependence leaders in a number of key Francophone countries is certain to further the dissolution of France's currently close ties to Africa. Despite the institutional links and particularly the cultural affinities that French policy has deliberately sought to cultivate, French influence in Africa remains highly dependent upon the close personal ties forged during the period of decolonization. As experience with such states as Benin, Congo, Central Africa, and Madagascar has shown, the second generation of leaders in such countries as Senegal, Ivory Coast, Gabon, and Cameroon is unlikely for very long to accept the continuation of existing arrangements. The pressures already building in those societies for greater independence from pervasive French economic influence are virtually certain to be accompanied by similar pressures for a recasting of military relationships as well.

Like Giscard before him, Mitterrand and his close African advisers in the Élysée are not insensitive to the limitations and liabilities, both domestic and international, of France's activist military policies. The commitment to assist friendly countries in maintaining their security and stability has not been withdrawn, but the record reveals considerable case-by-case flexibility as to when and how that commitment is carried out. Clearly the French decision to limit its military commitments in Chad while encouraging negotiations among the various factions reflects an awareness of the limits of French military power. Similarly, the effort to ease Mauritania out of the Saharan conflict and to promote

49. "Ivory Coast Looks to the Future," *West Africa*, no. 3250 (October 29, 1979):1977–79.

negotiations between Morocco and Algeria reflects the importance France attaches to continuing good relations with both moderate and radical regimes in North Africa, as well as recognition of the need for a political solution that leaves the balance of power between them essentially intact. The evidence suggests that France is prepared to accommodate itself to changing African realities—provided these changes do not seriously disrupt its principal clients or directly threaten important French interests.

Multilateralization. Efforts to compensate for the limitations on France's ability to respond directly to what it perceives as destabilizing events in Africa have thus far met with mixed success. A notable example is the attempt begun by Giscard and continued by Mitterrand to "multilateralize" African security problems. The idea of a permanent pan-African force, first suggested publicly by Giscard at the 1977 Franco-African summit in Dakar, seemed at first glance to offer a number of advantages to both France and its African allies. Presumably it would enable participating African states to strengthen their defenses through a collective security arrangement, while at the same time reducing the necessity for, or at least the visibility of, outside actors, that is, France. However, with the exception of Senegal's President Senghor, who perhaps deserves the status of co-author, the proposal was received with little enthusiasm by the Francophone states it was intended to benefit.

There were, first, a host of practical and technical problems. Not the least of these was that the effectiveness of such a force depended in the first instance on the indigenous military capabilities of the states that might become party to the arrangement. But the examples of Chad, Mauritania, and Central Africa—despite more than a decade of French military training and assistance—inspired little confidence in local military capabilities, either individually or collectively. Thus such a force would ultimately have to depend on whatever backing and support it received from external sources. But a collective security arrangement that required an outside backer would only amplify the same political liabilities that the Francophone states already faced by virtue of their separate military ties to France—and with no appreciable improvement in their security. Thus, when the proposal again came up for discussion at the 1978 summit meeting in Paris, a number of Francophone leaders, led by Mali's President Traoré, joined in opposing the idea.[50] The only concession Giscard was able to win was the agreement of Senegal, Ivory Coast, Morocco, and Gabon to a one-time participation in a joint security force to replace French and Belgian troops in Shaba.

Giscard was similarly unsuccessful in winning Western support for the other half of his multilateral scheme: namely, a coordinated Western response to destabilization in Africa. When proposed by Giscard in the wake of Shaba II, the United States, Britain, Germany, and Belgium reacted with skepticism and reserve. For its part, the United States saw the proposal as risking a further polarization of Africa along East-West lines, with the likely consequence of increasing both tensions and the opportunities for Soviet troublemaking. Such an outcome, unwelcome though it would have been in all but the most extreme circumstances, was even more undesirable at a time when the United States was seeking broad African and Third World support for its settlement initiatives in southern Africa, as well as proposals on global issues. For their part, the other Europeans were inclined to see Giscard's proposal as a means by which France could get them to underwrite the cost of defending French—as opposed to more broadly Western—interests in Africa, with France reaping both the political credit and the material benefits. In view of the outpouring of African criticism that followed the coordinated Western military action in Shaba and given the reserve with which even the most moderate African leaders were responding to the proposal, the lack of support from the allies was both understandable and inevitable.

Mitterrand applied the multilateral approach in an attempt to find a solution to the Chadian imbroglio in 1981–82. He proceeded with a style quite different from that of Giscard, but ultimately with no clearer pattern of success. At the meeting of world heads of state in Cancun, Mexico, in October 1981, Mitterrand urged deployment of a force from the OAU to keep the peace. His government further supported African efforts to remove Libyan troops, which were assuring some modicum of order in the country and propping up the government of Goukouni Oeddei, in part by promising Qaddafi to resume arms shipments and full-scale diplo-

---

50. Lellouche and Moisi, "French Policy in Africa," p. 28.

matic relations once the Libyans withdrew. Mitterrand emphasized that France sought only to play a disinterested role and was
inspired "by principles identical to those of the OAU."[51]

Along with the United States, France contributed heavily to
underwriting the OAU peacekeeping force, notably by providing
logistical support and paying the expenses of the Senegalese battalion. Perhaps equally important in the eyes of many, French support allowed an important part of the OAU force to operate with
some independence from the Nigerians, who provided the largest
contingent and the general in charge of the operation. As it turned
out, the multilateral OAU force was able to play only a
minor role in succeeding events. Troops of Hissene Habre (backed
notably by Sudan, Egypt, and Saudi Arabia) swept into the Chadian capital and sent Goukouni into exile. The OAU troops stood
aside from the fighting and were rather lamely withdrawn by the
OAU's president at the end of June 1982. The Habre military victory could hardly be considered an unalloyed triumph for multilateral intervention, nor as one that provided France with either a
graceful exit or a particularly friendly regime.

The foregoing analysis has attempted to show the constraints
and limitations on France's ability to conduct an activist military
policy in Africa. Moreover, it suggests that despite past examples
of French interventionism—and, indeed, because of them—those
constraints are likely to grow. That does not suggest, however, the
likelihood of any imminent or dramatic shifts in French policy or
aims nor any rapid dilution of French influence. French interests in
Africa, political and economic, are real and enduring, as is the
French determination to use all available means, including military ones, to protect them. France has demonstrated over the years
both a singular persistence and a remarkable flexibility in adjusting to changing African conditions. Just as de Gaulle was able to
accommodate African demands for political sovereignty without
diminishing—but indeed, enhancing—French influence, his successors have exhibited notable adroitness in modifying the specific
applications of French policy so as to preserve France's privileged
position.

51. *Marchés Tropicaux*, April 2, 1982, p. 916.

Likewise, French policy continues to strike a responsive chord among a number of Africans. Even the most moderate may be led over time by their occasional embarrassment over French zeal to seek greater distance in their relations with France. And most clearly prefer discreet bilateral arrangements to participation in grander designs. But their own insecurities, not only with respect to possible Soviet troublemaking but also vis-à-vis other major actors on the scene—Nigeria, Algeria, Libya—will undoubtedly cause them to welcome the counterbalance of a continuing French role, at least in the near term.

Finally, for all their disdain for French pretensions and distrust of French maneuvering in Africa, France's Western allies will undoubtedly continue to find some assurance in France's continued involvement on the continent. And to the extent that French actions are perceived to serve broader Western interests, they can be expected to encourage and, where appropriate, lend active support to French efforts.

4

Changing Military Capabilities in Black Africa

WALTER L. BARROWS

Black Africa's armed forces are almost as diverse as its cultures, geography, and political systems.[1] They range in size from Sierra Leone's two light infantry battalions to Ethiopia's huge military establishment equipped with modern Soviet weapons systems. They also vary in effectiveness from the highly disciplined Malawi army to the newly recruited troops of strife-torn Uganda. Moreover, they contrast sharply in political character from Guinea's commissar-controlled military through Senegal's Western-style apolitical armed services to what many observers consider Zaire's uniformed predators.

Change, however, is common to most Black African armed forces, particularly in the years since 1975, when the Angolan civil war focused unprecedented attention on Africa and precipitated intensified East-West competition throughout the continent. Most black armies have grown at least moderately, and some have undergone extraordinary expansion. Ground forces have accounted for most of the manpower change (see table 4.1). But a comparison of major African military establishments shows that tanks and other armored vehicles, artillery, jet fighters, and naval craft have

1. The countries treated here include all those on the African continent except South Africa and its homelands, Sudan, and the Mediterranean littoral states. Only the military forces of states are considered here; insurgent forces are not treated, although much of the analysis in this study dealing with the "elements of military capabilities" for states applies as well for insurgents.

Table 4.1. Regular Armed Forces Personnel in Black Africa,
1975 and 1982

| Country | Personnel Strength[a] | | Percent Change[b] |
	1975	1982	
Zimbabwe (Rhodesia)	5,700	41,300	625%
Mauritania	1,300	8,470	552
Ethiopia	45,000	250,500	457
Somalia	20,000	62,550	213
Malawi	1,600	4,650	191
Togo	1,800	5,080	182
Tanzania	14,600	40,350	176
Zambia	5,800	14,300	147
CAR	1,200[c]	2,300	92
Benin	1,700	3,150	86
Upper Volta (Bourkina Fasso)	2,100	3,775	80
Guinea	5,700	9,900	74
Kenya	9,600	16,000	67
Senegal	5,900	9,700	64
Congo	5,500	8,000	45
Rwanda	3,800	5,150	36
Cameroon	5,600	7,300	30
Ivory Coast	4,100	5,070	24
Angola	31,500[c]	37,500	19
Mali	4,200	4,950	18
Liberia	5,200	5,550	07
Sierra Leone	3,000	3,100	03
Niger	2,200	2,220	01
Chad	4,200	4,200	00
Ghana	15,500	12,600	−19
Burundi	7,000[c]	5,200	−26
Mozambique	19,000[c]	12,650	−33
Nigeria	208,000	133,000	−36
Zaire[d]	43,000	26,000	−40

Source: The Military Balance 1975–1976, 1977–1978, 1982–1983, 1983–1984
(London: International Institute for Strategic Studies; 1975, 1977, 1982, and
1983).

a. Total armed forces. Paramilitary units not included. These personnel
strengths should be considered rough approximations.

b. $\frac{1982-1975}{1975} \times 100 = \%$ change.

c. 1977.

d. The sharp drop in the size of the armed forces in Zaire was due less to a
reduction of uniformed manpower than to a 1977 reorganization that separated the National Gendarmerie from the military.

increased in numbers and levels of sophistication, sometimes dramatically, although in a few cases, such as Somalia and Uganda, inventories were reduced or depleted by defeat in war.

Some of this growth and change is accounted for by changes in mission. In the years following independence, most African states expected their forces to do little more than establish a fitful official presence in outlying areas and to control potential disruption in the principal cities. Major secessionist movements, as represented by the Nigerian civil war or Ethiopia's Eritrean rebellions have provoked dramatic increases in size and armaments. So, too, have threats from neighbors, as when Tanzania armed heavily in response to Idi Amin's menaces. As this example shows, increased military capabilities have led to new missions. In 1979 Tanzania's forces pushed across the border and overthrew Uganda's mercurial dictator.

Manpower and matériel figures provide only rough—and often deceptive—indicators of military capabilities, however, and changes in the size and equipment inventories of African armed forces do not necessarily signify like changes in effectiveness. For instance, the dramatic manpower increases registered by Mauritania and Ethiopia were not matched by proportionate increases in capabilities. Although in the Ethiopian case military effectiveness did indeed rise as new units equipped with modern weapons were integrated into the ground forces, the growth of capability has not been commensurate with the numbers involved. Near the other end of the spectrum, efforts to reduce the size of the Nigerian army have enhanced its capabilities by creating a more manageable organization that can allocate a greater portion of its resources to training and replacement of obsolescent equipment.

In Black Africa, moreover, human resources play a greater role in developing military capabilities than material resources. Almost all matériel is imported from more technologically advanced countries. A few Black African states can produce small arms ammunition, but weapons, vehicles, spare parts, and other items of equipment are obtained almost entirely from abroad. From this standpoint, therefore, all Black African states are on roughly an equal footing. Some (for example, Nigeria) can afford to pay more for matériel than their neighbors; some (for example, Angola) are more willing than others to grant military access rights to outside powers in return for arms; and some (for example, Senegal) have profited from closer military relations with former colonial rulers than more independent-minded counterparts. But once the matériel is delivered, whatever its quantity, all states are confronted by the same basic problem—shortages of personnel skilled in using hardware and in managing the complex organizations required to operate modern weapons systems.

The problem of inadequate human resources is not unique to Africa. All military organizations devote considerable attention to the never-ending task of training and retaining skilled personnel. In poor countries, however, the challenge is especially acute because of the generally low educational and technological development of the skills required for military organizations; this, therefore, accounts for wide variations in military capabilities, both over time in the same country and among countries. It is also the case, even more dramatically in Africa than elsewhere in the world, that a major sustained increase in a state's military capabilities requires further development of its educational resources, within both the armed forces establishment itself and society in general.

THE ELEMENTS OF MILITARY CAPABILITIES

In rough order of importance, the following appear to be the key ingredients that determine the levels of military capability in Black African states:

- Human resources (skills, leadership, morale)
- Logistics (supply, maintenance)
- Mobility (rapid movement of men and matériel)
- Firepower (quality and quantity of arms)
- Manpower (numbers of personnel)

Other factors such as command and control, communications, or intelligence are of course important, but they seem less potent in distinguishing the capable from the incapable than do the five main elements.

The elements of military capability are closely interrelated and difficult to separate even analytically. Leadership has a crucial impact on all aspects of military operations. Troop morale—and therefore skills and leadership—are heavily dependent upon logistical supply. Morale is also affected by firepower, modern weapons being objects of pride and esprit de corps. Logistics and mobility are mutually dependent; poorly maintained trucks soon become more a burden than a help, and a well-organized supply depot is useless if troops in the field cannot be fed because of vehicle shortages. Firepower likewise depends upon a constant supply of fuel, ammunition, and spare parts, not to speak of skilled personnel.

Beyond their interconnections, the elements of military capability are affected by domestic and international political considerations.

Human Resources: Skills, Leadership and Morale. Modern military forces are complex organizations that require specialists as well as leaders capable of coordinating and motivating them. Obtaining adequate numbers of specialists—from riflemen to radar repairmen to planners—entails not only elaborate training programs but command and organizational procedures that will deploy and use skills effectively and that will maintain and refurbish them over time. The armed forces of most Black African countries perform poorly on both counts, in part because of the sheer difficulty of developing modern organizations within a milieu that offers limited educational and technical resources. Industries, political parties, and educational systems face problems similar to military organizations in this respect and compete with them for talent. In some countries the concentration of human talent and other scarce resources in the military has probably contributed to economic stagnation within the wider society. Although Somalia, for instance, mobilized a large portion of its population to achieve a notable, albeit temporary, feat of arms, as one of the poorest countries in the world it lacks the societal infrastructure to sustain a high tempo of military activity and expansion without detriment to economic development.

Whatever the overall level of skills and training within a state's armed forces, effective leadership is required to deploy resources effectively. Few African regimes, whatever their ideology, feel secure enough to encourage such leaders within the military, whether or not the political incumbents themselves wear uniforms. The fear of a coup d'etat leads many political leaders to take measures designed to keep potential rivals within the armed services off balance and deprived of a power base. Competence usually takes second place to loyalty, and in some cases it is discouraged altogether.[2] Officers tagged as being too bright or too popular for their own good may find themselves shunted aside to a military attaché job abroad, relegated to an obscure administrative post with no troops to command, cashiered, or—as in Mengistu's Ethiopia, Idi Amin's Uganda, or Guinea during the long period of the *complot permanent*—physically eliminated. Whatever the cost to the individual officer of such self-protective tendencies among political incumbents, the military itself is likely to pay a high cost in effectiveness, as mediocrity is perceived by young officers to be the safest way to the top. As Decalo has shown, the more adventurous among their number are likely to dissimulate their skills and ambition until they feel in a position to strike preemptively against the regime and their own superiors.[3]

As is true in almost every armed service throughout the world, intelligence organizations reporting directly to top officials are used to keep an eye on would-be troublemakers. As much as any ideological indoctrination, this is the principal function of political commissars in military services built on a socialist or revolutionary model. The militaries of Angola, Sekou Touré's Guinea, Ethiopia, and Mozambique are examples. As in such parent models as the Soviet Red Army, political commissars are rarely viewed with enthusiasm by professionally oriented regular officers. In addition to such surveillance, most Black African regimes use one or more political techniques to reduce the threat of a takeover by ambitious military leaders.

Ethnic favoritism or balancing is an important tool for commanding allegiance. At one extreme, recruitment and personnel assignments for key positions favor the group considered most loyal to top leaders, whereas at the other extreme a careful balance is maintained in the officer corps to prevent any one group from

2. For a fuller treatment of the survival techniques used by the typical soldier-politician and their deleterious effects upon military capabilities, see Walter L. Barrows, "Dynamics of Military Rule in Black Africa," paper presented to the conference on How to Look at Africa in the 1980s, Washington, D.C., September 1982.

3. Samuel Decalo, *Coups and Army Rule in Africa: Studies in Military Style* (New Haven and London: Yale University Press, 1976), pp. 7–22.

dominating. Both policies emanate from recognition of the military's potential for overturning the political order. Until the old regime in Liberia was overthrown in April 1980, the senior officer corps was still dominated by members of the Americo-Liberian elite even though the rest of the military and much of civilian life had been thoroughly penetrated by sons of the hinterland. As the Liberian example attests, however, exclusivist policies have their shortcomings, and many regimes prefer to deal with the sensitive if unpublicized issue of the military's ethnic make-up by balancing key groups within the top echelons. Nigeria is a good example. The First Nigerian Republic collapsed in large part as the result of ethnic tensions that were played out within the army's officer corps. Heavy-handed attempts to correct an overrepresentation of Ibos by promoting less well-educated northerners helped spur the 1966 coup. Since the civil war, successive regimes have striven to avoid even the impression that one group is favored in the officer corps lest restiveness in the ranks threaten the delicate quiltwork of recent nation-building efforts. Nigeria benefits in this from its relatively extensive system of secondary and university education, which allows drawing qualified officer candidates from most parts of the country.

Ethnic tension within the armed forces of Zimbabwe poses a severe challenge to the regime of Prime Minister Robert Mugabe. The new army is composed largely of former guerrillas from Mugabe's Zimbabwe African National Union and Joshua Nkomo's Zimbabwe African People's Union, rival black nationalist movements. This political cleavage coincides closely with differentiation between the Shona and Ndebele peoples. Zimbabwe's future stability will in good measure hinge on Mugabe's success in managing—through ethnic balancing or other techniques—this highly charged situation.

Divide-and-rule personnel policies complement balancing efforts. Officers are played off against one another or reassigned frequently lest a position of strength become established. Mobutu of Zaire is famous for such rapid shuffling of military leaders—a technique applied to his political subordinates as well. Even so temperamentally and ideologically dissimilar a chief of state as Tanzania's Nyerere has made liberal use of this technique.

Loyalty may also be elicited in return for opportunities to use public positions for private benefit—in other words, through corruption. Zaire is often accused of allowing the soldiers free rein, but corruption in the military is widespread throughout Africa. In some countries the complicity of the ruling class is thoroughgoing, while in others there is less outright encouragement of corruption than apprehension that firm corrective measures could precipitate a counterreaction or at least a withdrawal of loyalty on the part of officers and men accustomed to an array of unofficial perquisites. Wholesale corruption within the armed forces of such countries as Zaire, Uganda, and Ghana not only has undermined military professionalism but has contributed to economic decline as well. The population at large usually suffers considerably from soldiers on the take, and alienation of key sectors of society represents the major risk to a regime that uses this method for gaining support from the military.

African regimes sometimes counterbalance their armies by paramilitary units, which in some cases are larger and better equipped than the regular forces. (Table 4.2 compares army and paramilitary manpower strengths for 1982.) The gendarmerie in Francophone Africa, for example, is often explicitly intended as a potential counterweight, an alternative source of armed support for a chief of state should the regular armed forces come under the sway of disloyal or overly ambitious leaders. An extreme case is found in Gabon, where the Presidential Guard is considerably more capable than the army. At the very least, the existence of such alternative forces complicates the task of anyone planning a military coup. The utility of this technique was demonstrated in August 1982 when Kenya's General Services Unit, a specially equipped and trained element of the police force, helped put down a coup attempt by junior officers and enlisted men of the Kenya Air Force.

However politically attractive or indeed necessary these techniques for enhancing the survivability of regimes may be, they have a deleterious effect on military capabilities. They create shortages of skilled personnel, deflate morale and dedication among officers, frustrate professionalism, undermine discipline, invite duplication of effort, and deflect energies from strictly military pursuits. The more solidly established the regime, the more it can afford to concentrate the talents and energies of uniformed per-

Table 4.2. Regular Forces and Paramilitary Personnel Strengths in
Black Africa, 1982

COUNTRY	REGULAR FORCES	PARAMILITARY
Angola	37,500	10,000
Benin	3,150	1,100
Botswana	3,000	1,260
Burundi	5,200	1,500
Cape Verde	1,000	
CAR	2,300	1,500
Chad	4,200	6,000
Cameroon	7,300	5,000
Congo (Brazzaville)	8,700	3,000
Djibouti	2,700	2,100
Equatorial Guinea	1,550	2,000
Ethiopia	250,500	3,000
Gabon	2,200	2,800
Gambia	475	
Ghana	12,600	5,000
Guinea	9,900	9,000
Guinea-Bissau	6,050	5,000
Ivory Coast	5,070	3,000
Liberia	5,550	1,750
Madagascar	21,100	8,000
Malawi	4,650	1,000
Mali	4,950	5,000
Mauritania	8,470	2,500
Mozambique	12,650	6,000
Niger	2,150	2,550
Nigeria	133,000	
Rwanda	5,150	1,200
Senegal	9,700	6,800
Seychelles	1,000	900
Sierra Leone	3,100	800
Somalia	62,550	29,500
Togo	5,080	750
Tanzania	40,350	51,400
Uganda	15,000	2,000
Upper Volta (Bourkina Fasso)	3,700	900
Zaire	26,000	22,000
Zambia	14,300	1,200
Zimbabwe (Rhodesia)	41,300	13,000

Source: The Military Balance 1983–84 (London: International Institute of
Strategic Studies, 1983), pp. 67–81.

sonnel on solely military tasks and delegate to them the authority needed to raise military capabilities.

Within the political and educational constraints faced by virtually all African countries, a few military establishments have managed, usually with considerable outside assistance, to make appreciable progress in developing their human resources. Because of perceived necessity—Ethiopia, Zimbabwe, Kenya—or a sense of domestic security—Tanzania, Malawi, Senegal—political restraints have been relaxed to permit more emphasis on competence and correspondingly less on ideological or ethnic purity or on loyalty to a specific individual. Other countries—Nigeria and Botswana come to mind—have in recent years raised somewhat the level of skills, leadership ability, or morale within their military establishments. Even then, the underdeveloped nature of society as a whole limits what can be done: human resource shortcomings continue to be the principal drag on improvement of combat capability.

In an African situation, rapid development of human resources within the military inevitably requires heavy dependence on external powers—with all the drawbacks such dependence entails. Indigenous programs only occasionally provide training above basic levels, so foreign advisers, instructors, and schools become essential for upgrading military capabilities. Sending military officers abroad for several years incurs political risks, as does hosting a foreign military presence at home. In either case, the inculcation of military skills may be accompanied by unwanted political influences, if not outright subversive indoctrination. The risks of foreign involvement can be reduced by spreading training assistance programs among several external sources, as is done by Zambia, Zaire, and Nigeria among other African countries. But this stratagem creates a hodgepodge of doctrines and practices that adversely affects military capabilities by facilitating rivalries among those trained by different foreign countries and by adding to what are usually already formidable logistics complications.

Black African states have sought foreign military training from a variety of sources—former colonial powers, other African states, Third World leaders such as India or Yugoslavia, and a variety of North African and Middle Eastern countries whose quest for advantage over one another has included wooing clients in Black Africa. But especially since 1975 most attention has focused on the superpowers and their competition for influence.

As tables 4.3 and 4.4 demonstrate, both the United States and the Soviet Union have increased their training programs for African military personnel during the past five years or so. These efforts, which include in-country training as well as military schooling and specialized instruction within the United States or USSR, are undertaken for a variety of reasons. Training programs are usually relatively inexpensive yet often quite effective in increasing military capabilities through the development of key skills. For little cost, the donor state can contribute—perhaps dramatically—to the security of a client regime and thereby gain credit for providing an essential service.

Moreover, training often complements other programs such as equipment deliveries. The overall effectiveness of a military assistance relationship depends upon provision of adequate training, since weaponry or equipment without manpower capable of operating, maintaining, and repairing it will soon become more a burden than a benefit. In this respect, the United States enjoys a far better reputation in the developing world than the USSR. The American total-package concept, by which equipment deliveries are integrated with appropriate training, ample supplies of spare parts, and provision of follow-on support, is widely appreciated.

Table 4.3. Soviet and Eastern European Military Personnel in Sub-Saharan Africa[a]

COUNTRY	1978	1981
Angola	1,300	1,600
Ethiopia	1,400	1,900
Guinea	100	50
Guinea-Bissau	65	50
Mali	180	205
Mozambique	230	550
Other	540	945
Total	3,815	5,300

Source: U.S. Department of State, *Communism in Africa,* Bureau of Public Affairs, Current Policy no. 99 (Washington, D.C., 1979), p. 2; and *Soviet and East European Aid to the Third World, 1981,* Department of State Publication 9345, Bureau of Intelligence and Research (Washington, D.C., 1983), p. 14.

a. Minimum estimates of the number of persons present for one month or more. Most of these personnel were Soviets; for instance, of the 1981 total, 4,535 were Soviets. They were engaged primarily as military advisers, instructors, and technicians.

Table 4.4. U.S. International Military Education and Training
(IMET) Programs in Sub-Saharan Africa

	FY1978	FY1979	FY1980	FY1981	FY1982
Allocation					
(U.S. $ in Thousands)	2,654	2,976	2,707	3,939	5,196
Students trained	196	202	184	309	392
No. of countries with IMET program	6	8	15	19	27[a]

Source: U.S. Department of Defense, Defense Security Assistance Agency,
*Foreign Military Sales, Foreign Military Construction Sales, and Military Assistance
Facts as of September 1982* (Washington, D.C., n.d.), pp. 64–65 and p. 76.

a. Botswana, Burundi, Cameroon, Central African Republic, Congo, Djibouti, Equatorial Guinea, Gabon, Ghana, Guinea-Bissau, Ivory Coast,
Kenya, Liberia, Malawi, Mali, Mauritania, Niger, Rwanda, Senegal, Sierra
Leone, Somalia, Sudan, Togo, Uganda, Upper Volta (Bourkina Fasso), Zaire,
and Zimbabwe.

The Soviets, in contrast, are often accused of attempting to gain
undue influence over clients by, for instance, refusing to allow students to retain key manuals, closely controlling supplies of spare
parts, and failing to develop depot-level repair capabilities so that
major items of Soviet-supplied equipment must often go back to
the USSR for overhaul. These practices may increase the short-
term dependence of clients upon Moscow, but they also constitute
irritants that undermine long-term influence. Gaining or retaining influence is, of course, an important reason for extending
military assistance to a recipient state. Training programs are
especially appealing in this respect, because they entail face-to-
face contacts with individuals some of whom may be the future
leaders of the military or even the state itself. Military-to-
military ties are strengthened by the friendships formed, professional links forged, and attitudes shaped through such personal
experiences.

Questions remain, however, regarding the durability of such
ties. They clearly were not resilient enough, for instance, to survive
the political sea changes that have engulfed the Horn of Africa
since the Ethiopian revolution in 1974. Military relationships between Ethiopians and Americans that went back to the early 1950s
dissolved fairly quickly once Haile Selassie was overthrown. His
successor, Lt. Col. Mengistu, had received ordnance training in the
United States, yet this did little to moderate his radical proclivi-

ties. And some fifteen years of Soviet tutelage did not prevent Somalia from severing all military ties with the Soviet Union once President Siad Barre decided in 1977 that Moscow was obstructing his political goals. These developments clearly demonstrate that military training programs, no matter how thoroughgoing, do not guarantee special entrée in perpetuity.

Nevertheless, despite the limitations illustrated by these extreme cases, training programs by and large effectively serve both donor and recipient, providing at relatively low cost a measure of contact and influence for the former and indispensable attention to the human resources problem for the latter. For instance, the goodwill, personal contacts, and military-to-military ties that had developed during several decades of U.S. training assistance to Liberia helped provide continuity in U.S-Liberian relations following the coup by enlisted men in 1980 that overthrew President William Tolbert. Building in part on these ties, the United States was able quickly to develop a working relationship with the new leadership, despite its inexperience and desire for radical changes, while simultaneously attending to the most critical training needs of the Liberian soldiery, thus helping the new regime in its effort to instill discipline and professionalism among troops.

U.S. military training programs in Africa are placing greater emphasis than in the past upon building skills in the field of logistics. Through addressing this key shortcoming, overall capabilities can be improved—and the pool of socially useful human resources incidentally enlarged—with little or no expenditure on expensive hardware.

Logistics: Supply and Maintenance. Shortages of skilled personnel and managerial talents probably are felt most severely in the field of logistics. Combat simply cannot be sustained without a well-developed logistics system. Feeding, clothing, housing, paying, and nursing large numbers of people as well as supplying, fueling, repairing, calibrating, and replacing their equipment is a complex task, one that more than any other criterion distinguishes greater from lesser capabilities in Black Africa. The poor communications infrastructure and the difficult terrain and climatic conditions characteristic of most of the continent add to the difficulties African armies face in moving and supporting men and matériel.

Ethiopia's dramatic gains against Somalia in the Ogaden and against insurgents in Eritrea have been widely attributed to massive Soviet arms deliveries and Cuban combat troops. But the Soviets and Cubans must have first laid a logistical foundation upon which their dramatic accomplishments were based; moreover, they likely have assisted the Ethiopian army in significantly improving its own logistical system, since it now seems able to carry out operations deep in the Ogaden and Eritrea, in contrast to the situation in 1977, when it had lost control of vast stretches of territory in the northern and southern parts of the country. Extended supply lines in rugged terrain, however, probably continues to account in large measure for Addis Ababa's inability to impose full government authority beyond the main population centers of Eritrea and Tigre provinces.

Organized resistance to Tanzania's advance into Uganda was minimal, particularly in the latter stages of the offensive. Even with this minor opposition, however, Tanzania's armed forces could have stumbled over self-inflicted supply and maintenance obstacles. That the advance did not grind to a halt is indicative of a basic accomplishment—setting up a logistical system that extended as much as one thousand miles from its tail in Dar es Salaam into the Ugandan hinterland. Logistical shortcomings do explain, however, why Tanzanian soldiers came to be resented by large segments of the Ugandan population. Dar es Salaam apparently decided it could not afford to supply food to its units in Uganda, but expected them to rely instead upon local resources. Without pay and provisions from home, Tanzanian troops, as could be expected under the circumstances, took to extracting goods from the people they were liberating.

Mobility. Closely related to logistics, the ability to quickly move troops, equipment, and supplies on a large scale requires physical, financial, and human resources that few African military organizations possess. Most can airlift very small units short distances; a few can airlift battalion-sized units over relatively great distances; and fewer still have even limited sealift capabilities.

Mobility shortcomings are not so restrictive as might appear at first blush. A country that lacks sufficient military transport equipment can commandeer civilian trucks and aircraft to move troops in an emergency. Moreover, with outside assistance transport equipment and crews can be acquired in a relatively short time. For instance, acquisition of a few C-130-type aircraft along with training and maintenance support can transform an army, as it has Nigeria's, from a largely homebound establishment to one capable of projecting at least limited force anywhere on the continent.

Mobility in combat is, however, considerably more demanding than simply delivering troops to a new location. Weapons systems designed for mobile warfare—combat aircraft, armored vehicles, self-propelled artillery, naval patrol craft—are complex, maintenance-intensive, and very expensive. They require heavy and continuous training efforts as well as effective command-and-control systems that add to the cost. It is, therefore, not surprising that only a few Black African countries are capable of conducting highly mobile combat operations. The white-led Rhodesian forces, which relied heavily upon air strikes and air mobile raids against guerrilla bases in neighboring countries, were unmatched in this respect. Several other states in the region possess components of combat mobility—an effective air force, for example—but none commands an all-around capacity for undertaking flexible and coordinated air, ground, and naval operations. Mobility in combat is among the most difficult military capacities to acquire, and the majority of African states will master it only slowly, if at all.

Firepower. The ability to direct more projectiles with more explosive power more accurately over greater distances than an opponent is certainly an advantage. In Black Africa it comes with a financial and political price tag, however. Since no country in the region can manufacture its own major weapons, outside suppliers are required, which in turn demands reciprocation, usually in money, political allegiance, or military access.

Some arms are delivered as a gift, but in most military assistance agreements cash is involved, either on liberal loan terms, as in the case of most Soviet contracts, or as strict commercial deals, in the manner of several West European countries. Needless to say, advanced weapons are expensive to purchase as well as to maintain. Ballpark cost figures for selected weapons systems are depicted in table 4.5.

Explicitly or implicitly, a military supply relationship carries with it political obligations. Dependence upon the supplier for a continuing flow of ammunition and spare parts as well as for tech-

Table 4.5. Approximate Costs of Weapons[a]

ITEM	PRICE (U.S.$)
M-60 machine gun (with accessories)	3,200
Scorpion tank (fully equipped)	350,000
M-60A3 tank	1,650,000
Chieftan tank[b]	650,000
Vickers tank (MBT)	1,600,000
AMX-30 tank	1,500,000
M-48 A3 Patton II (reconditioned)	515,000
M-113 armored personnel carrier	300,000
Erutu armored vehicle	225,000
Commando V-200 armored vehicle	190,000
M-109A2 Howitzer	900,000

Source: Gregory R. Copley, ed., *Defense and Foreign Affairs Handbook* (London, Washington, D.C., and Panama City, 1983), p. 929.

a. Market bulk rates in 1983. These sample figures should be regarded as rough approximations only. Costs of a particular weapons system vary considerably depending on its condition, ancillary equipment, amount of spare parts and ammunition, technical assistance from supplier, and other considerations.

b. Market bulk rate in 1981.

nicians and training assistance elicits at least caution if not outright realignment in the recipient's foreign policy dealings with its military patron.

Guinea, Angola, and Ethiopia have allowed the Soviets regular use of local facilities for their military ships and/or aircraft in partial return for arms assistance. French troops are stationed in several former African colonies as part of a general relationship that includes, within a network of ties, the supply of French matériel.

As with training, some African states avoid inordinate dependence upon any one source for matériel by securing a number of outside suppliers. This approach indeed limits external leverage, but it compounds logistical problems correspondingly by creating several supply and maintenance systems in each military service. Military effectiveness is often severely handicapped by such complications. In this way, too, a regime's concern with protecting itself against political pressures can contribute to lowering the capabilities of its armed forces.

Manpower. Although sheer size of one or another force rarely plays a decisive role in African military engagements, availability of manpower does offer an advantage. Personnel requirements balloon once a decision is taken to establish a specialized unit such as armor, artillery, or air transport. An array of secondary and tertiary personnel is essential for supporting the new unit. Moreover, specialized units create a demand for additional units—for example, tanks are most effective if used in conjunction with mechanized infantry, artillery, and, if possible, close air support units. In short, a well-rounded military imposes a greater need to recruit from the wider society than a simple force composed, say, predominantly of riflemen.

As in other regions of the world, a sense of threat is probably the most important catalyst for augmenting the size of military organizations in Black Africa. The greater the perceived external or internal threat to a regime, the more likely it is to expand its armed forces despite economic costs and political risks. A "ratchet effect" characterizes this relationship between threat and size, however. Even if the threat recedes, elements within the military and society will resist manpower reductions. Nigeria offers an example: only slowly and haltingly has it managed to cull surplus personnel from its ranks during the decade following the 1967–70 civil war, and only by the early 1980s did its demobilization effort bring the army down to the publicly announced goal of 150,000. Concerns about unemployment and disgruntlement among demobilized personnel were important factors that impeded force reduction plans. Zimbabwe faced similar pressures retarding the demobilization of excess personnel; the previous government's security forces were combined with two guerrilla armies to form a force larger and more expensive than the new Mugabe regime wanted.

Black Africa for the foreseeable future will probably move in fits and starts toward larger military forces. Despite some dilatory efforts to cut back personnel strengths, the general drift is likely to be expansionist, driven in some measure by an organizational imperative within military establishments to enlarge themselves, but even more so by episodic military encounters between and within societies.

CONSEQUENCES

Although increases in Black African military capabilities have not been so dramatic as might be suggested by changes in personnel strengths and equipment inventories, several countries have gradually improved the combat effectiveness of their armed forces in recent years. Examples are Ethiopia, Kenya, and Tanzania in East Africa, Senegal and Nigeria in West Africa, and Malawi and Botswana in the South. With occasional stagnation and even reversals in individual countries, prospects are for a continuation of this trend as African military establishments absorb additional weaponry and, more important, as some of them acquire the requisite organizational and technical skills. These rising military capabilities will have consequences for both domestic and international politics.

Domestic Affairs. In Africa, there seems to be no relationship between the capabilities of a military organization and its propensity to become politically involved. Weak, inept, unprofessional, ill-equipped, and tiny armies appear no less prone to staging coups than their more capable counterparts. Niger and Nigeria, or Sierra Leone and Somalia, seem no different in this respect. The trend toward more military effectiveness is therefore unlikely by itself to affect the incidence of coup attempts.

There is, however, one way in which the drive for greater military capability could raise Africa's coup quotient. Should some political leaders in an effort to enhance armed forces effectiveness relax the check-and-balance mechanisms that protect incumbents from potential rivals within the military, more power grabs could be expected. For instance, were an army to be strengthened without corresponding improvements in the paramilitary, or without compensating with other balancing techniques, a clique within the army could well become a threat to the regime.

Moreover, where civilian rule has replaced military rule, serious friction between newly established governments and the armed forces has sometimes developed over defense budgets. The civilians simply may not place the same priority upon upgrading military capabilities as their uniformed predecessors who, having given up political power, may become heavily committed to improving their own organizations. For the civilians, funds spent for equipment and training may be regarded as expensive bribes to keep the soldiers away from the political arena, while military leaders may chafe under what they regard as excessive and provocative budgetary cuts that dangerously impair the military's ability to carry out its duties. As indicated in the appendix, return to civilian rule rarely proves definitive.

Some regimes will, of course, view prospects for increased military capabilities with satisfaction. Greater combat effectiveness means greater ability to deter or defeat organized resistance. For example, an immediate consequence of boosting Ethiopia's capabilities was reestablishment of at least nominal central control in the Ogaden and much of Eritrea. Had Addis Ababa and its Soviet-bloc patrons not taken extraordinary steps to build up the armed forces, the map of Ethiopia would have been permanently redrawn and the Mengistu regime probably toppled. Other African countries threatened by secessionist or insurgent movements, latent or active, similarly regard military force as essential—although not necessarily sufficient—for controlling armed dissidence. The limitations of African military capabilities should be recognized, however. The major guerrilla movements active on the continent today—the Eritreans in Ethiopia, Polisario in Western Sahara, UNITA in Angola, the Resistência Nacional Moçambicana (MNR) in Mozambique, and SWAPO in Namibia—cannot be quashed by force of government arms. They are all well anchored in ethnic and regional groups that feel deeply aggrieved by the regime imposed upon them, and they enjoy significant external support. Political settlements are the only feasible route to ending these insurgencies. Nevertheless, the growth of military capability strengthens the hand of governments by making negotiations a more attractive option for guerrillas while at the same time increasing government bargaining power. Beyond this, lesser forms of disorder, such as riots, demonstrations, and ethnic clashes, can be contained all the more readily as police and army effectiveness improves. Simply put, the growth of central authority is for African states contingent in part upon gains in security force capabilities.

The broad trend toward strengthened security forces is, however, unlikely to apply equally among African states. Some will develop their military capabilities rapidly, in some cases far in excess of what is needed for meeting domestic challenges, whereas others will move at a slower pace, in some cases too slow to keep up with growing internal threats. Many states—Zimbabwe seems a good candidate—will likely experience at least temporary reductions in security force effectiveness. Indeed, viewed in long-term perspective, the volatile interaction of politics and martial affairs in Black Africa—and the deleterious effect this usually has on effectiveness—probably means that only a few states will sustain uninterrupted growth of military capabilities into the next century. Most will experience setbacks or reversals, in some cases for a long duration. This helps explain why the key to stability is found only partially in the growth of security forces capabilities. The more basic solution lies in the political realm, for with the growth of centralized political capabilities—the capacity to win loyalties and reconcile differences through patronage, persuasion, and inspiration—military capabilities are more able to flourish. Thus, while the relationship is reciprocal, political stability is likely to prove a more important precondition for an effective army than military capability for political stability.

International Affairs. Uneven rates of military development in Africa are likely to raise the chance of war between discordant neighboring states during the next several years. As a state improves the capabilities of its armed forces, it may at some stage pass the threshold beyond which their inadequacies no longer preclude carrying out sizable operations beyond its borders. In the past, only a few Black African states maintained levels of proficiency above this point, but in the future others can be expected to cross the minimum-competence threshold. They will be tempted to solve disputes by threats or use of force if their neighbors are weak. Thus, unless the drive toward enhanced military strength is carefully balanced among potentially antagonistic neighbors, the likelihood of armed conflict will increase.

East Africa is particularly susceptible to armed conflict encouraged by changing military imbalances. Ethiopia and Tanzania have been bolstering their capabilities at a faster pace than Kenya, Somalia, or Sudan. Djibouti without the French troops stationed there would be far weaker than its quarrelsome neighbors, Ethiopia and Somalia, and could count on little more than their mutual self-restraint for survival. Uganda, too, will be dependent for years to come upon the goodwill of its neighbors. While the Obote government has made surprising progress in containing armed dissident groups, internal conflicts could still get out of hand and invite external involvement by other states.

In general, East Africa is a region in which some governments will continue the time-honored practice of supporting dissident ethnic groups in bordering states. As armed forces develop, moreover, prospects for retaliatory strikes and conventional cross-border incursions will rise, particularly if the aggrieved state is militarily more capable than its rival.

In southern Africa, the Republic of South Africa has used its military and economic power to coerce its neighbors into at least temporary acquiescence in Pretoria's regional hegemony. The March 16, 1984, accord between Mozambique and South Africa is only one—if the most public and surprising—manifestation of this acquiescence.

Nevertheless, the slow, unsteady but nonetheless measurable improvement of the Frontline States' military capabilities will in time likely narrow South Africa's formidable advantage. South Africa will enjoy military superiority over its neighbors for at least the next decade and probably well into the next century, but as its lead slowly diminishes, one present constraint on Frontline support for anti–South African guerrillas will relax. That is, as the Frontline states (except for the weakest and most vulnerable among them) strengthen their defenses against cross-border strikes, their willingness and ability to assist guerrilla training and infiltration will increase. Insurgent activity will likely accelerate in response.

South Africa's lead would be cut severalfold if its opponents were to create an effective multinational force. The development of greater military capabilities among separate states adds to the technical feasibility of such a venture:

- Individual states can contribute contingents without decisively depleting their own defenses.
- Whatever new airlift (and perhaps even sealift) capabilities are acquired could provide an essential element that is now largely missing.
- In addition to supplying infantry troops, states could specialize among themselves, with, for instance, one providing an air defense unit and another an armored unit. Alternatively, and more realistically, states could stress developing capabilities for coordinated action as they build up their individual military establishments, encouraging common practices and communications networks as well as training exchanges and joint exercises.

Logistical and command-and-control problems would be daunting under the best of circumstances, but they could be kept manageable if the major contributors to the multinational force shared a common source of supply and military doctrine. The radical African countries supplied and trained principally by the Soviet bloc—from Algeria to Tanzania—would be the most likely candidates for undertaking such concerted action. Direct Soviet supply would of course enhance the effectiveness of the force and reinforce the commitment of its members, although currently Moscow is clearly reluctant to become involved in any large-scale direct undertaking against South Africa, notwithstanding its military assistance to most Frontline states and to anti–South African guerrillas.

The political and economic obstacles to greater military integration will quite likely prevent the formation of African multinational forces, even though the technical possibilities improve. Nonetheless, Africans are likely to devote increasing attention to the potential for joint military action. Confrontation with South Africa is not the only issue that will give rise to proposals for a combined force. There are and will be numerous domestic and international disturbances elsewhere in the continent that could invite outside intervention unless a concerted African effort were undertaken. The Peacekeeping Force (PKF) for Chad that was formed in 1982 under Organization for African Unity auspices by Nigeria, Zaire, and Senegal was criticized for ineffectuality. But with Western assistance, it was at least able to deploy troops to a harsh environment and support them. The PKF represents the kind of ad hoc arrangement that is likely to gain currency as Africa's security concerns grow more acute and the military capabilities of at least some states grow to the point where joint action is possible.

The world has grown accustomed to the role—often a dominant one—that African armies play in their countries' domestic political life. As these armies' military capabilities increase to the point where they can inflict serious damage on their neighbors, they are likely to play a commensurably greater role in Africa's international life. This new role will be more difficult for the international community to digest, but the manner in which outside nations react—particularly those nations in a position to supply military training and arms—will have important consequences both for Africa and for the broader international order.

5

South African Defense Strategy and the Growing Influence of the Military

ROBERT S. JASTER

STRATEGY AND SURVIVAL

South Africa carries little clout in world affairs. Only recently has it become the object of serious great-power concern. Yet, in thirty-five years of unbroken rule by the Afrikaner-dominated National party, its leaders have never accepted the notion of South Africa as a remote, third-rate power in the backwash of international politics. Indeed, they have consistently tended to think in strategic terms and to project an image of South Africa as a regional power with a significant strategic role to play in global as well as regional affairs.

Every National party administration has formulated foreign and defense policies in response to its perspective on global strategic trends and their implications for South Africa. Defense policies thus have seldom been an ad hoc reaction to particular local events, but rather a reflection of the leadership's worldview at the time.

In large part this is a function of the Afrikaners' very real concern with national survival—the dominant issue in Afrikaner political life for at least 150 years. As leaders of a white minority people ruling over an increasingly restive and militant black majority, the National party leadership has long recognized the need for allies. Hence over the years it has made persistent and often costly efforts to gain the protection of a Western defense umbrella and, more generally, to avoid being isolated internationally and cut off from the European mainstream.

As opposition to apartheid both within and outside South Africa has accelerated in the past few years, the white leadership has formulated an official ideology of survival against what it defines as a Communist-instigated "Total Onslaught" against South Africa. Its response to the Total Onslaught is the "Total National Strategy": a comprehensive plan to mobilize the society behind the government. This has led, inter alia, to efforts to broaden its support among nonwhites, to a rapid expansion of its military capabilities, and to an active and often interventionist policy vis-à-vis neighboring states. Nor has the Botha leadership despaired of winning Western—especially U.S.—support for its self-proclaimed anti-Communist struggle at the tip of Africa.

The leadership's preoccupation with strategic issues has only recently led to an influential policy role for the South African military. The tension and hostility prevailing between the Afrikaans- and English-speaking communities in the 1950s ruled out any close consultation between the Afrikaner government and the general staff and officer corps, which were predominantly English speaking. Moreover, until the early sixties the only real threat to security was seen as coming from within; hence the military establishment was small and weak and essentially viewed as a local adjunct to Western defense forces. Even the major defense buildup by the mid-sixties did not lead to significant military participation in the policy process. Indeed, as argued in this chapter, only in the late seventies—following a dramatic shift in the balance of power in southern Africa and a marked deterioration, both in South Africa's relations with the West and in its external security situation—has the South African military establishment suddenly emerged on the political scene to pursue and protect policy interests of its own. With the growing mobilization of the society in response to the concept of Total National Strategy, the military has come to exert a major, and at times decisive, influence on policy. And this, in turn, has important implications for South Africa, the subregion, and the West.

SHIFTING THREAT PERCEPTIONS AND RESPONSE

Internal Security and the Search for Allies, 1950s. During roughly the first decade of National party (NP) rule (1948–58), domestic security issues predominated. The very early apartheid measures, which the government put through chiefly as a means of consolidating the support of the Afrikaner electorate behind the party, quickly led to organized resistance, including civil disobedience, by nonwhites. The government saw this as Communist instigated and responded with massive arrests and detentions, together with a succession of Draconian security laws. But the threat remained, as sporadic resistance continued through the decade, leading successive NP administrations to reaffirm that the *primary* responsibility of the South African Defence Force was to maintain internal security.

The early NP leaders also evolved a basic strategy for external defense. They saw no immediate threat of outside attack, but were much concerned over the growing political upheaval as black nationalism spread through Africa, a development they saw as part of a global Communist plan to weaken the West by wresting Africa and its riches from Western control. Hence it was necessary to keep radical black nationalism from spilling over South Africa's borders and infecting its black population.

The strategy of the fifties had three major objectives:

- South Africa should enter a formal defense alliance with the West.
- The West should be committed to the defense of Africa.
- In the event of general war against Communism, the enemy should be engaged as far away as possible from South Africa.

The first objective was seen chiefly as a means of achieving the second, which the South Africans considered vital to their national defense. Neither was achieved, however; simply put, the Western powers never came to perceive Africa or its defense to be as vital to Western security as the South Africans had. The nearest South Africa came to such a pact was the Simonstown Accord with the United Kingdom in 1955 (since terminated by the United Kingdom), in which both states agreed in very broad terms to defend southern Africa against external aggression.

South Africa's leaders also were frustrated in their efforts to persuade the Western powers not to decolonize Africa—a line the South Africans pursued virtually to the end of the decade. Indeed, the emergence of independent black states at that time found the

South African government unprepared with any policy toward them. Similarly, although aware of the problems that apartheid was creating for Pretoria's relations with Africa and the West, the South African leadership nevertheless continued throughout the decade to nurture serious hopes that the West would acknowledge a guiding role for South Africa in regional African affairs. From the security standpoint, the really important issue was the fate of the three British High Commission Territories, which South Africa had hoped to incorporate into South Africa proper. Since the three achieved independence (as Botswana, Lesotho, and Swaziland), South Africa became increasingly concerned at the possibility of their being used as bases for infiltration of terrorists into the Republic.

In spite of the government's growing concern over external security, defense outlays remained low through the decade. Even by 1960 the defense budget amounted to less than 1 percent of GNP. Demobilization after 1945 had sharply reduced the South African Defence Force (SADF), which remained very small until the sixties. In the decade following the 1948 victory of the NP, the SADF was further weakened by wholesale dismissals of English-speaking officers in favor of Afrikaners and by the resignation of the chief of the general staff in protest. Arms purchases were small and were made not for local defense needs but to enhance South Africa's credibility as a military partner of the West. All this is consistent with the leadership's threat perception; Communist aggression was seen as a remote threat for which the Western powers would bear major defense responsibility, with only token participation by South Africa (for example, SAAF airmen took part in the Berlin airlift and a squadron served with UN forces in Korea). As yet there was no threat of attack by African states.

The Growing External Threat and the Defense Buildup, 1960–74. As the sixties opened, South Africa's security situation deteriorated sharply. Internal resistance suddenly came to life, leading to the tragic shooting of African protesters at Sharpeville. Violent offshoots of the two major (and banned) African nationalist groups, the African National Congress (ANC) and Pan African Congress (PAC), turned to sabotage. In spite of a spate of tough new security laws and increasingly effective police work, it took the government over five years to crush the internal resistance.

Outside developments were also alarming. South Africa was forced to leave the Commonwealth (1961), and both Western and African states began voting against South Africa in the United Nations. The start of the Angolan uprising prompted the Verwoerd administration to initiate patrols of the Namibian coast and to enlarge the garrison at Walvis Bay. Verwoerd warned Parliament that the major threat was now an "Afro-Asian" attack. Although he thought such an attack unlikely, if it were to come, South Africa could not count on Western help. Hence, the Republic must develop its own striking power and be able to stand on its own feet, he said.

Accordingly the sixties saw a rapid buildup of South African defense. The Permanent Force—the "regulars"—was expanded from 9,000 in 1960 to 15,000 in 1964, while the number of national servicemen trained each year grew from 2,000 to 20,000 during the same period. By 1964 South Africa had approximately 120,000 men under arms:

Permanent Force	15,000
National Service Trainees	20,000
Commandos (home guard)	51,000
Police	34,000
	120,000

At the same time South Africa launched a massive program to modernize its armaments. In nine years more than $800 million was spent on major purchases of aircraft, ships, armor, rockets, artillery, and a range of radar, sonar, and navigational equipment. The purchase of naval frigates from the United Kingdom and three French submarines, together with reconnaissance aircraft, gave South Africa a creditable maritime strike capability. Consonant with the perceived dual threat of conventional land attack and growing guerrilla warfare, the lion's share of new purchases went to ground defense, including new equipment for the army.

In 1964, spurred by the United Kingdom's announced termination of arms sales to South Africa, the government undertook an ambitious program aimed ultimately at achieving self-sufficiency in arms. A state board, with wide powers to develop, manufacture, and procure arms, soon administered a variety of weapons-producing facilities within the country. By 1971 South Africa's defense minister could point to local production of a wide range of infantry weapons, armored cars, ammunition, explosives, and simple communications equipment.

In spite of impressive results over the years, however, South Africa remains dependent on foreign suppliers for tanks, aircraft, helicopters, advanced naval vessels, and sophisticated electronics, among others. And key components in several locally produced weapons continue to come from abroad.

As South Africa's defense capabilities increased during the sixties, the threat of direct conventional attack across the border faded rapidly. Toward the end of the decade, attack from the weak states to the north was out of the question, and the chief threat was seen to be "small wars"—growing guerrilla incursions. The SADF's first large-scale military exercise, Operation Sibasa in 1968, involved a force of mock terrorists entering the Transvaal from Mozambique. The South Africans concluded that they could handle such small-scale attacks alone; hence the need for military alliances diminished. The defense minister, P. W. Botha, declared, however, that the instigation of local wars was but one stage in the Communist grand strategy: if it eventually succeeded, then "a final conventional confrontation" would take place.

Defense costs rose rapidly in the early sixties (see table 5.1). Since this was a period of record-breaking economic growth and heavy exchange earnings, the defense buildup caused no severe economic strains. As the threat of direct attack faded and inflation accelerated, the defense minister came under strong pressure to hold down spending; hence the defense vote leveled off, averaging some 285 million rand (at the time, 1 rand = $1.20) between 1968 and 1973.

South Africa's burgeoning economy, together with its enhanced military might and the apparent end to internal resistance, made it by far the dominant power in a region of weak new states and gave the leadership a new self-confidence in the late sixties. With an anxious eye to future guerrilla threats, South Africa decided to use its new power to strengthen political and economic links to nearby states, especially Botswana, Lesotho, and Swaziland. This outward thrust of power was also reflected in a more interventionist foreign policy, particularly in Rhodesia, where several thousand South African troops engaged in counterinsur-

Table 5.1. South Africa: The Defense Vote, 1960–61 to 1982–83[a]

Financial Year	Defense Vote, Mill. Current Rand	As % of Budget	As % of GNP	% Rise Over Past Year
1960–61	44	6.6	0.9	
1961–62	61	10.0		38
1962–63	120			96
1963–64	120			0
1964–65	230	21.0		92
1965–66	219			(−)
1966–67	248	19.0		13
1967–68	256			3
1968–69	252	16.1	2.5	(−)
1969–70	272	16.8	2.4	8
1970–71	257	13.0		(−)
1971–72	317	12.0	2.6	23
1972–73	335	12.0	2.3	6
1973–74	472	13.7	2.6	41
1974–75	692	16.0	3.2	47
1975–76	948	18.5	3.7	37
1976–77	1400	17.0	4.1	48
1977–78	1526	19.0	5.1	9
1978–79	1682	16.6	4.2	10
1979–80	1857		5.0	10
1980–81	1890			2
1981–82	2459			30
1982–83	3100	20.0	4.0	
1983–84	4000[b]			
1984–85	4950[c]	15.0		21+

a. From official data. Excludes defense spending by other departments, as well as DoD expenditure on loan account.

b. Derived figure.

c. Preliminary total.

gency operations from 1968 to 1975, and in Angola, where the South Africans conducted joint antiguerrilla operations with the Portuguese.

Toward Fortress South Africa, 1975–84.

The Deteriorating Security Situation. The overthrow of the conservative Portuguese government in April 1974 led to a dramatic shift in the balance of power in southern Africa. As the only remaining white-ruled states in the region, South Africa and Rhodesia no longer could launch joint counterinsurgency operations with a friendly Portuguese administration in Angola and Mozambique. Instead Pretoria's leaders faced the prospect that self-declared Marxist regimes in these territories would support guerrillas operating against Rhodesia, Namibia, and South Africa itself. Above all, however, the Vorster government was apprehensive over the dangers inherent in prolonged chaos and political turmoil just across its borders.

Pretoria's response to the new situation was détente. Its essence was that South Africa must assert a vigorous leadership role in regional affairs and must win the cooperation of African states—conservative states, in particular—to bring stability to the region and prevent the further spread of radicalism and chaos. South Africa offered friendship and technical assistance to the new government in Maputo, among others. But the main test for détente was Rhodesia, where Vorster personally took charge of a major South African peace initiative that involved six months of high-level talks with African leaders and considerable arm-twisting of Ian Smith. In the event, détente came to a halt in August 1975, when a crucial meeting between Smith and the black nationalists collapsed in rancor.

By then, however, South Africa had already become militarily involved in Angola. South Africa had no advance master plan for its Angolan venture. Like other intervening countries, it seems to have been drawn into a step-by-step escalation, mostly through a series of ad hoc responses to growing fears and tactical opportunities. By early summer, heavy fighting among rival nationalist groups throughout Angola had led to a rapid breakdown in order, and southern Angola had become a no-man's-land, where South Africa was soon engaged in guarding joint hydroelectric projects, establishing centers to stem the flow of Angolan refugees into Namibia, and seeking out SWAPO guerrilla bases for destruction.

At least by June 1975, Vorster, apparently at the urging of the military, had decided to play a far more active role by helping two guerrilla groups, UNITA and FNLA, to block the more Marxist MPLA's efforts to gain control over Angola. This course was the more attractive since the United States and several African states already were helping the two anti-MPLA groups. By September or

October the South Africans had organized UNITA and FNLA troops into several combat groups, led by SADF officials and equipped with South African armored cars, mortars, and artillery. Within weeks the southern half of Angola had been cleared of MPLA and its Cuban advisers, and a South African-led force advanced five hundred miles toward Luanda. The combined force continued fighting through December.

But on January 22, 1976—almost six months after its initial involvement—South Africa withdrew all its forces, except those patrolling just over the border. Political factors were crucial to the decision; a U.S. congressional mandate against continued American involvement, plus South Africa's failure to win either Western or African endorsement of its intervention, left South Africa in an extremely exposed and isolated position and with no clear idea of what might happen were its forces to enter Luanda. But there were military considerations as well. Soviet weapons and Cuban troops, introduced on a small scale in early summer, were pouring into Angola by October. The SADF's overextended supply lines, together with the absence of support units, particularly engineers to bridge Angola's large rivers, began to slow the South African advance. By December, the South Africans were finding the fighting far tougher than the easy sweep through the South a few months earlier. As Vorster told the press in late December, the Russians were bringing in tanks, 122mm rockets in clusters, and infantry-borne SAMs. "Only big powers can affect this arsenal . . . it is certainly beyond our limits." Without broad military cooperation from the West, South Africa's (officially claimed) two thousand troops in Angola faced a bleak future.

Yet, in spite of all these developments, South Africa's military leaders are said to have urged Vorster to let them launch an assault on Luanda, the capital, and presumably occupy it. The military's frustration at what they termed a "political decision" to withdraw from Angola is reflected in the official SADF account of the Angola venture, entitled "We Could Have Gone All the Way."

The Angola venture was costly for South Africa. It put paid to détente, led to widespread international condemnation, and brought further strains to Pretoria's relations with the West. Most important, it gave the USSR and Cuba a pretext for massive Cuban military intervention, thereby bringing about the very situation that South Africa's leaders have always most dreaded: a strong Communist conventional military presence—twenty thousand Cubans—on its borders.

There were domestic costs, too. The military grumbled openly at the politicians' handling of the war. And South African casualties, light as they were—forty-three killed and a hundred wounded—came as a shock to South African whites. For one thing, they had been told nothing of their country's intervention until the troops were about to be withdrawn. For another, South Africa's long-simmering counterinsurgency had cost almost no South African lives up to that time. Parents complained to their MPs about young national servicemen sent without parental permission to fight in a foreign country. In the end, however, the government managed to survive the Angolan debacle with surprisingly little public outcry and no evident political casualties.

In June 1976 South Africa's internal security was suddenly shaken by the country's most serious racial disturbances of this century. By November the so-called Soweto riots—South Africa's most serious and violent outbreak of black protest in this century—had struck almost every black township and campus in South Africa, leaving some six hundred dead (including a handful of whites) and thousands injured, plus widespread property damage. The immediate cause of the protest was government insistence that African students do much of their schoolwork in Afrikaans— for most a third or fourth language and one with objectionable associations—but behind that lay the whole gamut of black grievances against white domination. In spite of the government's massive and prolonged security crackdown, the depth of black grievances revealed at the time bodes ill for long-term racial peace. But Soweto had a more immediate impact on external security. Several thousand blacks, mostly young students, fled South Africa during the Soweto troubles and have since swelled the ranks of South African black nationalist groups in exile. Indeed, the Soweto refugees already have been explicitly linked to the sharp rise in guerrilla incidents inside South Africa during the past few years. In addition, Soweto contributed to the growing antiapartheid sentiment that resulted in a mandatory UN arms embargo against South Africa in November 1977.

Repercussions from the Angolan and more particularly the

Soweto developments were significant factors in South Africa's deteriorating relations with the West after 1976. But there were others. The advent of the Carter administration signaled a new, tougher U.S. stance toward Pretoria. In the summer of 1977 Western suspicions that South Africa was planning to test a nuclear weapon led to cool, mostly low-key exchanges that left each side unsatisfied and uncompromising. In 1979 U.S. military attachés in Pretoria were ousted for spying. Namibia, too, had contributed to strained relations by 1979, when the South Africans denounced the Western Five for allegedly showing bad faith and conniving with UN officials to install SWAPO in power.

Approaching the Garrison State. In early 1976, as the last South African troops were withdrawing from Angola, the defense minister warned Parliament that the presence of Cuban troops and sophisticated weapons in Angola had "introduced a completely new factor . . . virtually overnight." As a result, he said, South Africa now "must have a deterrent to be able to resist a fairly heavy *conventional attack* on South Africa" (italics added). In line with this new threat, South Africa by 1977 had procured antitank missiles, naval attack craft, and long-range strike aircraft. Most revealing was a large-scale military exercise held in September 1977 when, for the first time, the object was to test a mechanized combat group in conventional warfare. Artillery, armored cars, tanks, and mortar units repulsed the "enemy": an armored division supported by aircraft that had entered the country via Namibia. The 1982 White Paper on Defence noted that the increase in Soviet-supplied heavy weapons to nearby states had increased the prospect of a conventional attack, "even in the short or medium term."

Clearly South Africa's heightened threat perception has led it to prepare for a worst-case contingency: a substantial conventional attack from the North. But how real is this threat? It seems extremely unlikely on the face of it that the Cubans—or the East German military personnel, whose arrival in Angola in the late seventies caused much concern in Pretoria—at any time contemplated taking part in an invasion of Namibia or South Africa. The explanation for South African apprehensions probably lies in the range of tactical responses the SADF thinks might be necessary in the future. Its ability to keep SWAPO off balance and unable to organize a large-scale operation against Namibia depended on hard-hitting preemptive strikes at SWAPO bases and supply centers, as well as at the Soviet-supplied missile and radar complexes deep within Angola that threatened to interfere with South African air strikes. As Angolan defenses improved, increasingly heavy South African strikes were called for. South Africa also carried out several surprise armed raids against suspected ANC targets inside the capital cities of Mozambique and Lesotho. It has threatened Zimbabwe with similar attacks.

South Africa's military leaders have prepared the SADF to take even bolder preemptive measures in the future—for example, taking and holding sizable pieces of neighboring territory for prolonged periods if necessary. Thus in 1982 the SADF established a unit that would be able to set up within forty-eight hours a fully operational advanced tactical air base to serve a South African air force (SAAF) squadron. South Africa's military leaders thus seem to have gamed out a future scenario in which increasingly heavy SADF responses would be called for and against which the target countries would at some point be provoked into calling on outside forces to intervene on a large scale. In short, the perceived conventional threat against which South Africa has been preparing appears to be that of a massive retaliation by radical black states and their Cuban and Soviet supporters against future preemptive attacks by the SADF.

Defense budgets in the last few years are consistent with South Africa's heightened threat perception. After remaining stable at 300 to 400 million rand in the early seventies, the defense appropriation rose steeply to 700 million rand in 1974–75 with the initiation of a five-year program to expand and modernize the SADF. Two years later the defense budget had doubled. In 1981–82, it rose 40 percent to almost 2.5 billion rand ($2.75 billion), and in 1982–83 it totaled more than 3 billion rand. In March 1984 South African officials announced that military spending would increase by over 21 percent in 1984–85 and that it would be "unrealistic" to expect the recent peace initiatives in the region to lead to a defense cut in the near future.

Implementation of the Total National Strategy has been accompanied by a steady intrusion of military and security matters into everyday life in South Africa. In January 1978 the initial period of military service for draftees was raised from one year to two.

Subsequent legislation provides that, after serving two years, ex-servicemen automatically are placed on active reserve for twelve years, during which they can be recalled to active duty for up to 90 days a year for a maximum of 720 days' total service in that period. The number of school cadets was doubled to more than three hundred thousand, with training to take place during school hours and summer holidays. Local authorities throughout South Africa have created committees for the adjustment of servicemen to civilian life, and the SADF has been pressing for larger pensions for the war-disabled. To stem the exodus of white farmers from border areas subject to terrorist incursions, the government subsidizes the purchase of unoccupied white farms. It has been proposed that ex-servicemen be encouraged to settle in these areas so as to create a chain of protected villages that could double as military bases in times of national emergency.

Meanwhile security legislation introduced in 1981 would require *all* South Africans to be fingerprinted and to carry identification cards. In 1982 the government revised its internal security laws to provide somewhat greater protection to detainees, but indefinite detention without access to family or a lawyer remains. Other recent legislation imposes vague restrictions on publishing, conveying, or compiling information deemed prejudicial to the state.

The Military's Influence on Policy. The growing security threat since 1976, and particularly the growth of the SWAPO insurgency, has been accompanied by the emergence of the military as a major force in the policy process. In October 1978, when the Western Five foreign ministers arrived in Pretoria to take up the Namibian issue with the new prime minster, P. W. Botha, the South African side was joined for the first time by General Magnus Malan, then chief of the defense staff. Malan, who was subsequently named minister of defense, has continued to play a major role in the negotiations and to express strong views in public and private on the Namibian issue. He is believed to have strongly opposed the Western proposals for a demilitarized zone straddling the Angolan border and has been outspoken in his opposition to any settlement terms that might lead to future SWAPO domination over Namibia.

Botha's reliance on military men and military advice has been shown on various occasions. Following the recent collapse of the internal Namibian political alliance favored by Pretoria, the head of military intelligence personally intervened to help establish a new political grouping. The State Security Council (SSC), South Africa's top policymaking body, has become a sort of supercabinet under Botha's administration. Made up of a handful of senior cabinet members, including the prime minister, the ministers of defense, foreign affairs, justice and peace, and occasional ad hoc members, the SSC thus concentrates top decision making in very few hands. Some of those represented have indicated their frustration over what they see as the predominant influence of the defense minister on SSC decisions. At a lower level, too, Botha has arranged for the military to become broadly engaged in the planning process through its representation on all interdepartmental committees.

In the spring of 1980 the SADF was involved in an unprecedented move to influence the internal political process. The South African press surfaced a classified SADF document entitled *Psychological Plan: Defence Budget Debate,* which assigned to various military departments a mission "to nullify the parliamentary Opposition's attack on the Prime Minister during the budget debate." The object was to blunt the opposition's attacks on government policy in several vulnerable target areas: the role of nonwhites in the armed forces, the complaint that most of the fighting along the Angolan border is borne by the Citizens' Force (active reservists), treatment of conscientious objectors, and pay. Botha and General Malan dissociated themselves from the document. An SADF inquiry was promised, and the prime minister reiterated his commitment to keep the military out of politics. But suspicions linger that more was involved than a random act by an overeager underling; particularly when at about the same time, it was disclosed that SADF officers had been pressuring television producers at the South African Broadcasting Corporation to produce "sabre-rattling films."

All this is consistent with Botha's own hawkish inclinations and with his close ties to the military as defense minister for more than a decade. During that period he promoted and directed the rapid expansion and modernization of South Africa's armed forces. It was Malan who sold Botha on the ideology of the Total National Strategy: an ideology that by definition implies a leading role for the military.

Although the military has taken an extremely hawkish position on external matters, it has at the same time taken a leading role in promoting domestic race reform and nonwhite advancement. The SADF has been in the vanguard in recruiting, training, and promoting nonwhites. Military bases in the combat zone are said to have fully integrated accommodations and facilities. The military's pro-reform position reflects two major institutional concerns. First, it is the view of the military leadership that, although the SADF can continue for some time to hold the fort against any likely threat from without or within, ultimately a political solution—a resolution of South Africa's internal race problem—must be found. Thus the military strongly backs Botha's controversial program of constitutional and labor reform, modest though it appears to outside observers. A second military concern is the need for healthy, educated recruits to meet future SADF skilled manpower requirements. Since this need cannot be filled from the limited pool of available white manpower, the SADF has a strong interest in seeing improved health and educational standards for the nonwhite majority.

Thus, as Botha relies on the military, so the military relies on Botha to press forward with domestic race reforms. Indeed, it is not too farfetched to suggest that ultimate failure on the part of the government to accommodate nonwhites could lead to a military takover, with or without Botha, in which a military dictatorship would take the necessary steps to ram through a series of reform measures over the stubborn opposition of right-wing whites.

It seems unlikely, however, that the growing political influence of the military depends exclusively on its having as patron a prime minister. As the government faces increasingly complex military and military-technical questions concerning Namibia, weapons procurement, counterinsurgency warfare, and so on, any leadership in Pretoria will be likely to continue to rely on military expertise and counsel as essential inputs to policy. And the military will continue to have major interests to protect through the policy-making process.

In Pursuit of Regional Security, 1979–84. During 1979 an abrupt hardening appeared in official South African attitudes toward the West, particularly the United States. A number of major policy statements depicted the West as being both unwilling to challenge Soviet military expansionism and dishonest in its dealings with the Republic. This shift reflected Pretoria's growing isolation from the West during the previous few years. The first blow had been U.S. withdrawal from support of South Africa's invasion of Angola in the summer of 1975. The Soweto uprising of 1976 and South Africa's subsequent harsh security crackdown had led to sharp criticism from Western leaders and a UN arms embargo in 1977. In Rhodesia, too, South African support for Ian Smith's internal settlement initiative in 1978 meant a departure from Western efforts to reach a settlement that would include the guerrillas. Worsening relations with the Carter administration culminated in Prime Minister Botha's angry denunciation of U.S. and UN duplicity in the Namibian negotiations early in 1979.

Thus Pretoria's leaders asserted that South Africa could no longer look to the West for help in solving southern African problems but must itself take the lead in seeking peaceful solutions and preventing further Communist inroads in the region. This theme was elaborated in major speeches by South Africa's foreign minister in early 1979. Outlining a new dispensation for southern Africa, he said that Pretoria would:

- Adopt a position of greater neutrality between East and West.
- Work at solving regional problems through local leaders.
- Consider organizing a constellation of seven to ten southern African states. "International secretariats" might be established to regulate the affairs of the people in these states.
- Establish its own independent national goals, including the attainment of peace and stability in the area and the promotion of a "sub-continental solidarity," which could be the basis for close collaboration in various spheres of activity.

Joint military action was to occupy a central place in the proposed constellation. The regional security theme appeared in the 1979 White Paper on Defence, which called for "mutual defence against a common enemy"—the latter defined as the spread of Marxist influence. Botha also proposed a nonaggression treaty, in which regional states would pledge themselves to combat terrorism and to respect existing national borders.

To assess this policy—if indeed such general statements of intent add up to a policy—its various elements must be examined and the soft elements separated from the hard.

First, neutrality is not a serious option for Pretoria, which ultimately must depend on the West for capital, technology, manpower, and arms. No Communist state would believe a South African declaration of neutrality, let alone adopt a less hostile policy toward Pretoria because of it. Nor would Africa's nonaligned states be impressed. The white minority's best hope for retaining power is to win Western support, whether in the form of secret arms deals, technical cooperation, or joint measures to avert punitive international sanctions. Threats to remain neutral thus appear no more than a gesture of defiance—a way to show the electorate that its leaders were being tough and uncompromising in the face of external pressure and hostility.

Similarly the notion of a broad constellation linking the other regional states to apartheid South Africa economically, politically, and militarily must be seen as the Botha administration's reaction to its growing estrangement from the West and as a sign of its decision to adopt its own regional policy, independent of the West. It is doubtful that South Africa really expected seven to ten nearby states to show any interest in its constellation proposal. Predictably, there were no takers at the time. Indeed, the immediate response of the region's nine black-ruled states was to form their own organization for regional economic cooperation, the Southern African Development Coordination Conference (SADCC), a major objective of which is to reduce member states' dependence on South Africa.

What, then, was the real significance of the constellation proposal? Most likely South Africa's leadership sought to give an aura of grand strategy and larger purpose to a policy that in fact was based on narrow, pragmatic self-interest. What remained of the constellation once its soft, rhetorical parts had been excised was a plan to strengthen the defense perimeter, or *laager;* but a laager redrawn to include a friendly dependency of Namibia and a dependent Muzorewa government in Rhodesia in which power would remain in white hands.

Concrete policy moves in 1979–80 were consistent with the idea of such an extended defense perimeter. In Namibia the South

Africans, hostile to the idea of a SWAPO-dominated government and skeptical of the outcome of the Western Five negotiations, nonetheless continued to negotiate an internationally sponsored settlement; but they also worked assiduously, though without success, to establish a broadly based political structure inside Namibia that could either compete effectively against SWAPO in an election or, if necessary, govern the territory under an internal settlement.

There had been similar hopes for Rhodesia. The Botha administration gave heavy military and financial support to the Muzorewa government. Prime Minister Botha and other South African officials threatened to intervene militarily in its behalf if the London peace talks led to "confusion and civil war." Indeed, Botha acknowledged in late 1979 that South African troops already had been operating for some time inside Rhodesia. But hopes for a defense alliance collapsed with Mugabe's election victory in March 1980 and his subsequent policy statements of adopting nonalignment and a cool but correct line of noninterference in South Africa's affairs.

As the prospects for a constellation faded, South Africa was already embarking on a hard-hitting campaign of preemptive and punitive attacks, both covert and overt, against neighboring states allowing sanctuary to ANC and SWAPO guerrillas. SADF ground units were already operating permanently along a thirty-mile-wide zone *above* the Angolan border. The Angolans estimate that, by 1982, these operations, together with SADF deep-penetration raids, had caused $7 billion in damage. Between 1981 and 1983, South African forces carried out three armed attacks against suspected ANC offices in Maputo, Mozambique's capital city. In 1982 a similar surprise SADF raid on alleged ANC-occupied buildings in Maseru, Lesotho's capital, took thirty-seven lives, including a number of innocent Lesotho citizens.

South Africa also organized, trained, and equipped guerrilla groups to act as its proxies in exerting military pressure against neighboring states. The longest-standing and most effective of these is UNITA, which was an authentic national movement fighting for Angolan independence from Portugal. Since 1975 it has fought against the MPLA government. In addition to maintaining its own forces in Angola, the SADF has conducted regular liaison with UNITA and has supplied the guerrilla forces with weapons from its own stocks and with arms captured by the SADF from Angolan and Cuban troops. Irregular SADF units have supported UNITA on the ground, and the SAAF has sometimes flown air cover for UNITA operations.

Against Mozambique, South Africa has until recently sponsored and apparently directed the activities of a shadowy force of mercenaries known as Renamo, or the MNR: the Resistência Nacional Moçambicana. The MNR's origins go back to groups recruited by the Portuguese to fight Machel's Frelimo guerrillas. Many fled to Rhodesia when Frelimo came to power in Mozambique; they were reconstituted as the MNR by the Rhodesian intelligence services and used to disrupt the activities of Rhodesian guerrillas operating from Mozambican bases. With the advent of an independent Zimbabwe in 1980, the MNR crossed into South Africa, where the SADF trained, equipped, and sent them into Mozambique once again to carry out sabotage and armed attacks on isolated army and police posts and villages. Despite the lack of a political program, the MNR's eight thousand to ten thousand guerrillas have won at least some local support and have frequently disrupted transport and communications in various parts of the country.

Zimbabwe, too, has lived with the threat of covert military action by South African–supported guerrillas. Zimbabwe's leaders have offered documentary evidence of South African recruitment and training of Zimbabwean dissidents—ex-guerrillas from Nkomo's disbanded ZIPRA forces and former members of Bishop Muzorewa's auxiliary troops—who are alleged to be operating now as numbered SADF battalions stationed along the Transvaal-Zimbabwe frontier. Zimbabwe authorities have charged these forces with acts of sabotage and with secreting large arms caches inside Zimbabwe in preparation for a campaign to foment political dissidence and disrupt forthcoming elections.

By early 1984 South Africa's aggressive policy toward neighboring states had scored some remarkable successes. Lesotho responded to South African pressure by forcing refugees linked to the ANC to leave the country in late 1983. Following South Africa's offer of a trial SADF withdrawal from Angola, that country accepted Botha's bid for a cease-fire and agreed in February 1984 to join the SADF in a joint commission to monitor compliance with its terms. In March South Africa and Mozambique signed a mutual nonaggression pact. Without mentioning any group by name, the agreement called for a halt to Pretoria's support of the MNR in exchange for Mozambique's expulsion of active ANC military personnel. At about the same time, it was revealed that South Africa and Swaziland had signed a secret nonaggression treaty in 1982.

Other factors contributed to these developments. U.S. pressure on Botha to offer Angola a cease-fire and withdrawal from its territory was one. U.S. intermediaries were also involved in moving Botha and Machel toward an understanding. Moreover, Mozambique, suffering its third year of disastrous drought, badly needed relief from guerrilla depredations and looked for South African economic and technical aid as a by-product of its accord with Pretoria.

There is no doubt, however, that South African leaders correctly perceive the recent moves toward regional détente to be the direct result of their policy of clubbing their neighbors into submission. While the results are far from the benevolent constellation of states envisaged in 1979, the latest developments have given the Botha administration great confidence in its capability to exert its will in the region and ultimately to bring about the conditions it seeks, *independently* of the West. Thus buoyed by recent successes, in March 1984 South Africa proposed a regional peace conference on Namibia that would exclude the West and the United Nations.

The search for security has an internal dimension as well. While taking a hard line toward the outside world and trying to promote a regional security arrangement, Botha has also been moving to enlarge the domestic laager to attract the support of South Africa's Coloureds, Asians, and ultimately an urban black elite. His motive is clear: military power alone cannot guarantee the future security of South Africa's white minority; its survival requires a political solution in which South African nonwhites gain a sufficient stake in the society to support the government and provide the manpower needed by the SADF. This is a view that South Africa's military leadership has been pressing on the government for several years.

It remains to be seen how far the Botha program—which contains proposals in such diverse areas as constitutional reform, extension of black trade union rights, and review of the Land Act—will be implemented and, if implemented, how effective these measures will be in co-opting nonwhites into continued support of white domination. The 1982 defection from the National party of seventeen members of Parliament to form a new right-wing opposition and their leader's successful challenge in a May 1983 by-election show that many Afrikaners will oppose some of the proposals as going too far. Most black leaders already have criticized them for leaving the basic structure of apartheid intact.

FUTURE CONSTRAINTS AND VULNERABILITIES

As South Africa has moved toward a war footing, the problem of manpower has continued to be the greatest constraint on government policies. Since only whites can be drafted, the SADF must draw heavily on the country's pool of 750,000 white males between the ages of eighteen and thirty-five. Moreover, this same group accounts for 40 percent of South Africa's economically active whites—hence the continuing tension between the manpower needs of the armed forces and those of the private sector.

Until 1977 South Africa could count on a substantial inflow of white immigrants each year to meet its growing manpower requirements. Indeed, economic growth targets were based on an assumed net inflow of thirty thousand whites annually. But following the Soweto riots South Africa suffered a net loss of twelve hundred whites in 1977 and two thousand in 1978. Thanks to the U.K. recession and a large influx of whites leaving Zimbabwe, gross immigration totaled over thirty thousand in 1982. Since both these sources seem likely to dry up in a short time, the long-term outlook remains cloudy. Military authorities note that military service is no longer popular among whites, and the SADF has difficulty retaining skilled personnel.

The government has taken a number of steps to make military service more attractive and to make better use of available manpower. Its boldest move has been to expand the participation of nonwhite volunteers, particularly Coloureds and Asians. By 1979 these two groups together made up 20 percent of the navy's permanent force. The arming of blacks remains a touchy political issue among the white electorate; hence Botha has moved with great caution. By 1982, eight years after the army had quietly begun to train black volunteers, its black component had grown into two battalions, probably numbering under a thousand through the rank of corporal. The army plans to train at least three more black battalions, but this will take time. Clearly a combat failure, or worse still a mutiny, would spell the end of Botha's scheme.

South African security policies are also vulnerable to actions by other countries. First, of course, is direct attack by a superior military force. South Africa, however, would offer formidable opposition. At any moment it has over 60,000 servicemen on active duty; another 100,000 to 150,000 trained active reservists could be quickly called up. The active police force numbers some 35,000 and the commandos, or home guard, 90,000. Recent legislation will enable the government to mobilize a force of over a million. The army has 270 tanks, 1,600 armored cars, over 1,700 armored personnel carriers, and two types of surface-to-air missiles. In May 1980 Botha announced that South Africa had developed an "artillery missile," a 127mm rocket designed to counter the Soviet 122mm multiple rocket. The navy is equipped with three submarines, five new missile patrol craft, plus frigates, minesweepers, and other craft. Aircraft include vintage Canberras, Buccaneers, and Shackletons, reinforced by Mirage jet fighters. South Africa should be able to cope effectively with any attack by other African states during the next few years, at least.

South Africa would be in deep trouble if an external attack were coordinated with a massive internal uprising. The recent history of violent protest in South Africa suggests, however, that the chances of a large-scale armed insurrection in the next few years are slim. White unity, the disunity and geographic isolation of black communities, the distance of major cities from the border, and the effectiveness of the police are all factors in the government's favor for the time being. Yet the balance has begun to shift gradually away from the state. Black leadership and organization improved markedly in the past decade. So did the strategy and tactics of black protest. Another factor to reckon with is the growing muscle of black labor unions, which have been expanding their membership and their recognition by both government and industry in the past few years. It seems inevitable that their strength will ultimately be directed toward achieving political objectives.

In spite of the absence of massive domestic upheavals since 1977, there is no reason to believe that the experiences of the seventies have faded from the black communal memory. The inevitable next round of protest will not start from square one, but will reflect the collective experience of the recent past. Meanwhile, Soweto lingers on in the growing incidents of urban terrorism laid to the students who fled in 1976 and who now return as ANC saboteurs.

South Africa would be particularly vulnerable to an assault involving one or more major powers. This, too, seems remote, however. The high costs of launching an invasion several thousand miles away, where it would be necessary to use inadequate (and vulnerable) roads, ports, and airfields in nearby states would be a serious inhibition. Moreover, barring some extreme provocation by Pretoria, any Western government would find it politically unthinkable to attack South Africa. For the USSR and its Communist allies, it is a long step from arming and training guerrilla groups and the armed forces of pro-socialist states in Africa to launching a conventional attack on South Africa. Even the support of African proxies in such an attack carries serious risks—for example, what to do if the attackers face defeat—which the USSR would have to balance against possible gains. The mild Soviet response to South Africa's armed raid on an ANC-occupied building in Mozambique's capital in 1981 is but one of several indicators that the USSR is not eager for a fight with the South Africans. In the aftermath of the raid, Soviet warships visited Mozambican ports—a move that a Soviet official was at pains to say was not meant to threaten anyone.

Economic warfare against South Africa could also pose a military challenge if the international community sought to enforce sanctions on the spot. An international blockade of South Africa's coasts could lead to serious incidents, and it seems doubtful that even the USSR, let alone the West, would be eager to incur the costs of an extended blockade of a long and distant coastline that would probably be less than completely effective. Moreover, the ports of Walvis Bay, Capetown, Durban, Richards Bay, Maputo, and Beira are important not only to South Africa: they are the economic lifeline of Botswana, Swaziland, Zambia, Malawi, and Mozambique. A total blockade of these ports seems out of the question; yet a random or selective stop-and-search among the two thousand ships a month passing the Cape would be costly and less than fully effective. Presumably such an arrangement would allow South Africa enough slippage so that it would choose to live with the blockade and avoid belligerent acts, but this is by no means certain.

A more pertinent question is how international sanctions might affect South Africa's security. From the security standpoint, weapons and weapons technology and oil remain the most serious vulnerabilities. The government's efforts over the past fifteen years to achieve a high degree of self-sufficiency in arms and ammunition have been discussed. The mandatory arms embargo of 1977 already has hurt, but the South Africans' greater concern is for the future. It simply is not feasible for so small a country with a limited capital equipment industry, a small domestic market, and a restricted pool of technically skilled manpower to attempt to produce models of fighter aircraft, missiles, and complex communications and radar, all of which rapidly become obsolescent. Already, South Africa has begun retiring its aged Shackletons, used for maritime patrol, without evident replacements. Yet if the arms ban is strictly enforced, a prolonged denial of access to new developments in Western military technology could cause South Africa to fall behind technologically. This would not be critical for a few years; but eventually it might lead to an important technical advantage on the part of a hostile neighboring state—an advanced radar or ground-to-air missile capability, for example—that would tip the scales away from South Africa militarily.

If the recent history of sanctions breaking is a fair guide to the future, South Africa's acquisition of sophisticated weapons from commercial arms dealers, sometimes working closely with a sympathetic foreign defense establishment, is likely to continue. But the arms embargo and the media exposure of illicit arms traffic to South Africa will make such transactions more difficult and more costly than in the past. And the weapons South Africa needs the most are the complex systems that will be the most difficult to acquire.

In regard to petroleum, South Africa is believed to have stockpiled on the order of 40 million tons, or roughly two to two and one half years' requirements at recent consumption levels. It has extensive (if expensive) capacity to refine oil from its abundant coal deposits. In gross terms, oil accounts for only 20 percent of South

Africa's total energy requirements and less than 10 percent of the energy needs of commerce and industry. The transport sector alone takes two-thirds of the total.

Since the cutoff in supplies from Iran, which formerly supplied 90 percent of South African needs, the South Africans have been forced to buy on the spot market initially at steep premiums. Shortages have appeared from time to time in certain products, particularly diesel fuel. Since, in a crisis, priority allocations of diesel would go to South Africa's highly mechanized armed forces, the burden of a continuing shortage would undoubtedly fall on the commercial trucking industry. Presumably, however, South Africa has taken advantage of the present world oil glut to add to its stockpile. For the time being, at least, oil is not a vulnerability. Only a complete and prolonged cutoff in supplies would cause severe problems.

South Africa's leaders acknowledge, however, that *any* interference in trade and finance would have serious consequences for the Republic. They are anxious to escape the imposition of such measures. Nonetheless, both the leadership and the electorate seem prepared to face sanctions as long as the alternative is seen to be acceptance of the principle of black majority rule. Indeed the government has tried—apparently with some success—to persuade its constituents that they face an even starker choice: hold out against foreign pressures or give in to one-man, one-vote rule.

PROSPECTS AND FUTURE STRATEGIES

South Africa entered the 1980s more concerned about its isolation and the threats to its security than at any time in the past. Its formerly close military ties to the West had eroded and were proscribed by the 1977 UN arms embargo. A similar falling-off had occurred in its scientific-technical exchanges, which were particularly valuable in such areas as nuclear fuel and energy development. Botha's efforts to attract nearby black states into a defense alliance and a formal economic grouping lay dead in the water, torpedoed by the Mugabe election victory in Zimbabwe and by decisions of the black-ruled states to try jointly to reorient their economies away from South Africa. The South African government expressed great hope that a Reagan administration in Washington would lead to a substantial inflow of Western support.

This hope has been only partially fulfilled. While the American administration's policy of "constructive engagement" has relaxed restrictions on the sale of "gray area" equipment (which has both civilian and military uses) and has expanded diplomatic contacts to include visits by South African military leaders to Washington, the changes have fallen short of South Africa's early expectations and in any case have been too marginal to change South Africa's security outlook.

Guerrilla attacks inside the Republic have grown in frequency and sophistication and are unlikely to be halted for long by South Africa's recent pacts with its neighbors. Minor incidents occur almost weekly, and major incidents show increasing boldness. In 1980 the African National Congress blew up oil storage tanks at the SASOL oil-from-coal complex; in 1981 it launched a brief rocket attack on a major South African military base near Pretoria. The following year the ANC seriously damaged a major nuclear reactor that had supposedly been under heavy guard. These incidents were designed primarily for symbolic effect and to minimize loss of life. In May 1983, however, the ANC—in an act declared to be a reprisal for an SADF attack on ANC personnel in Lesotho—planted a large bomb outside air force headquarters in downtown Pretoria that killed eighteen persons and wounded two hundred. This was viewed as a major escalation and perhaps as heralding a shift toward systematic urban terrorism. Such guerrilla attacks are still on too small a scale, however, to pose a threat to the government.

Moreover, the guerrilla threat, though the most imminent, is not the only one. South Africa's leaders continue to anticipate a worst-case scenario: a conventional attack from the North by Cuban-and-Soviet-supported African forces, possibly coordinated with an armed insurrection within.

And, of course, another Soweto can occur at any time. Given the continuing absence of effective dialogue between the black and white communities, the chances are better than even that the government will again be taken by surprise, as it was in June 1976. Until the event, there is little basis for assessing whether South Africa's blacks will be able to achieve the unity, organization, means, and outside support necessary to stage a nationwide industrial shutdown, let alone a successful armed insurrection. Based on what is known of the current situation—the unity, will, and awesome power of the white community against the isolation, weakness, and disarray of the black—it seems unlikely that the latter could bring about industrial paralysis or widespread revolt in the next few years. But it also is unlikely that South Africa will be able to avoid a rising incidence of violent episodes, some perhaps more widespread and lasting than those of 1976.

Not all recent developments have been unfavorable to Pretoria's immediate security interests, however. The prospect that the end of white rule in Rhodesia would quickly bring an upsurge in African states' militancy directed against South Africa has, for the time being, faded in the glow of Pretoria's recent success in forcing neighboring states to expel ANC activists. Meanwhile, a new African strategy for bringing an end to apartheid has yet to emerge. When it does, it will likely place much greater emphasis on internal black organizations—particularly those of industrial workers—with less reliance on guerrilla infiltration across borders.

In Namibia, too, the long impasse in negotiations between Pretoria and the United Nations seems to have worked to South Africa's advantage. South Africa's astute diplomacy has enabled it to delay for five years putting its name to a settlement that in all probability would have resulted in a SWAPO electoral victory and a SWAPO-dominated Namibia. During that time, South Africa carried out a highly aggressive counterinsurgency that all but wiped out SWAPO's basis for claiming to be an effective guerrilla movement. South Africa also used those years to train and expand indigenous Namibian military units to take over some of the fighting against SWAPO. Most important, of course, South African intransigence has prompted the United States to link a Namibian settlement to the parallel withdrawal of Cuban troops from Angola as a final inducement to win Pretoria's agreement to implement the UN settlement plan for Namibia.

On a couple of important counts, however, South Africa has failed in Namibia. In its concern to avoid offending Namibia's seventy-two thousand whites, the Botha government has blocked desegregation in the territory, thereby undermining its own efforts to establish a moderate, multiethnic alliance of political parties that might pose a credible alternative to SWAPO in an election. In a larger sense, South Africa's greatest failure has been its inability to offer a coherent blueprint for Namibia's future.

If roughly the above set of conditions persists in the coming decade, South Africa's total-defense strategy is likely to consist of several key components:

1. *First priority will be to enhance the country's defense potential against all possible contingencies.* The leaders have expressed confidence in their ability to contain guerrilla attacks from without and to suppress insurrection within. They are far less confident of their capability to defend against conventional attack. Indeed, defense spokesmen have noted that South Africa could not by itself prevail against an all-out attack involving one or more of the industrial powers.

Until the mid-seventies such an attack was considered to be an extremely remote possibility. Moreover, it was assumed that an attack by the USSR—which was seen as the only potential source of such an assault—would bring the Western powers to South Africa's defense. Now the situation is different. Not only is a conventional attack viewed in Pretoria as a very real, though not imminent, threat; it is assumed that South Africa would have to fight alone. Hence, the recent strategy has been to develop and maintain a credible national deterrent—a force capable of inflicting sufficient damage in conventional warfare to discourage potential attackers.

This, of course, raises the question of the ultimate deterrent—a nuclear weapon. The acquisition of such a weapon would be consistent with the leaders' perceived need to be capable of deterring a conventional attack and with their defiant go-it-alone defense posture. It also would be compatible with their commitment to assure the survival of the Afrikaner people.

Officially the government denies any intention of developing a nuclear weapon. Yet circumstantial evidence suggests that South Africa has reached the weapons-testing stage and may, indeed, already have detonated a nuclear device. After studying satellite photographs of a suspected South African test site in 1977, U.S. technical experts were reported to have ruled out all other possible explanations of its intended use. Similarly, informed technical opinion appears to lean heavily toward the view that a nuclear device was exploded off South Africa's Atlantic coast in September 1979.

If the South Africans have, as suspected, decided to go for a nuclear weapon, there is little doubt that the defense chiefs were directly involved in the decision. South Africa's tough security laws virtually rule out any open discussion of defense issues. But several years ago Admiral Hugo Bierman, chief of the defense staff at the time, warned that although national defense efforts and regional security arrangements were important and necessary, South Africa's security could be guaranteed only by bringing it under the Western nuclear umbrella. Failing that, presumably the second best option—though Admiral Bierman did not go so far as to say so—would be to develop a unilateral nuclear capability. More recently, SADF officers have discussed informally and privately the hypothetical possibility of using tactical nuclear weapons to defend the Namibian border. Indirect evidence that South Africa's military is actually involved in nuclear developments is the fact that its military attaché in Washington was the only foreign official to order, at a price of $1,200 a year, an unclassified U.S. government series of reports on the detection of nuclear explosions.

2. *The government will continue to undertake initiatives designed to win the support, or at least the acquiescence, of black groups.* Prime Minister Botha and his military leaders appear to have been convinced for some time that South Africa's security in the long run cannot be assured unless its African, Coloured, and Asian peoples are offered a better political and economic dispensation. His various initiatives in such areas as black union rights have run into serious opposition from the National party's right wing, however, and his ability—or will—to prevail against such opposition is uncertain.

The Botha administration has been somewhat more astute than its predecessor in recognizing and reacting to black grievances. But a wide gulf remains between black demands, which are virtually certain to escalate, and the maximal concessions that Botha or a like-minded reformer may be able to ram through the National party caucus. The balance of power in the party now seems to rest with a group of middle-of-the-road pragmatists who are likely to weigh each issue primarily in terms of its likely impact on party unity. It is this group that will decide the fate of the Botha reforms.

Meanwhile, incidents of right-wing white terrorism—at least one of which involved off-duty policemen—have become part of the South African political landscape. Escalating white violence of the Argentinian variety would inevitably radicalize an increasing number of blacks, the great majority of whom so far have remained nonviolent. Such incidents are also an indication of serious divisions in the white community and suggest the difficulties faced by those white leaders favoring concessions to black grievances.

3. *The leaders will be ready to seize opportunities to restore or enhance South Africa's foreign relations, particularly with the industrial Western states.* During the late seventies growing international antipathy toward South Africa was reflected in the increasingly lopsided UN votes on apartheid and Namibia, South Africa's ouster from a number of important international bodies, and the imposition of a mandatory UN arms embargo in 1977. From Pretoria's standpoint, the most serious development was its deteriorating relations with the Western industrial powers, which had been the crucial source of arms, technology, capital, and skilled labor (in the form of some thirty thousand European immigrants each year), as well as providing a moderating influence on Third World initiatives against South Africa.

Because of the potential role of the industrial Western states in providing diplomatic, military, and technical/economic support to South Africa—a role no other state or group of states can fill—Pretoria's leaders will give particular attention to improving ties with the West. Undoubtedly the military, which needs access to developments in Western military technology, will heavily support overtures to the West. In return for concrete measures of Western support, South Africa would almost certainly be prepared to make concessions on specific issues, but separate development remains nonnegotiable. The leadership was hopeful that political changes in the West—for example, the Reagan election victory or growing Western alarm over Soviet expansionism—would lead to a softening in Western attitudes toward South Africa and a desire for closer relations with Pretoria. This hope has survived South African disappointment that the advent of a Tory government in the

United Kingdom has so far produced no measurable improvement in Britain's ties with South Africa. Nor have Pretoria's appeals to the more conservative members of the Reagan administration brought any sharp change in U.S. policy. In 1981, Botha seized on the Reagan administration's near-obsession with the Cuban presence in Angola to try to convince the United States that the real issue in Namibia is not South Africa's illegal occupation and refusal to negotiate a settlement but a war against Soviet expansionism. His efforts did not succeed. The linkage of a Cuban troop withdrawal to a Namibian settlement seems to have been a reflection of the Reagan administration's need to placate right-wing critics at home, as well as an honest belief that a Cuban departure would remove what was seen as a critical obstacle to a settlement. The administration has not shown any interest in subscribing to Pretoria's declared anti-Communist crusade.

South Africa's relations with so-called Fifth World states— those not belonging to any alliance or other grouping—continue to be pursued, in part for public relations purposes and in part with specific technical or other benefits in mind. An exchange of diplomatic representatives is considered useful in demonstrating that South Africa is not totally shunned or isolated. In the case of Israel and Taiwan, however, important pragmatic objectives are involved. Both Israel and Taiwan have substantial achievements and capabilities in military technology and nuclear energy development. Since Pretoria's exchanges with the West in these areas have been largely cut off, those with Taiwan and Israel have become more important.

4. *Relations with nearby states will continue to be marked by quiet offers of carrots, backed up by willingness to use a club.* Should the recent détente initiative unravel, the South African leadership is committed to resuming its preemptive and retaliatory strikes against suspected guerrilla installations in neighboring countries and its support of dissidents and guerrillas. Although the goal of these actions may be merely to intimidate neighboring governments into refusing sanctuary to ANC guerrillas, the distinction between such aggressive bargaining and a concerted effort to destroy independent governments on South Africa's borders is not likely to be a clear one. Such a South African response to a perceived total on-

slaught would again raise the prospect of a wider war for which the SADF clearly feels it must be prepared.

South Africa's strategy for the rest of the eighties is thus likely to be a continuation of that developed by the Botha administration since 1978. The military establishment will almost certainly continue to play a forceful and visible political role as South Africa copes with internal and external security problems in the years immediately ahead. Botha may win the support of the party leadership for further political and economic dispensations for nonwhites. This program would suffer a severe setback, however, if black protest should suddenly turn to large-scale violence against whites, leading to a massive white reaction. Indeed, in that event, both the reform program and the prime minister would probably be jettisoned by the white electorate. There is also a good probability that, one way or another, South Africa will be confirmed in the next few years to have a nuclear weapons capability. This will be Pretoria's ace in the hole, its insurance against external attack or blackmail, its ultimate club to back up a tough, go-it-alone stance in a hostile world. But South Africa will also continue to seek close economic, technical aid, and other links to other states, particularly the United States.

By playing all these cards—a mobilization of the society, limited concessions to nonwhites, and the threat of heavy armed attacks against nearby states suspected of supporting the ANC and other guerrillas targeted against the Republic—South Africa's leaders will hope to postpone Armageddon. They will be under no illusion, however, that this strategy will solve the problem of trying to exist as an apartheid state in a world that condemns apartheid as morally unacceptable.

6

African Militaries as Foreign Policy Actors

HENRY S. BIENEN

What difference does it make for Africa's international relations that so many of its states have military governments or governments strongly influenced by the military (see appendix)? The question is of obvious importance, but answering it carefully requires exploring many facets of African states' political performance that are not well understood.

The answers to several initial questions can shed some light on the subject. Do African armed forces "make" foreign policy in distinctive ways? Do they favor particular types of foreign policy? Do they perceive the role of superpowers in Africa differently from civilian leaders? Are African soldiers more disposed to look to resolve conflict through military means and thus more inclined to lean toward the Soviet Union, which has been willing to project its military might to Africa, or toward France, which has done so on a smaller scale? Are African military rulers more, rather than less, dependent on non-African countries because they are large importers of hardware and expertise and/or because they may have narrow political bases? Although an examination of the evidence does not reveal very sharp distinctions between civilian and military leadership in African countries, it does provide some interesting insights into the workings of policy processes—under both military and civilians. It may be useful first to consider the particular characteristics of armed forces as policy actors in the African context.

In trying to understand what is distinctive about military rule as compared to civilian rule in Africa, observers have focused more on policy outcomes that are measurable, such as rates of economic growth, rates of inflation, and structure of government spending, than on the political process.[1] Obviously, it is harder to devise measures of popular representation, nature of authority, patterns of decision making, ways information is gathered and processed than it is to measure rates of literacy or patterns of investment.

What does emerge from the studies done is that (1) military regimes cannot easily be distinguished from civilian regimes by their economic and social policies or abilities, (2) the degree of diversity among military regimes is similar to the diversity found among civilian regimes, and (3) the general degree of similarity or dissimilarity between military and civilian regimes varies from one variable, or one category of variables, to another.[2] Still, the presence or absence of military rule does not explain a great deal about how regimes affect social and economic life. This is not surprising because military regimes, like that large residual category, civilian regimes, cover such a multitude of types; because time lags exist between military takeover and ability to influence social and economic change; because change may be more responsive to external factors, for example, prices of exports or imports, than anything that can be done domestically; because any regime operates under constraints set by the past and by the present environment and resources. Furthermore, African military regimes are internally fragmented and differ in the extent of civilian authority, the size and capabilities of armed forces, policy outlooks, willingness to use coercion, and the role of civil service.

Once researchers abandoned the simple dichotomies between military and civilian regimes, the pendulum swung too far in the

1. See Henry Bienen, *Armies and Parties in Africa* (New York: Africana Publishing Co., 1978), esp. pp. 7–18 and 193–96.
2. See especially Robert Jackman, "Politicians in Uniform: Military Governments and Social Change in the Third World," *American Political Science Review* 70 (December 1976); R. D. McKinlay and A. S. Cohan, "A Comparative Analysis of Political and Economic Performance of Military and Civilian Regimes," *Comparative Politics* 8, no. 1 (October 1975); McKinlay and Cohan, "The Economic Performance of Military Regimes: A Cross-National Aggregate Data Study," *British Journal of Politics* 6, no. 3 (July 1976).

other direction, as it almost always does in African studies. The new argument contended that the nature of civil-military relations was irrelevant to a nation's stability or level of development. Whatever abilities or disabilities the military might have was overwhelmed, in this view, by the determinancy of large forces. Some saw those forces as a manifestation of the world capitalist system, which maintained African countries in a structured dependence that was much more important than indigenous institutions in influencing political and economic development. The "political economy of dependence" became a framework that told us to look away from the peculiar and specific features of a given domestic politics to the worldwide forces of trade and investment and cultural diffusion. Others, starting from the premise that all is chaos and disorder in African politics, saw institutions of all sorts overwhelmed by ethnicity and interest groups that clash directly with one another over a small and often dwindling pie.

The idea that there are important differences between military and civilian regimes should not be abandoned. The evidence we have shows that there are distinctive norms attached to armed forces in Africa and that recruitment and socialization processes create institutions that have distinctive boundaries and personnel.[3] African armies are, within their societies, relatively insular communities; they have a greater concern for hierarchy, chain of command, and corporate cohesion and a greater fear of faction than have civilian bureaucracies. It is the structural adaptation to fulfill a unique, primary function, that of combat, that gives militaries their distinctiveness, their special concerns for corporate autonomy, and their emphasis on hierarchy and chain of command. Even when the possibility of combat seems remote, even when African armies have a hard time maintaining equipment and depend upon foreigners for hardware and training, African armies still feel the need for cohesion, corporate identity, and chain of command.

3. Among the case studies, see Robin Luckham, *The Nigerian Military* (Cambridge: Cambridge University Press, 1971); Ali A. Mazrui, *Soldiers and Kinsmen in Uganda* (Beverly Hills: Sage Publications, 1975); Thomas Cox, *Civil-Military Relations in Sierra Leone* (Cambridge: Harvard University Press, 1976). Also see the various memoirs by African military men, for example, A. A. Afrifa, *The Ghana Coup* (New York: Humanities Press, 1966).

Of course, cohesion and chain of command frequently break down. Junior officers and even NCOs have staged coups. Many armies are rife with ethnic factionalism. In several extreme cases, breakdowns in civil order under military rule have had consequential effects on governance. First, under some military regimes in Africa, accountability has disappeared. Thus, Amin simply ended organizational controls over the armed forces in Uganda. His was a military regime that lived off the land. Second, where there are military regimes without any bureaucratic or political checks on actions of the armed forces save the internal factionalism of the military itself, then policy is determined narrowly by internal military politics. Rivalries between service branches, between junior and senior officers, and between officers and enlisted men may be played out in policy disputes. As each of these categories may be drawn disproportionately from specific regions or strata of society, the rivalries have larger societal consequences. Still, we see that even in the extreme cases, the definition of militaries, their internal and external legitimacy, their understanding of themselves, the socialization process that soldiers undergo, no matter how imperfectly, lead them to aspire to cohesion and corporate identity. In Africa, as elsewhere, norms and realities frequently conflict and create special tensions.

In what way? Not necessarily for rates of growth or growth versus equity. Rather, it is more rewarding to look for differences between regimes and for distinctive aspects of military rule in the process of politics itself. Differences appear in the ways decisions are made by military as compared to civilian elites. Military elites have different links to their populations compared to the links that elites with other organizational bases have. Under military rule, distinctive patterns of political participation evolve. Military regimes, by definition, lack the direct and legitimate links with the population provided by political parties—even by a single, authoritarian party. Under the military, public political participation tends to take ritualistic forms of orchestrated demonstrations of support or alternatively to express itself in anomic violence. More sophisticated participation is likely to take place behind the scenes in the form of pressures on the civil service to provide policy and more direct payoffs to particularistic interests. Indeed, this is not surprising. We might expect that the institutional characteristics of armed forces would have an impact on political processes greater than their impact on social change or economic outcomes.[4]

MILITARY REGIMES AND FOREIGN POLICY FACTORS: THE BACKGROUND

Can we isolate any distinctive relationships between military regimes and foreign policy? Do certain foreign policy stances characterize African militaries in or out of power? Do African militaries have a tendency to be more or less nationalistic or autarkic? Are they more or less willing to use force to achieve foreign policy goals? Are there any institutional features peculiar to armed forces' recruitment, socialization, and operations that lead military organizations to process information, make foreign policy decisions, or implement foreign policy decisions in distinctive ways? In short, does the presumed special concern with the capabilities of the state and the integrity of national borders lead military governments to take foreign policy postures different from civilian regimes?

In dealing with these questions, it is necessary to consider willingness to spend more on defense, to enter into military assistance agreements, to commit forces outside their own borders, to enter cartels, and to seek special relationships with one or another of the major powers.

What emerges quite clearly from a tentative investigation of these questions is that foreign policy decisions do not seem to change much when national leadership is in the hands of the military. Military officers appear to set their nation's international course according to much the same criteria of national interest as civilians.

Until recently, it was commonly assumed that the former colonial powers' control over the training of African armies or the dependence of those armies on continued relations with outside suppliers would ensure that African armies would remain oriented to the West. Ernest Lefever, for one, believed that African mili-

4. See Bienen, *Armies and Parties*, and Henry Bienen and David Morell, eds., *Political Participation under Military Rule* (Beverly Hills: Sage Publications, 1976).

taries' interests in foreign and domestic policy paralleled those of the West.[5] On the other side of the political spectrum, Ruth First argued that African militaries would become instruments to protect Western economic and security interests.[6] Analysts who saw African armies acting to protect middle-class interests or multinational corporations' interests maintained that these armies were surrogates for an absent middle class.

Recent events have invalidated these arguments. African military rulers, like civilians, now have wide options for external relations. Military regimes, including Somalia, Ethiopia, and Mali, have chosen to depend on the USSR or China when their leaders have thought it advantageous to do so. Some have sought their supplies from multiple sources, in particular Nigeria, Zambia, and Congo (Brazzaville). Nor are these commitments permanent. Despite their long relationship with the United States military, which included training for virtually the entire senior officer corps, the Ethiopian officers who overthrew Haile Selassie refused to see their interests as aligned with U.S. interests. Of course, officers who maintain their pro-Western views can be eliminated (as was the case in Ethiopia) and an army can be internally transformed by purges, by new functions, and by new alliances with domestic groups.

In Africa, where class divisions are blurred and interest groups (except for ethnic groups) are poorly organized, the state has greater autonomy than elsewhere. The military's corporate power, status, and material well-being depend on its relationship to a strong state of whatever ideological stripe.[7] It is true that individual officers may in effect destroy a government in order to stay in power. Or a military might turn into a band of thugs. Factions within the military may deliberately weaken the state in order to preserve their own power, as in the case of Uganda under Amin, but the destruction of the state cannot be beneficial to the military's concern for its corporate power or even for the stability of a

5. Ernest W. Lefever, *Spear and Sceptre: Army, Police and Politics in Tropical Africa* (Washington: Brookings Institution, 1970).

6. Ruth First, *Power in Africa* (New York: Pantheon Books, 1970). See Aristide Zolberg's review article, "The Military Decade in Africa," *World Politics* 25, no. 2 (January 1973), esp. pp. 320–31.

7. Henry Bienen, "State and Revolution: The Work of Amilcar Cabral," *Journal of Modern African Studies* 15, no. 4 (1977):555–56.

particular military faction's power. Most African armies are not bent on transforming their societies. The Nigerian military did so in the 1960s when it pulled down the old Nigeria of the regions, created a multistate structure, and then tried to centralize within it, but its December 1983 coup appears intended to preserve structures, not disrupt them. Most armed forces are content to use the state bureaucracy to stay in power and to use the apparatus of the state to appropriate resources from society. Even the up-country military regime of Liberia's Sergeant Doe, which seized the state from the long-dominant Americo-Liberian elite, has found it necessary to use the bureaucratic skills of many members of the old families. The armed forces cannot destroy the state and remain intact themselves.

Few African armies possess firm ideological commitments or allegiances. Generally, officers and enlisted men are not recruited from well-formed social classes. They do not have ingrained alliances with domestic businessmen or with trade unionists, who are themselves politically weak in Africa. Some officers may have ties to traditional leaders in particular societies, but rarely do African officers come from a traditional leadership structure. They are situational, not class elites; [8] that is, they depend on their own institutionally derived power and on their corporate identity. Without ties to particular interest groups, armies have flexibility of action in both domestic and foreign policy realms. These advantages are counterbalanced by the military leaders' comparative isolation from the population as a whole. Without the experience of grassroots political organization, they lack information about local conditions, needs, and sensitivities. They may issue orders, but find that only their troops follow them. If in addition they are preoccupied with maintaining the military's own corporate cohesion, they may find their freedom of action more theoretical than real.

DEFENSE EXPENDITURES

If the distinctiveness of the armed forces as an interest group has affected the policies military regimes have adopted, the conse-

8. Alfred Stepan, *State and Society in Contemporary Peru* (Princeton: Princeton University Press, 1978).

quences of what Chester Crocker has called "a remarkably low level of defense capability" in Africa have had much greater "direct implications for the continent's international relations."[9] Until recently, the legacy of colonial military policy in Africa and African dependence on outsiders for military wherewithal narrowed foreign policy options. But African nations are acquiring new military capabilities at uneven rates, and this trend, together with the increasing number of non-African countries intervening on the continent, spells more, rather than fewer, interstate military conflicts.[10]

Although defense expenditures have increased in Africa, the rise is not a consequence of the increasing number of military regimes. Defense spending has gone up rapidly under civilian regimes. Somalia was a big spender long before the 1969 coup, and neither Tanzania's Julius Nyerere nor Morocco's King Hassan has refused to sacrifice domestic development spending when he deemed it necessary to expand military expenditure to secure important foreign policy goals. Although defense spending may be responsive to short-run demands of armed forces organizations and these organizations may be better able to enforce demands after their representatives take over the highest offices in government, defense spending appears to be related more to factors outside the borders of a given country. Marc Howard Ross and Elizabeth Homer have tested the effects of internal characteristics of states on military spending. They conclude that "in African nations, the size of defense budget as a proportion of government expenditure is predicted by a diffusion variable: the size of a neighbor's defense budget as a proportion of his government spending."[11] Thus, a change from civilian government to military rule in Kenya or in Zambia would not necessarily lead to different defense policies or different foreign policies more generally.

9. Chester A. Crocker, "Military Dependence: The Colonial Legacy," *Journal of Modern African Studies* 12, no. 2 (June 1974):284.

10. See Henry Bienen, "United States Policy in a Changing Africa," *Political Science Quarterly* (Fall 1978):443–464.

11. Marc Howard Ross and Elizabeth Homer, "Galton's Problem in Cross-National Research," *World Politics* 29, no. 1 (October 1976):1–29. For Latin America, Philippe Schmitter found no consistency in direction of defense spending after changes from civilian to military rule. See Philippe Schmitter, "Foreign Military Assistance, National Military Spending and Military Rule in Latin America," in Philippe Schmitter, ed., *Military Rule in Latin America* (Beverly Hills: Sage Publications, 1973), pp. 117–88.

LEADERSHIP AND INTEREST GROUPS IN FOREIGN
POLICY MAKING IN AFRICA

Foreign policy making, whether under civilian or military regimes, is usually personalistic and removed from public view. In content, style, or process, are there distinctive foreign policy styles in military regimes? Again the answer must be: not really.

Leadership change can be consequential for foreign policy in Africa, perhaps more so than in other areas of the world, but this is equally true in military and civilian regimes. One reason for the strong impact of leadership in Africa is that the number of domestic interest groups with foreign policy concerns is small except when ethnic-language groups spill over the border of a country. Economic interest groups and interests have not played a critical role in foreign relations among African states so far. Nigeria has sought to influence domestic policies in Chad and Ghana by withholding oil supplies. And in specific situations, access to the sea or need for shipment of goods across another country determine foreign policy positions. Thus, Zambia's Angolan policy was affected by the need to ship copper via railroad through territory held by Jonas Savimbi's UNITA group, and its policy toward Zimbabwe was affected by Lusaka's need to import from that country.

But even where economic interests have been crucial, leaders and their regimes have not always been highly constrained by relationships of dependence. "Radical" leaders (such as Touré, Nkrumah) did not rupture economic links to the West, but they took independent stances on many issues. Tanzania, which remains a large importer of capital, technical assistance, and foodstuffs, has had a very independent foreign policy. Although dependent on South Africa to provide jobs for many of its workers and for maintenance of ports and railroads, Mozambique until 1980 supported guerrillas in Rhodesia, regularly denounced South Africa, and harbored military as well as political cadres of the African National Congress (ANC). It took substantial military pressure from South Africa—not economic threats—to persuade the Mozambique government to restrict the ANC's freedom of movement. Throughout Africa, simple economic dependence is a poor predictor of foreign policy positions.

African leaders have been relatively free to "make" foreign policy, especially in non-African contexts, partly because their countries have been marginal international actors and partly because most countries do not have articulate interest groups that bring pressure to bear on their foreign policy decisions. Further, foreign policy bureaucracies are generally weak in Africa. Intelligence services and foreign services exercise few constraints on high-level decision makers.

Nigeria is, in great degree, the exception that proves the rule. Few African countries have had the personnel or resources to elaborate foreign policy structures to the extent the Nigerians have. Few have also had a relatively large, informed public that follows foreign affairs, as has Nigeria. And it was a military government (under Murtala Mohammed) that greatly increased public input on foreign policy.[12] In fact, Nigeria's military leaders have shown more concern than most African leaders for broadening their public support of foreign policy stances. Soon after taking power in 1976, the Murtala Mohammed government brought in representatives from the press and universities as members of review committees on foreign policy. It tried to reorganize its foreign service. It created new structures parallel to the Ministry of External Affairs and reinforced old ones for national security advising. A policy-planning unit was set up within External Affairs. A think tank, the Nigerian Institute of International Affairs, was established and expanded.

At the same time, the Nigerian military leadership that replaced General Gowon was also atypical in that it reached out to a wide circle of military officers to include them in the foreign policy process. Officers engaged in a dialogue with the head of state, his deputy, the chief of army staff, and the commissioner of external affairs, who was a brigadier. There has not been extensive middle-level officer participation in foreign policy making under military regimes in other African countries (excepting Ethiopia with its ruling military committee, the *Derg*, composed of military person-

12. I am very grateful to Dr. Alaba Ogunsanwo for access to his "The Nigerian Military and Foreign Policy, 1975–1979: Processes, Principles, Performance and Contradictions," Princeton University, Center of International Studies, January 1980.

nel of various ranks). Extensive officer-civilian dialogues on foreign policy issues are also rare in other African countries.[13]

African regimes have occasionally changed their foreign policy directions after military coups, for example, in Ghana after Nkrumah, in Uganda under Amin, and in Ethiopia under Mengistu. It would be wrong, however, to argue that foreign policy considerations played a major role in triggering the Amin coup in Uganda. And in Ethiopia, the dramatic events unfolded over many months, and both domestic and external factors intertwined. Perhaps some Ethiopian coup makers from the start saw a need to break relations with the United States. The major thrust of their early statements and concerns was, however, in the domestic realm.[14]

We can find other examples of important foreign policy shifts after military regimes replaced civilians or after one military regime replaced another. In Mauritania, for instance, one regime was replaced by another that was committed to pulling the country away from involvement on the Moroccan side in the Western Sahara struggle. Although it would be hard to argue that foreign policy issues were primary in many cases, foreign and domestic affairs are often interrelated, especially when, as in the case of Ghana under Nkrumah, a foreign power assists a particular leader in developing alternative security forces to the regular armed forces. Or a foreign power may become so involved in domestic affairs that any change in factional alignments can lead quickly to foreign policy shifts, as is true in Angola, Mozambique, and Ethiopia today. Still, we cannot say of Africa, as one observer said of the Middle East, that "nearly one of every two [Arab] coups involved disputes over the direction of regime foreign policy orientations."[15] The direction of change after a coup has demonstrated neither that African militaries are invariably lackeys of foreign capitalism nor that

13. It may be that we see a more complicated foreign policy process in Nigeria because Nigerian commentators such as Ibrahim Gambari, Mazi Ray Ofoegbu, Olajide Aluko, Alaba Ogunsanwo, Bolaji Akinyemi, Adele Jinadu, and Adeoye Akinsanya have told us more about the Nigerian foreign policy process, some of them with insiders' views of the system, than other African analysts have been able to reveal about their own countries.

14. See David and Marina Ottaway, *Ethiopia: Empire in Revolution* (New York: Africana Press, 1978).

15. William R. Thompson, "Toward Explaining Arab Military Coups," in George A. Kourvertaris and Betty A. Dobratz, eds., *World Perspectives in the Sociology of the Military* (New Brunswick: Transaction Books, 1977), p. 179.

they are upholders of the interests of would-be middle-class ties to the West, any more than change has always been toward Marxist and radical military regimes.

NATIONALISM AND MODERNIZATION

It might be expected that military regimes would be particularly nationalistic because (1) armed forces see themselves as the carriers of nationalism, (2) they identify with the nation-state rather than with parochial interests, and (3) their mission is national security. Thus they would move to guarantee security through modernization, industrialization, and control of indigenous resources. This modernizing tendency may, however, arguably work against the nationalist impulse if the military is primarily concerned to guarantee foreign investors of capital the order they require.[16]

In fact, neither side of this dichotomy stands up to scrutiny. Comparative studies find no real correlations between industrial growth and/or modernization and military rule. It is difficult to see a constellation of interests between presumed middle classes and armed forces in Africa. Several African military regimes that have utilized an anticapitalist, anti-Western rhetoric have nonetheless maintained their ties with Western capital and have often tried to maintain their ties with ex-colonial rulers. For example, despite its rhetoric, Congo-Brazzaville has struck bargains with French expatriate interests strikingly less advantageous than many African conservative states have enjoyed.[17]

Some analysts point to Ghana as a country whose post-Nkrumah military regime reversed civilian foreign policies and was followed by a civilian regime, under Busia, that maintained the pro-Western orientation, only to have a partial return to Nkrumah's domestic and foreign policy stances under a new military leader, Acheampong. Although there were shifts in foreign policy positions under successive regimes after Nkrumah, the most

16. James H. Mittleman, "Dependency and Civil-Military Relations," paper presented to the conference, Civilian Control of the Military: Myth and Reality in Developing Countries, Buffalo, October 1974.

17. Samuel Decalo, *Coups and Army Rule in Africa* (New Haven: Yale University Press, 1976).

striking contrast was that under all post-Nkrumah regimes, Ghana was a much less visible international actor because its early leadership in Third Word forums was based on Nkrumah's personality, not on durable elements of national power. No Ghanaian regime of any stripe in the past fifteen years either altered the conditions of Ghana's economic and social life so that it could play important foreign policy roles or brought about any significant realignments within Africa.

Nigeria's military, on the other hand, altered Nigeria's political system and presided over a marked centralization of national power. And it is true that Nigeria, under military rule, staked out a much more activist set of international policies and moved to indigenize the Nigerian economy. But it was also during military rule that Nigeria became a major oil exporter. It is unlikely that a civilian regime that benefited from vastly increased oil revenues would have acted much differently.

Specifically, Nigeria did alter its position on the Israeli-Arab conflict. But so did most African countries after the 1973 war. The Nigerian military has not been unequivocally more pro-Arab than have civilian leaders. Both military and civilian leaders have been conscious of the potentially explosive issue of religion in Nigerian politics and have carefully decoupled Nigeria's position on Middle East conflict from domestic regional and religious factors. Nigeria has not joined the grouping of Islamic states, and military and civilian leaders have expressed equal reluctance to involve Nigeria in explicitly Islamic forums.

Prior to the Shagari regime, Nigeria under the military bargained more toughly over terms of investment generally and over investment in the petroleum sector specifically than it had under civilians. It could afford to bargain harder because of its growing economic strength, which the post-Shagari military leadership does not enjoy. But if we look closely at Nigeria under military regimes, we do not see an unambiguous posture against foreign capital. Under Gowon from 1967 to 1972, the stock of foreign investment in Nigeria nearly doubled. At different times, import duties were cut and foreign exchange controls were relaxed, not because the military regime became less militant, but because economic conditions allowed it. Economic nationalism has been more a response to changing economic and external conditions than to ideological biases of military men. There was as much shifting on activism and stance among generals Gowon, Mohammed, and Obasanjo as there had been between civilian and military regimes.

Perhaps the important distinction lies between nationalism as expressed in economic policies such as nationalization, self-sufficiency, indigenization, on the one hand, and nationalist styles, on the other. African armed forces frequently appear nationalistic. Nationalistic responses may indeed be necessary for military regimes that do not have broad support. Because real economic nationalism is constrained by economic structure and levels, however, they may rely mostly on rhetoric and symbolism.

The one place where style and economic policy seem to meet is in the indigenization of business. The easiest target for indigenization is not large-scale foreign enterprises and their managers, but African nonnationals or Asians who, as small businessmen and traders, are vulnerable. Military regimes have gone in for expulsions of nonnationals in Uganda, Ghana, Nigeria (where civilians have too), Congo-Brazzaville, and Togo. It might well be that if a Kenyan military regime came to power it would act less ambiguously against the Kenyan Asian community in order to have a piece of pie to distribute quickly. Obviously it is harder to strike at foreign large-scale capital and donors because the consequences of so doing make life difficult when it comes to new aid, loans, debt moratoriums, and investment.

Are African military regimes more nationalistic in other senses? It has been said that junior officers who take power are less concerned with the norms of international relations and with precedent than civilians. Junior officers who come to power (as in Ghana, Liberia, and Bourkina Fasso [Upper Volta]) do tend to utilize a nationalist rhetoric. (Young party leaders presumably would, too, if any young civilian leaders were coming to power.) Because African military rule has been personalistic, as is political party rule, foreign policy pendulums have swung wildly. Military leaders have often responded impetuously to foreign policy exigencies, verbally at least. And since much African foreign policy is a verbal matter, it may seem that junior officers are establishing radical and nationalistic foreign policies. But again, the nationalist rhetoric is infrequently followed up by radical change.

MILITARY RULE AND NEW INTERNATIONAL CONTEXTS

In the last decade, military intervention of outside countries has brought Africa openly into superpower rivalry. Non-African actors have become heavily involved in determining the internal alignments of African regimes as well as affecting their foreign policy stances. Outcomes of factional struggle in Angola, Zaire, Ethiopia, Zimbabwe, and Chad were all very much influenced by external, non-African participants. This new activism has coincided with military rule in many African countries. But it is not military rule but new possibilities for changing donors and partners and new military capabilities that have increased the potential for conflict in Africa. It was a civilian government in Tanzania that launched the first successful invasion of a neighbor aimed at bringing down its head of state—Idi Amin.

Again, as African countries have become more involved in foreign economic relations and in international arenas and as the wherewithal grows for some military actions within Africa, foreign policy becomes more consequential to African regimes. In the past, a country received its international definition by virtue of positions stated in the United Nations or the Organization of African Unity or Third World forums. Now, African countries are more involved in economic negotiations and in non-African conflict situations as new players intrude in the continent. But it is hard to see a set of outcomes in negotiations over African economic arrangements or links to European economic organizations or relations to OPEC that are affected by the fact of military rule.

There is, however, something relatively new under the African sun that may influence the links between militaries and foreign policy alignments. The great majority of African armies trace their origins to the forces organized by the colonial power. Some part of this European heritage remains, just as it remains to influence the actions of postcolonial civilian governments. Militaries, however, that come to power through an anticolonial struggle or conceivably in the future might come to power through secessionist and/or guerrilla struggle against an African regime will not have these ties. Previously, large-scale violence against a colonial regime did not always leave the independent African regime dominated by the military or by freedom fighters. In Kenya, those who were active Mau Mau lost out in the factional fighting before and after independence. In Madagascar, the large-scale anticolonial violence did not give rise to a military regime at the time of independence. In Algeria, a military regime did come to power, but the fighters who carried the brunt of the battle in Algiers and the mountains played less of a role in the government than the military personnel who were encamped outside Algeria's borders during most of the struggle.

In Angola, however, the winners were determined through military struggle. This struggle was not only against the Portuguese but against other factions of the anti-Portuguese movement. And, of course, external support (principally from the Soviet Union and Cuba) helped determine the outcome. In Portuguese Guinea, too, those who took up arms became significant actors after the victory. In Mozambique, this pattern occurred as well. In Zimbabwe, military struggle ended in an electoral victory for one political-military group. Although the new prime minister, Robert Mugabe, was himself a political rather than a military leader, an ex-guerrilla commander now leads the regular Zimbabwean army, and several of his guerrilla colleagues now occupy cabinet positions. The claims of former rank-and-file guerrillas from Mugabe's movement—principally for education and good farmland—have been an important constraint on Mugabe's domestic policies, just as dissatisfied members of opposing guerrilla forces have contributed to dissidence in the countryside.

Here then are countries in which guerrilla struggle was and will be significant for determining leadership after independence. And the relationships of external military and political support were to some extent carried over. Change in Angolan foreign policy is likely to be possible within narrower limits with Cuban troops on Angolan soil. There has, however, already been a shift in Mozambique away from close relations with China and toward the USSR, which has been better able to equip the regular army. As regular armies develop, we may see cleavage between the original guerrilla base and the new regular formations; officers with different factional bases may have their own external patrons. The personal ties of the guerrilla leaders with outsiders, their experience as fighters, their relationships with other elites can be expected to be consequential for foreign and domestic politics.

MILITARY DIPLOMACY

To sum up, if there is a military mind or a military disposition in foreign policy matters, it is hard to discern. Militaries in Africa have not been more willing to use force across borders than civilian regimes. Somalia committed forces to fight in the Ogaden, and Amin's Uganda to Tanzania, but civilian-led Tanzania sent troops against Uganda and Morocco militarily occupied parts of Mauritania. Nor can we conclude that militaries in power necessarily could more easily dispatch troops abroad than civilians. The Nigerian military considered sending troops to Zambia during the Zimbabwe struggle. Elements within the military leadership strongly opposed this.

An important recent study has compared both the substance and the style of conflict resolution by the Ethiopian and Nigerian militaries. David Laitin and Drew Harker conclude that there was a behavioral difference between civilians and the militaries that replaced them in both countries during the initial period of military rule. "Both military regimes attempted to bring the issue of potential secession to a head, both being unhappy with the ambiguous situation of the peripheral provinces during the civilian period."[18] In general, militaries in power seem to have a style that shows less tolerance for ambiguity, less patience with sloppy political processes and messy outcomes. Surely, however, there have been vast differences between Ethiopian and Nigerian patterns of conflict resolution under military regimes, stemming from different domestic and external situations as well as differing ideologies and personality factors among the two military hierarchies. And style, although important in foreign affairs, is still subordinate to substance.

18. David Laitin and Drew Harker, "Military Rule and National Secession: Nigeria and Ethiopia," draft paper, May 1979. I am grateful for access to this paper.

When we look at substantive foreign policy outcomes, we do not find that African military regimes align themselves in clear-cut ways in either inter-African affairs or global politics. Nor do they seem to have a bias for particular policy stances. As we have seen, within a diversity of African regimes the foreign policy process is the domain of a small number of actors. That they are in many countries military actors is not decisive for understanding foreign policy in Africa or for making sound policy toward Africa.

7

The Militarization of Africa: Trends and Policy Problems

WILLIAM J. FOLTZ

As the preceding chapters have made clear, military factors have come to play an increasing role in Africa's international politics and have helped turn seemingly parochial African disputes into occasions for superpower competition. This concluding chapter attempts to look ahead to see what the rest of the decade will bring to provide some general guidance for Western, and particularly American, policymakers. In brief, this chapter will argue that over time African states are likely to become increasingly heavily armed and to spend more of their slender resources on armaments; although this is not in African or U.S. interests there is not much that the United States—or indeed the West as a whole—can do to reverse that trend. In that light, the task of U.S. policy might best be seen as one of reducing the political and human cost to Africa and to the United States of such armaments and of reducing and controlling the likelihood that they will actually be used on a larger scale. Failure to do so may be costly not only to Africa but to Western economic, political, and strategic interests as well.

SPACE FOR EXPANDING THE MILITARY

As the U.S. Congress discovers anew every year when it debates the American defense budget, there is no clear way to determine how much military power is enough. African governments are equally prey to doubts, conflicting demands, and budgetary counterpressures. The size and cost of the military in an African country ought reasonably to be related primarily to clear defensive needs—to the likelihood of threats from neighbors and from domestic dissidents—and, in a few cases at least, to adventurous foreign policy goals. Anecdotal observation tells us that these factors do play a role, but that many other factors also are involved. Among these are the political weight of the military establishment (coups often are followed by a short-run increase in expenditures on the military) and, of course, the ability to rely on an outside patron instead of one's own resources to meet one's defense needs (the case notably of the French client states and of a few utterly indefensible countries, such as Gambia). In the aggregate, though, there appears to be a tendency for the military and the military budget to expand to fill ill-defined space, the dimensions of which are likely to be set at least in part by comparison with what other countries do.

Two measures of such space are the size of a country's military and paramilitary forces in comparison with that of its population as a whole and in comparison with the area of the country they are engaged to defend. Table 7.1 presents such figures for African countries.[1] In each case the range is substantial, and the median figures may give the best summary idea for the continent as a whole. The median African country has three men (legally) under arms for every one thousand citizens. This is a slightly greater military presence than that evident in the most densely populated Asian countries, less than most South American countries, and of course but a tiny fraction of such highly militarized countries as Cuba, Taiwan, and Greece. In relation to area, the median African figure is 14.4 soldiers for every hundred square miles of national territory. This is substantially inferior to most non-African cases, including even sparsely populated Brazil.

To the degree that any sort of international norm exists in such

1. Each figure in table 7.1 should be treated with caution. African budgetary and census figures are often approximations, and any statistic dealing with the military is particularly problematical. In several instances, figures published by the International Institute of Strategic Studies and the Stockholm International Peace Research Institute differed from the U.S. Arms Control and Disarmament Agency figures used here (and with one another), but not consistently nor in a predictable direction. I am grateful to Laurence Lucas for his painstaking compilation and comparison of these data. In the discussion I rely on median figures, as the median is the most conservative statistic, least susceptible to distortion from a few wayward observations.

matters, a case can be made that most African militaries have space to grow. Such statistics by themselves have no force, but they do summarize a multiplicity of factors related to potential security needs—or at least to arguments military establishments make about such needs. Large tracts of unpopulated territory do not necessarily require a garrison of soldiers to watch over them, but they may lead an army to demand the logistic capability to mount surveillance operations and to send in columns when required. Large numbers of citizens are not by themselves threats to state security, but monitoring and policing them are considered essential tasks by most African regimes. African armies, since independence, have been slowly growing toward greater resemblance to other Third World military forces, and these figures suggest that their growth is unlikely to stop or be reversed.

It is not enough just to feel a need for more; a country has to pay for its protection, and armies—even small African armies—cost somebody money. Absolute expenditure figures are not much help in deciding whether a country is spending more or less than it can or should on the military. Were the world a different place, every kwacha, sily, naira, ouguiya, cedi, dinar, or dollar could more usefully be spent on civilian social services or on economic investment than on anything to do with the military. All expenditure benchmarks must be made in comparison to something. If one compares changes in total African expenditure on the military over time, one finds that, following an initial spurt of rapid growth in the 1960s when the new states shifted responsibility for their security from the former colonial metropole to themselves, *in constant dollars* military budgets have increased at a rate substantially exceeding the growth in either population or GNP. Thus between 1965 and 1970, aggregate military expenditures increased 74 percent in real terms; between 1970 and 1975 the increase was 25 percent, and between 1975 and 1980 (the last reasonably reliable figures available) the increase was 22 percent.[2] Having reached what appears to be an only modestly declining rate of increase, aggregate spending shows little sign of slowing down. In 1980 the

2. These figures are taken from the U.S. Arms Control and Disarmament Agency's *World Military Expenditures and Arms Transfers* reports for 1963–73, 1970–79, and 1971–80. SIPRI figures are consistently higher, but exhibit the same pattern of movement.

Table 7.1. African Military Comparison, 1980

Country	Size of Armed Forces (in Thousands)	Military Expenditure as Percent of GNP	Military Expenditure as Percent of Central Gov't. Expenditure	Armed Forces per 1,000 People	Armed Forces per 100 Sq. Miles
Algeria	101	2.2	7.6	5.4	11.0
Angola	53	NA	NA	8.2	10.6
Benin	7	2.2	15.3	2.0	15.6
Botswana	3	3.5	6.4	3.3	1.4
Burundi	8	2.6	22.2	1.9	74.3
Cameroon	14	1.5	9.9	1.6	7.6
CAR	5	1.8	8.9	2.2	2.1
Chad	NA	NA	NA	NA	NA
Congo	14	4.1	14.4	8.8	10.6
Egypt	340	6.0	16.4	8.1	88.1
Equatorial Guinea[a]	2	NA	NA	10.0	20.3
Ethiopia	240	9.7	42.6	8.1	60.8
Gabon	2	0.4	1.1	3.3	1.6
Gambia	1	0	0	1.7	25.0
Ghana	20	0.4	3.7	1.7	21.7
Guinea	18	NA	NA	3.6	18.9
Guinea-Bissau	12	6.4	6.6	15.0	85.9
Ivory Coast	11	1.2	3.6	1.4	8.6
Kenya	16	3.8	12.9	1.0	7.1
Lesotho	3	0	0	2.3	25.5
Liberia	5	1.5	5.1	2.6	11.4

Country					
Libya	53	1.7	4.5	17.7	7.8
Madagascar	28	4.1	13.5	3.3	12.1
Malawi	6	1.8	6.0	1.0	16.2
Mali	8	2.5	20.5	1.2	1.8
Mauritania	11	15.8	25.9	7.3	2.5
Morocco	117	6.1	17.8	5.6	46.0
Mozambique	27	NA	NA	2.2	8.9
Niger	6	1.0	4.8	1.1	1.4
Nigeria	222	2.6	9.3	2.9	62.1
Rwanda	6	2.0	15.3	1.2	59.0
Senegal	14	2.6	11.4	2.5	18.4
Sierra Leone	4	1.1	3.8	1.2	14.4
Somalia	54	6.2	18.4	10.0	21.9
South Africa	78	3.2	13.9	3.2	17.7
Sudan	68	3.0	12.2	3.6	7.0
Swaziland	3	2.5	6.2	5.0	44.7
Tanzania	57	5.0	16.3	3.1	15.7
Togo	8	2.4	7.0	3.1	23.8
Tunisia	29	1.4	4.5	4.5	45.8
Uganda	6	1.8	20.6	0.5	6.6
Upper Volta (Bourkina Fasso)	8	3.1	18.2	1.4	7.6
Zaire	42	3.1	12.4	1.5	4.8
Zambia	15	3.8	8.6	2.6	5.2
Zimbabwe (Rhodesia)	24	8.4	25.9	3.2	15.9

Source: U.S. Arms Control and Disarmament Agency, *World Military Expenditures and Arms Transfers, 1971–1980,* Washington, D.C., 1983.
a. 1979.

median African country spent 2.5 percent of its GNP on the military. In international comparison, 3 percent of GNP is what Argentina spent; the African median figure was more than Brazil's and Ecuador's, but less than those of Malaysia, India, and Indonesia, and much less than those of the heavily militarized Third World countries. It is also, of course, much less than the percentage that industrialized powers like the United States and the Soviet Union spend on their military establishments.

The final relationship that is useful in assessing the space for growth of African military establishments is that between the military budget and central government expenditure. Here the range is particularly great, going from next to zero for a few small countries to percentages in the twenties for such diverse countries as Mauritania, Zimbabwe, and Burundi, while Ethiopia, facing insurgencies on several fronts, spends over 40 percent of its national budget on the military. The median is 10.6 percent, with half the cases lying between 6 and 16 percent. If we take 16 percent of government expenditure as an upward limit within reach of a state whose government wishes to increase its military powers, seventeen states have space for increases equal at least to half their present spending on the military. These include such significant states as Cameroon, Nigeria, Algeria, and the Ivory Coast, all of whom have, or could have, the resources to make a considerable effort feasible. If more general patterns among developing countries hold, these are precisely the countries most likely to increase their military spending. As Benoit found in a wide-ranging comparative study, despite obvious exceptions those developing countries with a rapid rate of economic growth tend to assume a heavy defense burden, whereas those with the lowest growth rates tend to spend least on defense.[3] So far I have argued merely that African military

3. Emile Benoit, "Growth and Defense in Developing Countries," *Economic Development and Cultural Change* 26, no. 2 (January 1978):271. This does not mean, of course, that higher defense spending *produces* high growth rates. In developing countries, and industrialized ones as well, higher military burdens come at the expense of various forms of investment in future growth, particularly of human capital. See Saadet Deger, "Human Resources, Government Education Expenditure and the Military Burden in Less Developed Countries," Birkbeck College Discussion Paper no. 109 (November 1981), and Bruce M. Russett, *What Price Vigilance?* (New Haven: Yale University Press, 1970).

establishments and military budgets have increased regularly up to the present, and that viewed in comparison with other African and Third World countries, most African states still have space for further increase. Whether such space is taken—or exceeded—will depend on what military requirements and opportunities present themselves and how those are viewed by the regimes in power.

TECHNICAL REASONS FOR EXPANSION

As Walter Barrows argues in chapter 4, past increases in size of African armies have not translated directly into increases in military effectiveness. Lack of African management skills and logistical and transport capabilities have all impeded the ability of the military establishments to carry out their tasks. Although, viewed from a distance, these accurate observations would seem to be powerful arguments for restraining military growth, they may have opposite effects when weighed by African governments that are politically adventurous or under pressure from neighbors or their own military.

Rapid mobility of forces and of firepower is likely to be particularly highly prized for three reasons. First, as African armies become better established, their tasks are likely to be expanded beyond that of simply protecting the capital, a few other urban areas, and a few fixed border points. Second, recent important military confrontations in Africa have turned largely on questions of mobility. The conflicts in Chad, the Ogaden, and the western Sahara and above all the performance of the Rhodesian and South African armies have all provided powerful demonstration effects of how important it is to have modern equipment capable of moving men and firepower quickly. The lessons have not been lost on other countries. Third, as I shall argue more fully later in this chapter, Nigeria has discovered the advantages of substantial long-range transport capability. It is likely to want to increase this ability, and such action is likely to be imitated by others. Increased mobility of forces will in turn likely lead to a defensive response in the form of demand for ground-to-air and ground-to-ground heat-seeking and guided missiles, thus increasing the overall demand for new and fancier equipment.

There are, moreover, firm technical reasons for African armies to seek some of the very latest weapons systems.[4] Not only are these able to move faster and farther and to strike harder than previous generations of weapons; they are easier to operate. Furthermore, because these systems are modularized, or like the LAW antitank weapon designed to be thrown away after use, maintenance in the field is simpler. Fewer highly trained maintenance personnel would thus be required near the battlefield.

At the same time, most of the more sophisticated weapons also require a high level of discipline in use (since their cost per weapon is high and spares are likely to be at a premium in the field) and great sophistication and training on the part of the officers commanding their employment. Although the introduction of such sophisticated weapons may make the tasks of operational maintenance easier, it shifts the burden to the areas of central planning and supply where truly high-level managerial skills will be required. Some such skills can, of course, be hired from the outside. Because they are few in number and located at the rear, foreigners may be less visible, easier to recruit, and less politically objectionable than would a greater number involved more directly in operations. Furthermore, several African countries have by now turned out respectable numbers of university graduates with the background necessary for acquiring and exercising such skills. Nigeria, Kenya, Ivory Coast, Senegal, Ghana, Zimbabwe, and, in North Africa, Morocco, Algeria, and Egypt are all potentially in this position, though in most of these countries the military will have to compete with the civilian economy for such individuals. Such increase in technological sophistication would further augment the disparity in military capability between a few effective armies and the rest.

A final problem is whether outsiders will in fact supply such new weapons systems. This appears to be a theoretical problem only. Certainly, enough weapons to go around are being produced and by an increasing number of producers. As a senior U.S. official explained in mid-1980:

> Over 30 nations are now producing arms for their use, and the number is growing each year. This trend is . . . spreading to

4. I am grateful to Col. William J. Taylor, Jr., of Georgetown University, Center for Strategic and International Studies, for drawing my attention to this factor.

middle-tier and less developed countries. Major combat systems are now being produced by Argentina, Brazil, India, Israel, North Korea, South Korea, Pakistan, Singapore, South Africa, Taiwan, and Yugoslavia. Arms production by all LDCs is about 5% of the world's yearly total; it has grown from $1 billion in 1969 to a present figure of more than $5 billion. . . . Less developed countries are now building destroyers and frigates, jet fighters, antitank missiles, submarines, and main battle tanks. And some will soon be in the missile business.[5]

Nor do prospective buyers encounter serious problems persuading producers to sell their wares—quite the contrary. For most producers, including the United States' principal European allies, export sales are needed to establish a large enough production run to justify initial investment and maintain a viable industry.[6] As new arms-producing countries continue to enter the international market, the competition for clients intensifies and international agreements on restricting conventional arms transfers become more difficult to reach and impossible to enforce. As Nimetz put it, "Everyone wants a piece of the pie and will strike a deal that gives him the biggest slice."[7] As information provided by Louis Sarris in chapter 2 indicates, there is usually a five-year lag between the introduction of weapons systems in the Middle East and their introduction in sub-Saharan Africa. Even if this time discrepancy stretches out, at least a few African armies by the end of the 1980s should have made a major leap into sophisticated technology.

AFRICAN PERSPECTIVES ON ARMS

A significant proportion of African governments are unstable and insecure. Although outside observers may conclude that governments' policies and ineptitude are often the cause of their own problems, few African regimes, pursuing those policies with what-

5. Matthew Nimetz, under secretary of state for security assistance, science and technology, "Arms Coproduction," address before the American Defense Preparedness Association, July 15, 1980 (Washington: U.S. Department of State Bureau of Public Affairs, Current Policy No. 200, 1980), p. 2.
6. Ibid. The point is supported by a particularly well-informed European, France's Ingénieur-Général Cauchie, "Address at Symposium on European Armaments Policy, Paris, 3 March 1977," *Survival* 18, no. 4 (July–August 1977):180–84.
7. Nimetz, "Arms Coproduction," p. 1.

ever competence they can muster, are in a position to calculate coldly that their overall security needs have diminished. Most would be obliged to conclude that if their needs have changed at all, they have increased. On the continent as a whole, disruptions caused by internal dissidence have remained at least at the same level over the last five years, and armed rural banditry, with or without discernible political content, is on the upswing. Government response to such banditry has often involved considerably more than police action, as in the large-scale military reprisals carried out in Zaire and Cameroon during 1979, in Nigeria in 1981, and in Zimbabwe in 1983. During 1983, only eight of forty-two African states avoided some publicly reported active domestic or international involvement of their security forces.

Two patterns of cross-border action have increased security problems greatly in the most recent years—the transfer of arms by African states to dissident groups in neighboring countries and direct invasion or deep-penetration raids. To cite only the most obvious cases in which African states have transferred arms either on their own behalf or on that of outsiders, South Africa and Zaire have supplied arms to dissidents in Angola; South Africa, picking up where Rhodesia left off, has armed groups in Mozambique and probably Zambia; Tanzania, Zambia, and Mozambique, together with Nigeria and Ethiopia, helped the guerrilla forces in Rhodesia; Sudan and others have supported various groups in Eritrea and Chad; Somalia has supplied rebels in Ogaden; and Algeria has supplied and supported rebels against Mauritanian and Moroccan rule in the Western Sahara. Libya is a case unto itself, as Qaddafi has, with vast resources, taken over the role of regional trouble-maker that Nkrumah played to only minor effect in the early 1960s. Insurgent groups in Sudan, Western Sahara, and Chad have been the principal African beneficiaries of Libyan arms transfers, but in the spring of 1980 several Libyan armored cars turned up in Djibouti, seemingly as an unsolicited gift—one that shook the government and severely upset their French protectors—and more recently Benin and Bourkina Fasso (Upper Volta) have received Libyan military aid. Few African governments can rest assured that they will not someday attract Qaddafi's attention. All forms of support for dissident groups can be ideologically or pragmatically justified by the states transferring the arms, and most readers of this book will approve some of the cross-border support mentioned. Such legitimation only increases the likelihood that similar cases of support will occur in the future and that governments will take this likelihood into account when assessing their security needs.

A similar catalog may be elaborated for serious cross-border armed incursions: South Africa into Angola, Lesotho, Mozambique, Zambia, and Zimbabwe; Angola (or at least forces operating from Angola) into Zaire via Zambia; Libya into Chad and Tunisia; the Sahraoui out of Algeria into Morocco and Mauritania proper; and of course the two major cases, Somalia into Ethiopia and Tanzania into Uganda. The last of these, from Western points of view the most justified and welcome, has caused the biggest political stir within Africa as the first successful invasion of one African state by another. Of the two obvious lessons to be learned from it—that murderous dictators who menace the peace of the area may be overthrown from without and that it is now possible for African armies to carry out a successful invasion of a neighbor—the second seems to have made the greater impression and is most easily translated by African states into policy decisions.

Of the six large areas recently involved in cross-border military operations—the Horn, the Western Sahara, Zaire, anything in reach of Libya, southern Africa, and East Africa—only the last has even a slim chance of cooling down in the near future.

The Kenyan elections of 1983, which put President Moi in a commanding position, have led to a reopening of the border with Tanzania and an end to public recriminations, following several years of bickering over economic policy and relations with Uganda. In both countries, however, the tensions of the 1970s had led each country to double the size of its armed forces, and the military buildups will not easily be reversed. During the last five years, each military has significantly increased its political weight in government councils; unsuccessful coup attempts by disaffected units have led to a redeployment of military expenditures, but not their diminution.

For all that Kenyan-Tanzanian bilateral relations have improved, each country is subject to military pressures from wider regional involvements. Kenya's policy is affected by instability in the Horn and that area's wider role in great-power strategy. Not only are Somali claims to parts of northern Kenya still a latent concern, but U.S. acquisition of rapid deployment force staging and repair facilities in Mombasa have emphasized Kenya's strategic orientation toward the Persian Gulf and Red Sea. Tanzania, meanwhile, has provided troops to support threatened regimes in the Seychelles and Mozambique, and it is also concerned about acquiring a more serious seaward defense capability at a time when the Indian Ocean has become a focus of great-power naval competition.

In southern Africa, the hopes for a period of regional détente following the end of the Rhodesian civil war have proven evanescent. The experience of Zimbabwe since independence in 1980 demonstrates how difficult it is to reduce a military establishment once a liberation war is concluded. With help from a three hundred-man British training group, the Zimbabwean leadership began by amalgamating substantial portions of the ZANLA and ZIPRA guerrilla forces into the framework of the old Rhodesian army. Within a year the integration plan ran into difficulties. As relations began to fray between the political leaders of the two groups that had led the fight for independence, tensions between ex-ZANLA and ex-ZIPRA army personnel exploded in violence early in 1981. Although a major shoot-out was quelled by mixed battalions loyal to the central government, during the next year over a thousand ex-ZIPRA soliders, mostly Ndebele, deserted with their weapons and began marauding in their home region of Matabeleland, Joshua Nkomo's stronghold. The Mugabe government responded by deploying throughout Matabeleland five thousand members of the Fifth Brigade, all ex-ZANLA troops hurriedly trained by a North Korean team. The Fifth Brigade's brutal methods have, if anything, increased insecurity in the region and raised tensions along Zimbabwe's borders with Botswana and South Africa. Meanwhile, South African–backed sabotage of Zimbabwe's oil pipeline and direct rail link to the sea through Mozambique has required the posting of Zimbabwe troops at battalion strength at strategic points along the route. Additionally, sabotage of part of Zimbabwe's air force has led the government to purchase MIG-21s from China and to train new pilots and ground crews in their use and maintenance.

Although Prime Minister Robert Mugabe had once hoped to

emerge with an armed force of about thirty thousand men, the difficult security environment will probably mean that the Zimbabwean military will stabilize at twice that number. Although Zimbabwe will first have to overcome its domestic political and ethnic tensions, it is possible that the country will emerge as a minor military powerhouse by the end of the decade. It will, of course, remain well behind South Africa in military capability, but its strength will affect the military calculations of other states in the region, not all of which are likely in perpetuity to be close friends with any Zimbabwe regime.

Further in the future, one must expect that the French security umbrella that has allowed most of the smaller Francophone states to limit their own security forces will cease to provide such comprehensive coverage. As George Moose has shown, for the first time in almost a century French military involvement in Black Africa has become a political issue at home. It is a very minor issue as yet, but enough of one to make it more difficult for a French government to persist in a military presence when that presence is not welcomed by the people who are its alleged beneficiaries. The successors to Bongo, Houphouët, and confrères, lacking their predecessors' privileged personal positions, will have to confront the issue of redesigning their countries' relationship with France. Whatever the final shape of the new relationships may be, they will almost certainly have to take account of tremendous pressures from younger governmental cadres for greater autonomy from French tutelage. Military cadres will certainly join in these pressures. Whether or not the French umbrella is officially withdrawn, it is likely to be extended from a greater distance, and a domestic political condition of its remaining is likely to be a significant increase in the size of the local African military force. It would further seem likely that a successor regime in the Ivory Coast in particular would feel impelled to conduct a more adventurous foreign policy than Houphouët has favored. This, too, might provide an incentive to increased military spending.

So far, this has been a gloomy catalog, suggesting that African states are likely almost uniformly to increase their military expenditure as a result of both international and domestic developments. This does not by itself imply that violence is fated to increase on the continent. In many areas, including much of southern Africa, peace may indeed break out for a while, but it is likely to be an armed peace, and therefore expensive to maintain.

When an African government has been threatened by an external attack or internal revolt, Organization of African Unity (OAU) norms have countenanced each state's right to call in outside help on a one-to-one basis. This principle has legitimized most of the French interventions in their former colonies, the Cuban-Soviet intervention in Ethiopia, and in the eyes of many, their intervention in Angola as well. Pressures against such extracontinental recourse are mounting, though they will hardly dissuade a desperately beleaguered regime from turning to anyone it thinks likely to come to the rescue. Although the most spectacular and decisive interventions have involved forces brought in from outside Africa, concern over the use of extra-African forces has obscured a more significant trend: the increasing ability of a few states to loan—or rent—troops to other African regimes in trouble. The proclivity to provide battalions or palace guards on request follows no clear principle of ideology or alignment. Thus, since 1978, in response to appeals for help Tanzania has sent troops to Seychelles and Mozambique; Morocco to Zaire and Equatorial Guinea; Senegal to Gambia; Guinea to Sierra Leone; and Libya to Chad. The ability to provide or withhold provision of military force to neighbors in trouble has become a new currency of influence in African interstate politics, one that can establish credit and advantage not only with the recipient regime but also with outside powers interested in seeing that regime preserved. Rather than acting blindly as surrogates for outside powers, African states have responded selectively to appeals for military help according to their own calculations of advantage. Thus, Morocco, a frequent supporter of Western interests, declined Western urgings to send troops to Chad, thereby establishing a basis for Libya's reciprocal support for Moroccan claims to the Western Sahara.

The most theoretically acceptable means for meeting the extraordinary security needs of African states, and thereby, presumably, reducing the need for extraordinary levels of national armaments, is some form of collective security. The feeling that Africans ought collectively to take on the job of providing for Africa's security was articulated forcefully by Nigeria's General Obasanjo at the Khartoum OAU summit in 1978 and was optimistically enshrined in one of the concluding resolutions of the conference: "The summit officially announces that the responsibility for the safety of peace in Africa is the responsibility of Africans alone. No foreign country or group of countries may interfere in this matter." The conference further called for the reactivation of the OAU's moribund Defence Committee in preparation for the need to establish an African military force under the supervision of the OAU.[8]

The 1979 Monrovia summit echoed to further calls, led by the new chairman, Liberia's president William R. Tolbert, to establish a pan-African force as soon as possible. However, the report of the Defence Committee provoked such controversy that the matter was referred back for further study, with legal and financial experts assigned to the committee to assist its deliberations. Perhaps the principal encouragement their work received was the formal vote in which the assembled chiefs of state expressed their collective "political determination" that such a force be established.[9] Since then, a permanent pan-African force has come no nearer to fruition. The problems any such pan-African force faces are both technical and political. The technical problems of any broadly based OAU force are vast. In the extreme egalitarian version advanced by OAU secretary-general Edem Kodjo, forty African states would set aside special units of fifty men each so that the force would have on call some two thousand "casques verts."[10] The evident logistical and other technical problems of deploying and controlling such an improbable agglomerate demonstrate the depth of political suspicion impeding the creation of a credible force.

In effect, there are two competing visions of what an ideal pan-African force should be and who should control it. That which first came close to realization was the "Pan-African Force" of the conservative Francophone states discussed at the Franco-African meeting in Paris in June 1978, following Shaba II. This was torpedoed by objections from the more independently minded African chiefs of state present, put most cogently by Mali's Colonel Moussa Traoré: "The problems of security in Africa should only

---

8. The text may be found in *Africa Research Bulletin*, July 1–31, 1974, p. 4914.

9. See the report in *ARB*, July 1–31, 1979, pp. 5327ff.

10. See the interview in *Jeune Afrique* 966 (July 11, 1979):85.

and can only be dealt with in a bilateral framework, or in an exclusively African framework."[11] Opposed to the idea of an African force linked to the West is the vision shared by Qaddafi and others of a force under the control of the most activist members of the OAU and as much concerned with continuing the "liberation" of Africa as with protecting governments in power.

There is little likelihood that enough trust will develop to bridge the gap between these conceptions and great likelihood that the creation of one such force would spur the competitive creation of the other, with potentially disastrous results. This does not mean that multilateral African forces are impossible to mount, but as in the past they will presumably be ad hoc creations, put together at the invitation of a specific government for a specific and limited purpose. The joint force that in 1982 attempted the daunting task of keeping the peace in Chad is an example of the sort of force the OAU might in other circumstances be able to mount after all else had failed and of the limits on its effectiveness.

Not surprisingly, Nigeria has taken the greatest interest in developing a pan-African force; that interest goes back at least as far as 1971 when General Gowon told the OAU that within three years African forces should be prepared to join in the fight against Portuguese colonialism. The most thoughtful public analysis of what a pan-African force would require was presented in 1978 by the Nigerian chief of army staff, Lieutenant General Danjuma.[12] Chief among the requirements he foresaw were a clear and constant enemy against whom the force could be targeted, one "superstate—even if it is in relative terms only" to lead the military alliance, and a "standing force made up of contributions by member countries under a centralized command." The details of the third of these points might be unclear, but South Africa clearly was targeted as the necessary enemy and Nigeria as the "relative superstate." Although this vision of an OAU force is likely to be even further away from realization than Kodjo's egalitarian model, it is likely to contribute to the transformation of the Nigerian army in the direction of a more mobile, technologically so-

11. *Le Monde*, May 28–29, 1978.
12. Lt. Gen. T. Y. Danjuma, "In Search of an Enemy," address to seminar organized by the Nigerian Institute of International Affairs on the African High Command.

phisticated, and expensive military force. It is difficult to see any Nigerian government, civilian or military, resisting such a transformation for long, however much it may cavil at the cost.

For all the passion that Nigerians can develop on the subject of South Africa, it is clear that the army intends no direct military confrontation with the white regime, at least until the situation within South Africa has changed substantially. Nigerian officials assume that South Africa possesses the atomic bomb, and they take that very seriously. But in southern Africa the Nigerian army has already airlifted supplies and offered training to Zimbabwean guerrillas and to Namibia's SWAPO. At home, Nigeria was acquiring a significant population of young South African exiles. South Africa remains an intensely powerful symbolic issue for substantial portions of the Nigerian population, which raised over $15 million in public contributions for a Southern African Relief Fund.[13] The likelihood would seem to be Nigeria's government will cautiously encourage only peripheral involvement in southern African affairs through training and supply of guerrilla forces, but that in order to back up this involvement it will augment the long-distance transport capacity of its armed forces and also their ability, in time, to defend Nigeria against the eventuality of South African reprisal.[14] As in the past, a military government seems likely to attempt to acquire some domestic legitimacy by asserting a strong role in foreign affairs. Since Nigeria can be counted on to play such a role with a certain amount of fanfare, it is likely to attract competitors among African states seeking continent-wide leadership roles and some radical bona fides in a safely distant area. Algeria, Libya, and Egypt are prime candidates to offer Nigeria competition in this military-diplomatic sweepstakes. The entry price to the race will be high.

The final African state whose action will greatly affect the course of Africa's arming is South Africa itself. South Africa's mili-

13. In addition to the many articles in Nigerian newspapers, particularly those of Haroun Adamu in the *Daily Times*, see A. Bolaji Akinyemi and Margaret Vogt, "Nigeria and Southern Africa: The Policy Options," in Douglas Anglin, Timothy W. Shaw, and Carl G. Widstrand, eds., *Conflict and Change in Southern Africa* (University Press of America: Washington, D.C.).

14. See John M. Ostheimer and Gary J. Buckley, "Nigeria," in Edward A. Kolodziej and Robert E. Harkavy, eds., *Security Policies of Developing Countries* (Lexington, Mass.: Lexington Books, 1982), pp. 285–303.

tary thought is increasingly cast in a regional mold. The Botha government's idea of a constellation of states begins with the nucleus of South Africa and its Bantustans to embrace next the subcontinent. The 1979 White Paper on Defence—as always the best concise discussion of South African foreign policy—was for the first time openly based on planning for the defense of "southern Africa," which in subsequent commentaries appears to extend north to include at least Zaire's Shaba Province.[15] South Africa's goal is to build a zone of peace based on reinforced infrastructural and economic links and protected by a South African military umbrella. To those desirous of the peace and stability that South Africa promises, the idea might seem attractive—if it could work. There is little to suggest that it will, at least not without substantial violence.

As the events leading up to the Nkomati accords of March 16, 1984, have demonstrated, South Africa's regional hegemony is based on the use and threat of violence. Both are likely to continue. Present South African action indicates that for its peaceful constellation to work it must begin by inducing a certain amount of disorder in the area. Renewed support to Jonas Savimbi's UNITA forces in Angola is useful to South Africa not only because it complicates SWAPO's life and ties down Cuban troops; an active UNITA also guarantees that the Benguela railway remains out and that both Zaire and Zambia remain dependent on South Africa. The infrastructural integration forseen in the constellation now is effective to the extent that 95 percent of Zambia's copper exports pass through East London, and the same railroad line is the principal trading route for Zaire. South Africa's support for an armed resistance movement in Mozambique has put similar pressure on Zimbabwe by cutting its rail access to the port of Beira, thereby returning the southern route through South Africa to the importance it had during the Ian Smith years.

Further, regional stability over any extended period of time requires the acquiescence of the black population of South Africa itself. This is not the place to argue in detail that this is highly improbable. I would merely assert that there is no evidence that

15. See P. W. Botha, "Preface: 'Unity is Strength,' " in the South African government's *White Paper on Defence and Armaments Supply 1979* (Cape Town, April 4, 1979).

the quickest pace of domestic change held out by the most *verlig* members of government comes close to meeting present demands of most blacks, not to mention the rising expectations that would be engendered by beginning a serious course of reforms.[16] Any pattern of accommodation between South Africa and its black neighbors can be disrupted by a major disturbance created by South Africa's own black population. On past form, such disturbance will provoke outside opposition and augment domestic repression, at least in the short run.

In any eventuality, the progressive militarization of South Africa and the rise of military influence in the South African government seems likely to continue. An aggressive forward strategy is the most probable response to any setback in relations with South Africa's neighbors. This in turn may increase the military content of African opposition to South Africa and legitimate arms build-ups elsewhere on the continent, even in the absence of major direct military confrontations between South African and black African forces.

SOME THOUGHTS FOR U.S. POLICY

Over the years the United States has shown a reasonable reluctance to augment the arming of Africa. Even before the Carter administration proclaimed its devotion to restraining conventional arms transfers, the United States was a very weak third in transfers to Africa. The fact that the arming of Africans has been proceeding apace suggests that the African reasons and means for acquiring arms are such that the United States can have only a marginal influence in the matter.

Early in the Carter administration, the United States attempted to negotiate an agreement with the Soviet Union to limit arms transfers to Third World areas. It proposed Africa as the key area for mutual restraint. Without rejecting that proposal, the Soviet Union responded that it was even more interested in limit-

16. See Heribert Adam and Hermann Giliomee, *Ethnic Power Mobilized: Can South Africa Change?* (New Haven: Yale University Press, 1979), and William J. Foltz, "South Africa: What Kind of Change?" *CSIS Africa Notes*, Georgetown University, Center for Strategic and International Studies, November 1982.

ing deliveries to the Middle East; they emphasized, however, that the Europeans would have to be willing to cooperate with the superpowers in any understanding on restraint that might be reached. European reluctance to become engaged, clear reluctance by the United States to discuss arms sales restraint in the Middle East, and dissension within the Carter administration over the entire policy rapidly aborted the negotiations. The Africans themselves were indignant at the thought that the great powers would attempt to impose restrictions on their own efforts to ensure their security. In retrospect, it seems clear that comprehensive multilateral agreements restricting arms transfers to Third World areas, including Africa, are most unlikely.

The American public has demonstrated a general—and politically important—distaste for active involvement in things military (at least *foreign* things military).[17] Beyond that domestic political constraint, serious U.S. concern for the arming of Africans ought to focus on four points affecting its international interests.

First, however essential some level of armament may be, in and of themselves armaments are economically nonproductive. They use resources that otherwise could be used for development and siphon off talent and attention that ought to be more productively employed. As a major trading nation, concerned with developing lucrative markets and steady suppliers, the United States has a stake in African prosperity.

Second, the United States has a great stake in international stability, and beyond a point that in some cases has already been reached, the arming of African security forces can produce rather than reduce disruption.

Third, as armaments become more effective they threaten to do serious damage to economic installations in which the United States has an interest, both directly and indirectly through our general interest in African prosperity. Those areas whose disruption would make the greatest difference are the oil-producing areas of Nigeria, the copper belt of Zaire and Zambia, and the South

17. While foreign aid in general has become unpopular with the American public, foreign *military* assistance is appreciated even less, and by a substantial margin. See John E. Reilly, *American Public Opinion and U.S. Foreign Policy, 1983* (Chicago: Chicago Council on Foreign Relations, 1983), pp. 25–27.

African industrial enclaves, especially Port Elizabeth, East London, and the Vaal triangle. The ability of these regions physically to support and transport production is of considerably more importance to the West than the ideology or color of the governments that preside over them.

Fourth, military competition provides an easy way for the Soviet Union, which cannot compete effectively in the economic realm, to augment its political influence and physical presence in Africa. This hurts the United States in bilateral relations with African states and in international forums; above all, it increases Soviet leverage that can result in their receiving African base rights. These can affect, at least indirectly, America's national security.

United States policy will have to proceed from the premise that it alone cannot reverse most of the principal trends outlined in this chapter. There are, however, certain policy approaches that can shape these trends more in line with American interests.

First, it is clearly to the United States' advantage that the political and economic costs of modest increases in armaments be limited. The United States, ideally together with its principal allies, should consider developing inexpensive material adapted to African military needs. Or at least the United States should consider whether to encourage some African countries to procure such equipment from such countries as Israel, Brazil, or India when cost and simplicity are of clear importance. In the past the U.S. Defense Department has usually with strong congressional encouragement favored U.S. equipment for friendly countries regardless of cost factors. Although the African market is unlikely, even under the most dismal projections, to be large enough for American producers to justify a major R and D effort, simplicity of maintenance and operation of military equipment is a goal worth stressing for many other purposes as well. More effective training programs for African officers and men should be established, both those in Africa and those in the United States. As Barrows has pointed out, the development of human resources is most crucial at the highest levels of managerial and technical competence. The skills most needed are those that are as applicable to civilian as to military needs. Broadly based technical and managerial training for African officers who may in time return to the civilian sector makes good sense. Since the key in this is to permit African armies to avoid becoming dependent on the Soviet Union for training and equipment, encouraging other states—India and Brazil would be good examples—to participate in such training efforts would seem useful.

Second, the United States should pay particularly close attention to the African side effects of decisions taken for non-African reasons—most immediately the decisions involved in hunting for bases. These decisions are of course matters of global policy thought through in world geopolitical terms and in terms of American military technical requirements. However, the regional spin-offs of such decisions have a way of becoming, in time, global problems in their own right. Further development of the American facilities in Kenya and Somalia to the point where they become full-fledged military bases is likely not only to fuel an arms buildup in Africa, but to facilitate the Soviet Union's search for comparable bases as well. This latter is, presumably, not just a narrow regional concern.

Third, potentially the most disruptive political development on the continent would be the rigidification of a split between moderate and radical African states, clients of West and East, and its reinforcement in military terms. It is decidedly in America's interest to avoid forcing such polarization, which would have the effect of encouraging the more activist states to deal exclusively with the Soviet Union. Military assistance, which all too often is used to rigidify divisions, can also provide a symbolically potent tool for bridging the ideological gap. If the United States must provide defensive assistance to Morocco to shore up King Hassan, is there a good reason why some form of military assistance should not also be made available to Algeria or Mali? Mozambique, Zambia, and also Angola have legitimate security needs that we might want to be in a position to meet. Since there seems little chance that any permanent broadly based OAU peacekeeping force will come into being, we want to be certain that individual African states' appeals for outside help do not call forth a permanent, pan-African force controlled by a few ideologically cohesive and militant states. For the time being, selective French intervention may continue to be useful, and Nigeria and other individual African states may in time come to play a similar role; however, consistent with past African practice these should be kept as ad hoc arrangements.

Finally, in dealing with South Africa the United States must realize that it is that country's goal to polarize African affairs along an East-West dimension—in the conviction that this is the best way "to bring the West to its senses" and assure Western support for Pretoria. From virtually every point of view, and most certainly from any concern with military factors in Africa, that is not a game the United States should want to play. The United States does have considerable political and economic stakes in what happens to South Africa, though different Americans will assess those stakes differently. Perhaps the most important stake is in avoiding a direct cross-border military showdown and in facilitating what will have to be a complex pattern of change coming from within South Africa itself. It is highly probable that this will not be an entirely peaceful pattern of change, and in the future, policy may have to be directed toward holding the ring, so that the struggle remains as internal to the country as possible. Confining the struggle as much as possible to domestic forces would not be helped by a U.S. alignment, even a tacit one, with the South African government, nor by assisting that government in polarizing African states.

The military, one must conclude, seems here to stay as a permanent factor in the politics of Africa, just as it is a factor in the politics of other parts of the world. Increasingly, the focus is changing from concern with outside military forces to concern with African forces and from seeing those forces as factors in domestic politics to seeing them as factors in international politics. These developments will require thoughtful and creative responses from the United States to what is becoming a new and potentially dangerous game. Much of this game will be driven by local and regional aspirations, needs, and rivalries not directly subject to external control. Such a situation calls for an overall policy of restraint that avoids the gratuitous escalation of military means and the political escalation of African conflicts into tests of superpower strength and commitment.

CONTRIBUTORS

WALTER L. BARROWS, author of several published works on African politics, taught at Virginia Polytechnic Institute before entering government service, where he is currently in the office of the assistant secretary of defense for international security affairs.

HENRY S. BIENEN is William Stewart Tod Professor of Politics and International Affairs at Princeton University.

WILLIAM J. FOLTZ is professor of political science at Yale University, director of the Yale Center for International and Area Studies and associate director of the Yale-Wesleyan Southern African Research Program.

ROBERT S. JASTER has written extensively on African regional security matters at the International Institute for Security Studies in London and has taught courses on African politics and foreign relations at the Naval Post-Graduate School. As a fellow at the Woodrow Wilson Center, he has undertaken a major study of the Rhodesian crisis and peace settlement.

GEORGE E. MOOSE, a career foreign service officer, has been an International Affairs Fellow at the Council on Foreign Relations and is currently serving as ambassador to the Republic of Benin.

LOUIS GEORGE SARRIS, a career civil servant, is currently a divisional director within the Department of State's Bureau of Intelligence and Research.

Appendix:

Regime Changes and Coups

TABLE A–1.

Regime Changes and Coups in Africa, by country.

Algeria
    1962, July   Independence. Ahmed Ben Bella president.
    1965, June   Coup led by Col. Houari Boumedienne.
    1979, Feb   Col. Benjeddid Chadli elected president.

Angola
    1975, Nov   Independence. Government contested by MPLA (Agostinho
                  Neto) and coalition of FNLA (Holden Roberto) and
                  UNITA (Jonas Savimbi).
    1976, Feb   UNITA-FNLA defeated; MPLA forms government.
    1979, Sept   Neto dies, succeeded by José Eduardo dos Santos.

Benin
    1960, Aug   Independence as Republic of Dahomey. Coalition of
                  Hubert Maga, Sourou-Migan Apithy, and Justin
                  Ahomadegbe.
    1963, Oct   Coup led by Col. Christophe Soglo removes Maga.
    1965, Nov   Ahomadegbe forced out by Armed Forces Chief of Staff
                  Gen. Soglo.
         Dec   Soglo names "provisional" government, himself as
                  president.
    1967, Dec   Coup led by Maj. Kouandeté deposes Soglo. Ex-Armed
                  Forces Chief of Staff Lt. Col. Alley named
                  president with Kouandeté as prime minister.
    1968, Sept   Zinsou named president.
    1969, Dec   Armed Forces Chief of Staff Lt. Col. Kouandeté ousts
                  Zinsou. Triumvirate of Kouandeté, Lt. Col. De
                  Souza, and Lt. Col. Sinzogan.
    1972, Oct   Coup led by Maj. Mathieu Kerekou.
    1975, Oct   Dahomey becomes People's Republic of Benin.
         Dec   Kerekou launches a single-party state.
    1979, Nov   National Revolutionary Assembly elected as supreme
                  authority of the state.
    1980, Feb   Kerekou elected president.

Botswana
  1966, Sept   Independence. Sir Seretse Khama heads government.
  1980, July   Khama dies, Quett Masire elected president.

Bourkina Fasso
  1960, Aug   Independence as Upper Volta. Maurice Yaméogo
               president.
  1966, Jan   General strike brings military rule under Lt. Col.
               Sangoulé Lamizana.
  1970, Dec   Elections under new constitution; Lamizana president
               with civilian prime minister.
  1974, Feb   Lamizana installs military government.
  1978, May   Lamizana heads new civilian government.
  1980, Nov   Col. Sayé Zerbo leads military coup.
  1982, Oct   Noncommissioned officers coup.
  1983, Jan   Capt. Thomas Sankara named prime minister; Maj. Jean-
               Baptiste Ouédraogo president.
       May   Sankara purged as leftist.
       July   Sankara seizes power.
  1984, Aug   Upper Volta renamed Bourkina Fasso.

Burundi
  1962, July   Independence as monarchy. Six consecutive governments
               balance Hutu and Tutsi representation.
  1966, July   King deposed by son who reigns as Ntare V; Col. Michel
               Micombero becomes prime minister.
       Nov   Micombero declares a republic.
  1976, Nov   Col. Jean-Baptiste Bagaza seizes presidency in
               bloodless coup.
  1982, Oct   Elections held under new constitution.

Cameroon
  1960, Jan   Independence. Ahmadou Ahidjo president.
  1982, Nov   Ahidjo resigns, succeeded by Prime Minister Paul Biya.

Cape Verde
  1975, July   Independence in federation with Guinea-Bissau.
               Aristides Pereira president.
  1981, Jan   Coup in Guinea-Bissau severs link.

Central African Republic
  1960, Aug   Independence. David Dacko president.
  1965, Dec   Coup led by Col. Jean-Bedel Bokassa.
  1977, Dec   Bokassa crowned emperor of Central African Empire.
  1979, Sept   Coup led by Dacko with French assistance restores
               republic.
  1981, Sept   Coup led by André Kolingba establishes military
               regime.

Chad
  1960, Sept   Independence. François Tombalbaye president.
  1975, Apr   Tombalbaye killed in junior officers' coup; Brig. Gen.
               Félix Malloum becomes president.
  1978, Aug   Malloum and Hissene Habre form coalition government.
  1979, Feb   Troops loyal to Habre attack capital, leaving south
               under Malloum.
       Apr   Transitional Government of National Unity formed,
               fighting continues.

	Nov	Second National Unity Government formed under Goukouni Oueddei.
1982,	June	Habre's troops seize capital.
	Sept	Habre assumes presidency.

Comoros

1975,	July	Independence. Ahmed Abdallah president.
	Aug	Coup led by Ali Soilih; Prince Said Mohammed Jaffer takes over government.
1978,	May	Coup by mercenaries under Bob Denard.
	Oct	Abdallah elected president; new constitution creates Islamic Republic.

Congo-Brazzaville

1960,	Aug	Independence. Foulbert Youlou president.
1963,	Aug	Strikes force Youlou's resignation, army makes Alphonse Massamba-Débat president.
1968,	Aug	Coup by army. Capt. Raoul becomes head of state; Capt. Marien Ngouabi remains strongman.
1977,	Mar	Ngouabi assassinated; Col. Joachim Yhombi-Opango heads government.
1979,	Feb	Col. Denis Sassou-Nguesso takes control.
	July	Elections held for a People's National Assembly.

Djibouti

1977,	June	Independence. Hassan Gouled president.

Egypt

1951,	Oct	Egypt denounces 1936 treaty with Britain and 1899 agreement on the Sudan. Farouk takes title of King of Egypt and the Sudan.
1952,	July	Coup led by Gamel Abdul Nasser and Abdul al-Hakim. Maj. Gen. Mohamed Neguib made commander-in-chief.
1954,	Apr	Nasser becomes premier and military governor of Egypt.
	Nov	Nasser becomes head of state; Neguib arrested.
1956,	June	Nasser elected president of Egypt.
1958,	Mar	United Arab Republic proclaimed with Egypt and Syria as provinces.
1961,	Oct	Nasser recognizes Syria as a separate nation.
1970,	Sept	Nasser dies. Vice-President Anwar Sadat becomes president.
1981,	Oct	Sadat killed; Hosni Mubarak elected president.

Equatorial Guinea

1968,	Oct	Independence. Macias Nguema president.
1972,	June	Macias named president for life.
1973,	Aug	New constitution unifies previously autonomous provinces of Fernando Po and Rio Muni.
1979,	Aug	Coup led by president's nephew Col. Obiang Nguema, who becomes president.
1982,	Aug	New constitution provides for a return to civilian rule after seven years.

Ethiopia

1929,	Nov	Ras Tafari crowned as Emperor Haile Selassie.
1974,	Sept	Emperor deposed by military, Lt. Gen. Aman Andom heads military government.

	Nov	Aman shot, Maj. Mengistu Haile Mariam heads military government.
	Dec	Socialist state declared.
1977,	Feb	Mengistu formally made chief of staff.
1984,	Sept	New Marxist-Leninist party, The Worker's Party of Ethiopia, created under military auspices.

Gabon
1960,	Aug	Independence. Leon M'Ba president.
1964,	Feb	Coup gives power to J. H. Aubame; French troops quickly reinstall M'Ba.
1967,	Nov	M'Ba dies, succeeded by Omar Bongo.

Gambia
| 1965, | Feb | Independence. Government headed by Dawda Jawara. |

Ghana
1957,	Mar	Independence. Kwame Nkrumah heads government.
1966,	Feb	Coup; Gen. Joseph Ankrah heads military government.
1969,	Aug	General elections; civilian government under Kofi Busia.
1972,	Jan	Coup; military government under Gen. Ignatius Acheampong.
1978,	July	Lt. Gen. Frederick Akuffo ousts Acheampong.
1979,	June	Flight-Lt. Jerry Rawlings leads coup backed by NCO's.
	Sept	Hilla Limann heads civilian government.
1981,	Dec	Second Rawlings coup.

Guinea
| 1958, | Oct | Independence. Sekou Touré president. |
| 1984, | Apr | Sekou Touré dies; military seizes power under Col. Lansana Conté. |

Guinea-Bissau
| 1974, | Sept | Independence. Luiz Cabral president. |
| 1980, | Sept | Coup by military under João Bernardo Vieira breaks link with Cape Verde. |

Ivory Coast
| 1960, | Aug | Independence. Félix Houphouët-Boigny president. |

Kenya
| 1963, | Dec | Independence. Jomo Kenyatta president. |
| 1978, | Aug | Kenyatta dies. Vice-President Daniel arap Moi succeeds him. |

Lesotho
| 1966, | June | Independence. Chief Leabua Jonathan prime minister. |
| 1970, | Jan | Jonathan deposes king and suspends constitution when elections go against him. |

Liberia
1847,	Aug	Republic established.
1944,	Jan	William Tubman becomes president.
1971,	July	Vice-President William Tolbert succeeds on Tubman's death.
1980,	Apr	Master-Sgt. Samuel Doe leads coup; Tolbert killed.

Libya
    1951, Dec   Independence. King Idris rules.
    1969, Sept   Coup led by Col. Mu'ammar Mohamed al-Qaddafi who
                  becomes president and prime minister. Libya
                  renamed Libyan Arab Republic.
    1977, Mar   New constitution introduced. Country's name changed
                  to The Popular Libyan Socialist Arab Jamahiriya.

Malagasy Republic
    1960, June   Independence. Philibert Tsiranana president.
    1972, May   Tsiranana hands power to Gen. Gabriel Ramanantsoa
                  following serious riots.
    1975, Feb   Power handed over to Col. Ratsimandrava, who is
                  assassinated six days later. New leader is Gen.
                  Gilles Andria Mahazo.
         Mar   Lt.-Commander Didier Ratsiraka named president. All
                  but one of his cabinet is civilian.
         Dec   Ratsiraka wins seven-year presidency as new
                  constitution is approved.

Malawi
    1964, July   Independence. Hastings Banda president.
    1971, July   Banda named president for life.

Mali
    1960, June   Independence in federation with Senegal.
         Sept   Republic proclaimed with Modibo Keita as president
                  after Senegal withdraws.
    1968, Nov   Coup by junior officers, Lt. Moussa Traoré heads
                  military government.
    1979, Mar   Single-party system established with strong military
                  participation.

Mauritania
    1960, Nov   Independence. Moktar Ould Daddah president.
    1978, July   Coup establishes military government under Lt. Col.
                  Moustapha Ould Salek.
    1979, June   Ould Salek hands power to Lt. Col. Mohamed Louly.
    1980, Jan   Lt. Col. Mohamed Haidalla replaces Louly.

Mauritius
    1968, Mar   Independence. Seewoosegur Ramgoolam prime minister.
    1982, June   Opposition party wins general elections; Anerood
                  Jugnauth becomes prime minister.

Morocco
    1956, Mar   Independence under King Mohamed V.
    1958, May   Government reorganized as constitutional monarchy.
                  Ahmad Balafrej is prime minister.
    1960, May   Government dismissed; King Mohamed forms government
                  with himself as prime minister.
    1962, Feb   Mohamed V dies, succeeded by King Hassan II.
    1965, June   King Hassan suspends parliament and constitution while
                  governing under a "state of emergency."
    1977, June   Elections held for a national assembly.

Mozambique
1975, June   Independence. Samora Machel president.

Niger
1960, Aug   Independence. Hamani Diori president.
1974, Apr   Coup led by Lt. Col. Seyni Kountché.
1981, Feb   Government becomes increasingly civilian as number of
              soldiers in cabinet is reduced.
1983, Jan   Kountché asserts military's pre-eminence while
              appointing Oumarou Mamené, a civilian, as prime
              minister.

Nigeria
1960, Oct   Independence. Abubakar Tafewa Balewa prime minister.
1966, Jan   Coup by Ibo officers; Gen. Aguiyi-Ironsi takes control
              of government.
      July   Ironsi killed in coup; Lt. Col. Yakubu Gowon heads
              military government.
1975, July   Gowon ousted; Brig. Gen. Murtala Muhammed heads
              government.
1976, Feb   Murtala assassinated in coup attempt, succeeded by Lt.
              Gen. Olusegun Obasanjo.
1979, Oct   Return to civilian rule; Shehu Shagari elected
              president.
1983, Aug   Shagari re-elected.
      Dec   Coup led by Maj. Gen. Mohammed Buhari.

Rwanda
1962, July   Independence. Grégoire Kayibanda heads government.
1973, July   Bloodless coup brings Maj. Gen. Juvenal Habyarimana to
              power.
1978, Dec   New constitution brings civilian government under
              Habyarimana.

São Tomé and Príncipe
1975, July   Independence. Manuel Pinto da Costa president.

Senegal
1960, June   Independence in federation with Mali.
      Aug   Federation ends; Léopold Senghor becomes president.
1981, Jan   Senghor retires; succeeded by Abdou Diouf.

Seychelles
1976, June   Independence. James Mancham president.
1977, June   Armed coup by opposition; Albert René becomes
              president.
1979, Mar   Seychelles officially becomes a one-party state.

Sierra Leone
1961, May   Independence. Milton Margai heads government.
1964, May   Margai dies, succeeded by his half-brother Albert
              Margai.
1967, Mar   Elections won by Siaka Stevens; senior officers' coup
              establishes military government under Col. A. T.
              Juxon-Smith.
1968, Apr   Privates' coup hands government to Stevens.

Somalia
    1960, July   Independence. Abdirashid Ali Shirmarke prime
                  minister.
    1967, June   Shirmarke becomes president, Ibrahim Egal prime
                  minister.
    1969, Oct   Shirmarke assassinated; military coup a week later
                  under Maj. Gen. Mohamed Siad Barre.

South Africa
    1910, May   Union of South Africa proclaimed.
    1948, May   National party comes to power.
    1961, May   South Africa becomes a republic and leaves
                  Commonwealth.

Sudan
    1956, Jan   Independence. Abdalla Khalil heads government.
    1958, Nov   Military coup led by Gen. Ibrahim Abboud.
    1964, Oct   Widespread civil demonstrations divide army; Abboud
                  hands power to coalition civilian government.
    1965, May   Civilian government overthrown in bloodless coup led
                  by Gen. Gaafar Nimeiry.
    1971, July   Nimeiry overthrown by Communists; with Libyan help, he
                  is restored to power; Communists purged.
         Oct   Nimeiry wins general election, forms civilian
                  government with army support.

Swaziland
    1968, Sept   Independence. Makhosini Dlamini prime minister under
                  King Sobhuza II.
    1973, Apr   King abrogates constitution, rules through royal
                  family council.
    1982, Sept   King dies; Queen Mother Dzeliwe named regent.
    1983, Aug   Dzeliwe deposed; Prince Mahosetive (aged 15) named as
                  future king.

Tanzania
    1961, Dec   Independence of Tanganyika. Julius Nyerere heads
                  government.
    1963, Dec   Independence of Zanzibar under sultan.
    1964, Jan   Zanzibar revolution-armed insurrection drives the
                  sultan into exile. Abeid Karume becomes
                  president.
         Apr   Tanzania formed by uniting Tanganyika and Zanzibar;
                  Nyerere as president; Karume vice-president.
    1972, Apr   Vice-President Karume assassinated, succeeded by Aboud
                  Jumbe.

Togo
    1960, Apr   Independence. Sylvanus Olympio president.
    1963, Jan   Olympio shot; Sgt. Etienne Eyadema installs Nicholas
                  Grunitzky as civilian president.
    1967, Jan   Coup led by Col. Kleber Dadjo.
         Apr   Lt. Col. Eyadema takes control of military government.
    1980, Jan   Eyadema proclaims third republic with himself as
                  president.

Tunisia
 1956, Mar Independence. Habib Bourguiba prime minister.
 1957, July Bey of Tunis deposed as Tunisian republic created.
      Bourguiba is president.

Uganda
 1962, Oct Independence. Milton Obote prime minister. Kabaka of
      Buganda is president.
 1966, Apr Obote proclaims new constitution with himself as
      president.
 1971, Jan Coup by Maj. Gen. Idi Amin.
 1979, Mar Yusuf Lule chosen head of opposition executive
      council.
   Apr Tanzanian army occupies Kampala; Amin flees.
   June Godfrey Binaisa replaces Lule.
 1980, May Military overthrows Binaisa, announces elections.
   Dec Obote elected president.

Zaire
 1960, June Congo becomes independent. Joseph Kasavubu president
      and Patrice Lumumba prime minister. Army
      mutinies.
   Sept Col. Joseph Mobutu suspends constitution.
 1961, Jan Cyrille Adoula forms "national unity" government.
 1964, Apr Mobutu invites Moïse Tshombe to form government;
      Kasavubu tries to dismiss Tshombe.
   July Tshombe recalled as premier.
 1965, Oct Kasavubu dismisses Tshombe.
   Nov Gen. Mobutu seizes executive power and begins
      consolidating personal rule.
 1970, Dec Mobutu named party's founder-president as state
      institutions subordinated to party.
 1971, Oct Congo renamed Zaire.

Zambia
 1964, Oct Independence. Kenneth Kaunda president.

Zimbabwe
 1980, Apr Independence. Robert Mugabe prime minister.

TABLE A–2.

Regime Changes and Coups in Africa, by date.

1847, Aug	Liberia. Republic established.
1910, May	South Africa. Union of South Africa proclaimed.
1929, Nov	Ethiopia. Ras Tafari crowned as Emperor Haile Selassie.
1944, Jan	Liberia. William Tubman becomes president.
1948, May	South Africa. National party comes to power.
1951, Oct	Egypt. Egypt denounces 1936 treaty with Britain and 1899 agreement on the Sudan. Farouk takes title of King of Egypt and the Sudan.
Dec	Libya. Independence. King Idris rules.
1952, July	Egypt. Coup led by Gamel Abdul Nasser and Abdul al-Hakim. Maj. Gen. Mohamed Neguib made commander-in-chief.
1954, Apr	Egypt. Nasser becomes premier and military governor of Egypt.
Nov	Egypt. Nasser becomes head of state; Neguib arrested.
1956, Jan	Sudan. Independence. Abdalla Khalil heads government.
Mar	Morocco. Independence under King Mohamed V.
Mar	Tunisia. Independence. Habib Bourguiba prime minister.
June	Egypt. Nasser elected president of Egypt.
1957, Mar	Ghana. Independence. Kwame Nkrumah heads government.
July	Tunisia. Bey of Tunis deposed as Tunisian republic created. Bourguiba is president.
1958, Mar	Egypt. United Arab Republic proclaimed with Egypt and Syria as provinces.
May	Morocco. Government reorganized as constitutional monarchy. Ahmad Balafrej is prime minister.
Oct	Guinea. Independence. Sekou Touré president.
Nov	Sudan. Military coup led by Gen. Ibrahim Abboud.
1960, Jan	Cameroon. Independence. Ahmadou Ahidjo president.
Apr	Togo. Independence. Sylvanus Olympio president.
May	Morocco. Government dismissed; King Mohamed forms government with himself as prime minister.
June	Malagasy Republic. Independence. Philibert Tsiranana president.
June	Mali. Independence in federation with Senegal.
June	Senegal. Independence in federation with Mali.
June	Zaire. Congo becomes independent. Joseph Kasavubu president and Patrice Lumumba prime minister. Army mutinies.

July   Somalia. Independence. Abdirashid Ali Shirmarke prime
        minister.
Aug   Benin. Independence as Republic of Dahomey. Coalition of
        Hubert Maga, Sourou-Migan Apithy, and Justin
        Ahomadegbe.
Aug   Bourkina Fasso. Independence as Upper Volta. Maurice
        Yaméogo president.
Aug   Central African Republic. Independence. David Dacko
        president.
Aug   Congo-Brazzaville. Independence. Foulbert Youlou
        president.
Aug   Gabon. Independence. Leon M'Ba president.
Aug   Ivory Coast. Independence. Félix Houphouët-Boigny
        president.
Aug   Niger. Independence. Hamani Diori president.
Aug   Senegal. Federation ends; Léopold Senghor becomes
        president.
Sept   Chad. Independence. François Tombalbaye president.
Sept   Mali. Republic proclaimed with Modibo Keita as president
        after Senegal withdraws.
Sept   Zaire. Col. Joseph Mobutu suspends constitution.
Oct   Nigeria. Independence. Abubakar Tafewa Balewa prime
        minister.
Nov   Mauritania. Independence. Moktar Ould Daddah president.
1961, Jan Zaire. Cyrille Adoula forms "national unity" government.
May   Sierra Leone. Independence. Milton Margai heads
        government.
May   South Africa. South Africa becomes a republic and leaves
        Commonwealth.
Oct   Egypt. Nasser recognizes Syria as a separate nation.
Dec   Tanzania. Independence of Tanganyika. Julius Nyerere
        heads government.
1962, Feb Morocco. Mohamed V dies, succeeded by King Hassan II.
July   Algeria. Independence. Ahmed Ben Bella president.
July   Burundi. Independence as monarchy. Six consecutive
        governments balance Hutu and Tutsi representation.
July   Rwanda. Independence. Grégoire Kayibanda heads
        government.
Oct   Uganda. Independence. Milton Obote prime minister.
        Kabaka of Buganda is president.
1963, Jan Togo. Olympio shot; Sgt. Etienne Eyadema installs Nicholas
        Grunitzky as civilian president.
Aug   Congo-Brazzaville. Strikes force Youlou's resignation,
        army makes Alphonse Massamba-Débat president.
Oct   Benin. Coup led by Col. Christophe Soglo removes Maga.
Dec   Kenya. Independence. Jomo Kenyatta president.
Dec   Tanzania. Independence of Zanzibar under sultan.
1964, Jan Tanzania. Zanzibar revolution-armed insurrection drives
        the sultan into exile. Abeid Karume becomes president.
Feb   Gabon. Coup gives power to J. H. Aubame; French troops
        quickly reinstall M'Ba.
Apr   Tanzania. Tanzania formed by uniting Tanganyika and
        Zanzibar; Nyerere as president; Karume vice-president.
Apr   Zaire. Mobutu invites Moïse Tshombe to form government;
        Kasavubu tries to dismiss Tshombe.
May   Sierra Leone. Margai dies, succeeded by his half-brother
        Albert Margai.

	July	Malawi. Independence. Hastings Banda president.
	July	Zaire. Tshombe recalled as premier.
	Oct	Sudan. Widespread civil demonstrations divide army; Abboud hands power to coalition civilian government.
	Oct	Zambia. Independence. Kenneth Kaunda president.
1965,	Feb	Gambia. Independence. Government headed by Dawda Jawara.
	May	Sudan. Civilian government overthrown in bloodless coup led by Gen. Gaafar Nimeiry.
	June	Algeria. Coup led by Col. Houari Boumedienne.
	June	Morocco. King Hassan suspends parliament and constitution while governing under a "state of emergency."
	Oct	Zaire. Kasavubu dismisses Tshombe.
	Nov	Benin. Ahomadegbe forced out by Armed Forces Chief of Staff Gen. Soglo.
	Nov	Zaire. Gen. Mobutu seizes executive power and begins consolidating personal rule.
	Dec	Benin. Soglo names "provisional" government, himself as president.
	Dec	Central African Republic. Coup led by Col. Jean-Bedel Bokassa.
1966,	Jan	Bourkina Fasso. General strike brings military rule under Lt. Col. Sangoulé Lamizana.
	Jan	Nigeria. Coup by Ibo officers; Gen. Aguiyi-Ironsi takes control of government.
	Feb	Ghana. Coup; Gen. Joseph Ankrah heads military government.
	Apr	Uganda. Obote proclaims new constitution with himself as president.
	June	Lesotho. Independence. Chief Leabua Jonathan prime minister.
	July	Burundi. King deposed by son who reigns as Ntare V; Col. Michel Micombero becomes prime minister.
	July	Nigeria. Ironsi killed in coup; Lt. Col. Yakubu Gowon heads military government.
	Sept	Botswana. Independence. Sir Seretse Khama heads government.
	Nov	Burundi. Micombero declares a republic.
1967,	Jan	Togo. Coup led by Col. Kleber Dadjo.
	Mar	Sierra Leone. Elections won by Siaka Stevens; senior officers' coup establishes military government under Col. A. T. Juxon-Smith.
	Apr	Togo. Lt. Col. Eyadema takes control of military government.
	June	Somalia. Shirmarke becomes president, Ibrahim Egal prime minister.
	Nov	Gabon. M'Ba dies, succeeded by Omar Bongo.
	Dec	Benin. Coup led by Maj. Kouandeté deposes Soglo. Ex-Armed Forces Chief of Staff Lt. Col. Alley named president with Kouandeté as prime minister.
1968,	Mar	Mauritius. Independence. Seewoosegur Ramgoolam prime minister.
	Apr	Sierra Leone. Privates' coup hands government to Stevens.
	Aug	Congo-Brazzaville. Coup by army. Capt. Raoul becomes head of state; Capt. Marien Ngouabi remains strongman.
	Sept	Benin. Zinsou named president.
	Sept	Swaziland. Independence. Makhosini Dlamini prime minister under King Sobhuza II.
	Oct	Equatorial Guinea. Independence. Macias Nguema president.

	Nov	Mali. Coup by junior officers, Lt. Moussa Traoré heads military government.
1969,	Aug	Ghana. General elections; civilian government under Kofi Busia.
	Sept	Libya. Coup led by Col. Mu'ammar Mohamed al-Qaddafi who becomes president and prime minister. Libya renamed Libyan Arab Republic.
	Oct	Somalia. Shirmarke assassinated; military coup a week later under Maj. Gen. Mohamed Siad Barre.
	Dec	Benin. Armed Forces Chief of Staff Lt. Col. Kouandeté ousts Zinsou. Triumvirate of Kouandeté, Lt. Col. De Souza, and Lt. Col. Sinzogan.
1970,	Jan	Lesotho. Jonathan deposes king and suspends constitution when elections go against him.
	Sept	Egypt. Nasser dies.' Vice-President Anwar Sadat becomes president.
	Dec	Bourkina Fasso. Elections under new constitution; Lamizana president with civilian prime minister.
	Dec	Zaire. Mobutu named party's founder-president as state institutions subordinated to party.
1971,	Jan	Uganda. Coup by Maj. Gen. Idi Amin.
	July	Liberia. Vice-President William Tolbert succeeds on Tubman's death.
	July	Malawi. Banda named president for life.
	July	Sudan. Nimeiry overthrown by Communists; with Libyan help, he is restored to power; Communists purged.
	Oct	Sudan. Nimeiry wins general election, forms civilian government with army support.
	Oct	Zaire. Congo renamed Zaire.
1972,	Jan	Ghana. Coup; military government under Gen. Ignatius Acheampong.
	Apr	Tanzania. Vice-President Karume assassinated, succeeded by Aboud Jumbe.
	May	Malagasy Republic. Tsiranana hands power to Gen. Gabriel Ramanantsoa following serious riots.
	June	Equatorial Guinea. Macias named president for life.
	Oct	Benin. Coup led by Maj. Mathieu Kerekou.
1973,	Apr	Swaziland. King abrogates constitution, rules through royal family council.
	July	Rwanda. Bloodless coup brings Maj. Gen. Juvenal Habyarimana to power.
	Aug	Equatorial Guinea. New constitution unifies previously autonomous provinces of Fernando Po and Rio Muni.
1974,	Feb	Bourkina Fasso. Lamizana installs military government.
	Apr	Niger. Coup led by Lt. Col. Seyni Kountché.
	Sept	Ethiopia. Emperor deposed by military, Lt. Gen. Aman Andom heads military government.
	Sept	Guinea-Bissau. Independence. Luiz Cabral president.
	Nov	Ethiopia. Aman shot, Maj. Mengistu Haile Mariam heads military government.
	Dec	Ethiopia. Socialist state declared.
1975,	Feb	Malagasy Republic. Power handed over to Col. Ratsimandrava who is assassinated six days later. New leader is Gen. Gilles Andria Mahazo.
	Mar	Malagasy Republic. Lt.-Commander Didier Ratsiraka named president. All but one of his cabinet is civilian.

Apr	Chad. Tombalbaye killed in junior officers' coup; Brig. Gen. Félix Malloum becomes president.
June	Mozambique. Independence. Samora Machel president.
July	Cape Verde. Independence in federation with Guinea-Bissau. Aristides Pereira president.
July	Comoros. Independence. Ahmed Abdallah president.
July	Nigeria. Gowon ousted; Brig. Gen. Murtala Muhammed heads government.
July	São Tomé and Príncipe. Independence. Manuel Pinto da Costa president.
Aug	Comoros. Coup led by Ali Soilih; Prince Said Mohammed Jaffer takes over government.
Oct	Benin. Dahomey becomes People's Republic of Benin.
Nov	Angola. Independence. Government contested by MPLA (Agostinho Neto) and coalition of FNLA (Holden Roberto) and UNITA (Jonas Savimbi).
Dec	Benin. Kerekou launches a single-party state.
Dec	Malagasy Republic. Ratsiraka wins seven-year presidency as new constitution is approved.
1976, Feb	Angola. UNITA-FNLA defeated; MPLA forms government.
Feb	Nigeria. Murtala assassinated in coup attempt, succeeded by Lt. Gen. Olusegun Obasanjo.
June	Seychelles. Independence. James Mancham president.
Nov	Burundi. Col. Jean-Baptiste Bagaza seizes presidency in bloodless coup.
1977, Feb	Ethiopia. Mengistu formally made chief of staff.
Mar	Congo-Brazzaville. Ngouabi assassinated; Col. Joachim Yhombi-Opango heads government.
Mar	Libya. New constitution introduced. Country's name changed to The Popular Libyan Socialist Arab Jamahiriya.
June	Djibouti. Independence. Hassan Gouled president.
June	Morocco. Elections held for a national assembly.
June	Seychelles. Armed coup by opposition; Albert René becomes president.
Dec	Central African Republic. Bokassa crowned emperor of Central African Empire.
1978, May	Bourkina Fasso. Lamizana heads new civilian government.
May	Comoros. Coup by mercenaries under Bob Denard.
July	Ghana. Lt. Gen. Frederick Akuffo ousts Acheampong.
July	Mauritania. Coup establishes military government under Lt. Col. Moustapha Ould Salek.
Aug	Chad. Malloum and Hissene Habre form coalition government.
Aug	Kenya. Kenyatta dies. Vice-President Daniel arap Moi succeeds him.
Oct	Comoros. Abdallah elected president; new constitution creates Islamic Republic.
Dec	Rwanda. New constitution brings civilian government under Habyarimana.
1979, Feb	Algeria. Col. Benjeddid Chadli elected president.
Feb	Chad. Troops loyal to Habre attack capital, leaving south under Malloum.
Feb	Congo-Brazzaville. Col. Denis Sassou-Nguesso takes control.
Mar	Mali. Single-party system established with strong military participation.

Mar   Seychelles. Seychelles officially becomes a one-party
        state.
Mar   Uganda. Yusuf Lule chosen head of opposition executive
        council.
Apr   Chad. Transitional Government of National Unity formed,
        fighting continues.
Apr   Uganda. Tanzanian army occupies Kampala; Amin flees.
June   Ghana. Flight-Lt. Jerry Rawlings leads coup backed by
        NCO's.
June   Mauritania. Ould Salek hands power to Lt. Col. Mohamed
        Louly.
June   Uganda. Godfrey Binaisa replaces Lule.
July   Congo-Brazzaville. Elections held for a People's National
        Assembly.
Aug   Equatorial Guinea. Coup led by president's nephew Col.
        Obiang Nguema, who becomes president.
Sept   Angola. Neto dies, succeeded by José Eduardo dos Santos.
Sept   Central African Republic. Coup led by Dacko with French
        assistance restores republic.
Sept   Ghana. Hilla Limann heads civilian government.
Oct   Nigeria. Return to civilian rule; Shehu Shagari elected
        president.
Nov   Benin. National Revolutionary Assembly elected as supreme
        authority of the state.
Nov   Chad. Second National Unity Government formed under
        Goukouni Oueddei.
1980, Jan   Mauritania. Lt. Col. Mohamed Haidalla replaces Louly.
Jan   Togo. Eyadema proclaims third republic with himself as
        president.
Feb   Benin. Kerekou elected president.
Apr   Liberia. Master-Sgt. Samuel Doe leads coup; Tolbert
        killed.
Apr   Zimbabwe. Independence. Robert Mugabe prime minister.
May   Uganda. Military overthrows Binaisa, announces elections.
July   Botswana. Khama dies, Quett Masire elected president.
Sept   Guinea-Bissau. Coup by military under João Bernardo Vieira
        breaks link with Cape Verde.
Nov   Bourkina Fasso. Col. Sayé Zerbo leads military coup.
Dec   Uganda. Obote elected president.
1981, Jan   Cape Verde. Coup in Guinea-Bissau severs link.
Jan   Senegal. Senghor retires; succeeded by Abdou Diouf.
Feb   Niger. Government becomes increasingly civilian as number
        of soldiers in cabinet is reduced.
Sept   Central African Republic. Coup led by André Kolingba
        establishes military regime.
Oct   Egypt. Sadat killed; Hosni Mubarak elected president.
Dec   Ghana. Second Rawlings coup.
1982, June Chad. Habre's troops seize capital.
June   Mauritius. Opposition party wins general elections;
        Anerood Jugnauth becomes prime minister.
Aug   Equatorial Guinea. New constitution provides for a return
        to civilian rule after seven years.
Sept   Chad. Habre assumes presidency.
Sept   Swaziland. King dies; Queen Mother Dzeliwe named regent.
Oct   Bourkina Fasso. Noncommissioned officers coup.
Oct   Burundi. Elections held under new constitution.

Nov	Cameroon. Ahidjo resigns, succeeded by Prime Minister Paul Biya.
1983, Jan	Bourkina Fasso. Capt. Thomas Sankara named prime minister; Maj. Jean-Baptiste Ouédraogo president.
Jan	Niger. Kountché asserts military's pre-eminence while appointing Oumarou Mamené, a civilian, as prime minister.
May	Bourkina Fasso. Sankara purged as leftist.
July	Bourkina Fasso. Sankara seizes power.
Aug	Nigeria. Shagari re-elected.
Aug	Swaziland. Dzeliwe deposed; Prince Mahosetive (aged 15) named as future king.
Dec	Nigeria. Coup led by Maj. Gen. Mohammed Buhari.
1984, Apr	Guinea. Sekou Touré dies; military seizes power under Col. Lansana Conté.
Aug	Bourkina Fasso. Upper Volta renamed Bourkina Fasso.
Sept	Ethiopia. New Marxist-Leninist party, The Worker's Party of Ethiopia, created under military auspices.

Index

Africa: as physical obstacle to Asia, 2–3; as launching pad, 4–6, 11, 22; as rimland, 5; strategic resources in, 6–10; as surrogate terrain, 7–10. *See also individual African states*

African armed forces, 99–103, 153; corruption in, 106; paramilitary units, 106; training of, 108–11; size of, 172. *See also individual African states*

African armies, 173, 192; characteristics of, 155, 156, 159; and weapons systems, 177–79

African militaries: capabilities of, 104*n;* human resources of, 103–11; logistics, 111–12; mobility, 112–13; firepower, 113–14; manpower, 114–15

African nationalism, 65, 123; after World War II, 12; effects on great powers, 12–17; and military regimes, 164–67

African troops: in colonial armies, 7; morale, 102, 103

Algeria, 3, 78, 85, 93, 97, 187; colonial action in, 7; as supplier of petroleum, 20; French troops in, 64; relations with France, 65; military relations with Soviet Union, 120; anticolonial struggles of, 168; military budget, 176; military skills, 178; support of rebels, 180; and armed incursions, 181; military assistance to, 192

Amin, Idi, 101, 158, 163, 169; organization of armed forces by, 156; fall of, 167

ANC (African National Congress), 124, 138, 161; in Lesotho, 139; expulsion of activists, 139, 147; guerrillas, 146, 151, 152

Andropov, Yuri, 54

Angola, 91, 181, 183, 188, 192; relations with Soviet Union, 10–11, 37, 114; civil war, 12, 33, 65, 69, 99; relations with United States, 15; African nationalist movements in, 16; as petroleum producer, 20; UNITA insurgents in,